IMAGES
of America

Winona

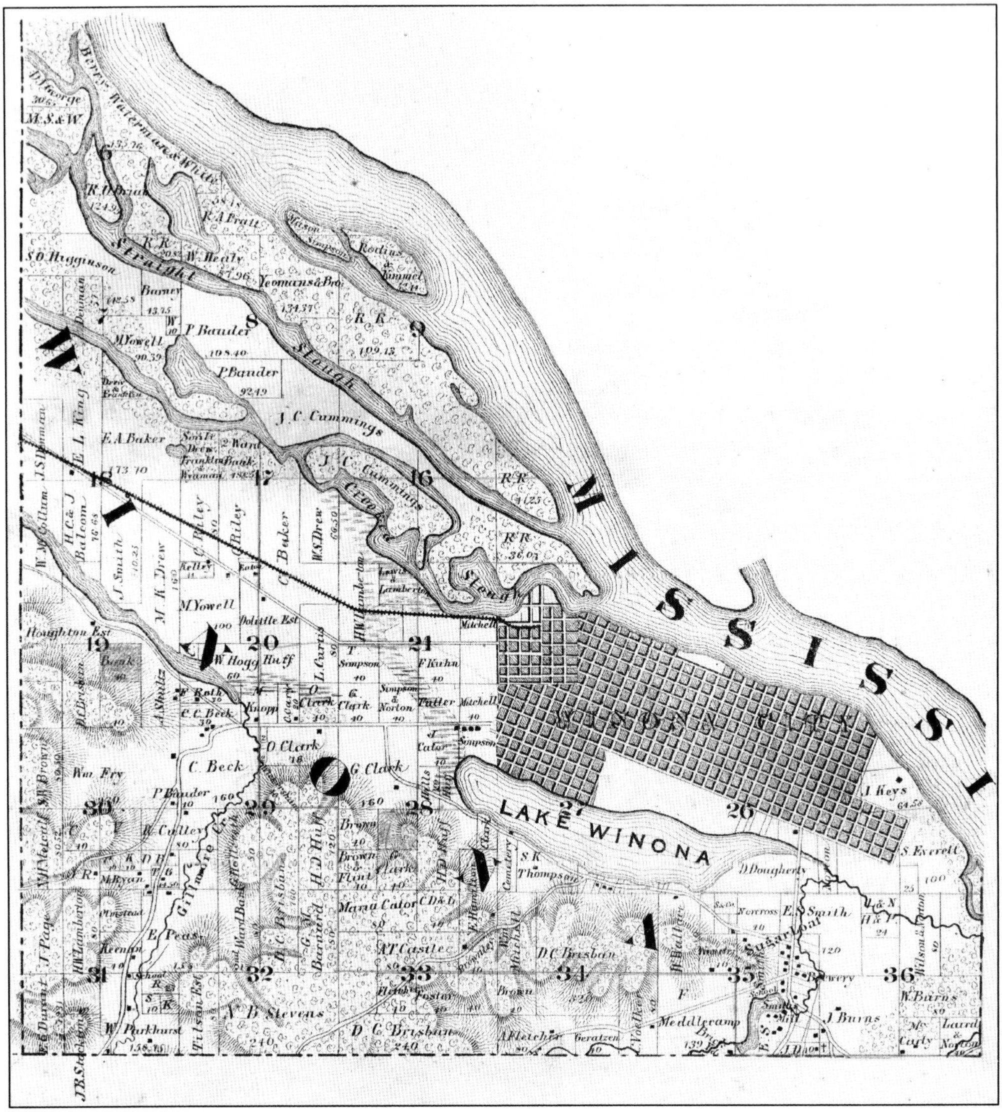

Pictured is a c. 1867 plat map of the southern half of Winona Township, located in Winona County, Minnesota. This map illustrates the placement, shape, and drainage of Lake Winona about 15 years after the settlement of Wapasha's Prairie. This map also shows the boundaries of the City of Winona and ownership of the land in a portion of Winona Township. In addition, the crosshatching illustrates the landscape's topography. (Bennett.)

ON THE COVER: The Chicago and North Western Railway Depot, located in Winona at the north end of Huff Street, was built in 1880 and is seen in its prime in the 1920s. The depot was considered one of the best in the upper Midwest. (Priewert.)

IMAGES
of America

WINONA

Walter Bennick

ARCADIA
PUBLISHING

ISBN 978-0-7385-9425-5

Published by Arcadia Publishing
Charleston, South Carolina

Printed in the United States of America

Library of Congress Control Number: 2012940908

For all general information, please contact Arcadia Publishing:
Telephone 843-853-2070
Fax 843-853-0044
E-mail sales@arcadiapublishing.com
For customer service and orders:
Toll-Free 1-888-313-2665

Visit us on the Internet at www.arcadiapublishing.com

To all the citizens of Winona, who make this history possible.

CONTENTS

ACKNOWLEDGMENTS

The images in this book were exclusively selected from the Winona County Historical Society's collection of photographs, lithographs, and albums, all of which have been donated to the society's archives. Many of these images were donated by the *Winona Daily News* and have appeared in print in the *Winona Argus*, *Winona Daily Republican*, *Winona Republican-Herald*, the *Winona Daily News*, or the *Winona Post*. Individuals, families, or a variety of community groups and/or organizations donated the remainder. The photograph of Wapasha II, which is in the collection, was included with permission of the Minnesota Historical Society. Several albums of photographs have been used in this book, including those by Ralph Boldt, Claude R. Graham, Angelyn de Groot, Orrin Fruit Smith, Charles A. Tenney, Clara (Sobotta) Evans, Gertrude Conaughty-Hardtke, Dr. Lewis I. Younger, Merritt W. Kelley, Kenneth M. Wright, Ben A. Huntley, and the American Legion.

Much of the history included in the captions of the selected photographs has been obtained from the county history books in the society's collection, from the local newspapers (on microfilm and courtesy of the *Winona Daily News*), or online through Winona State University's Winona Newspaper Project, which covers the period from 1857 through 1975.

Also, thanks go to the Winona County Historical Society for the opportunity to utilize its collection of photographs in this project and to the staff for its encouragement. In addition, thanks also go to Mark Peterson, the society's director, for his assistance and direction.

Introduction

Prior to the last ice age, the land where present-day Winona is located was relatively flat lowland that drained toward the north. The ice-age glaciers were deflected around parts of Minnesota and Wisconsin, leaving a region untouched by the ice. The Mississippi River was formed along the western edge of the glaciers as melting caused sediment-laden water to flow southward. This flow of water formed a valley over 1,000 feet deep. As the flow diminished, the sediment was dropped, filling the valley with hundreds of feet of sand and gravel and leaving a large floodplain.

After later flooding, the river would entrench itself, but between the flooding the valley floor was built up with more sediment than could be carried away. This caused the main channel to be diverted from side to side. One result of this meandering was that a large sandbar formed in the river. Gradually, sediments filled the channel between the south wall of the valley and the sandbar, forcing the channel to the north side of the sandbar and leaving a large lake and marshland in its place.

Numerous explorers passed by the island in the Mississippi River that later became Winona. In their journals, Fr. Louis Hennepin and André Penicaut described the Mississippi River Valley. Archaeological evidence and various journal accounts place the Native Americans in the vicinity of Winona well before the 17th century. Following the French and Indian War, the English took control of Wisconsin and parts of Minnesota, and after the Louisiana Purchase, Pres. Thomas Jefferson sent Lt. Zebulon Pike to explore the Mississippi River. As he traveled, Pike wrote in his journal after stopping on the prairie just past the Black River:

> We crossed first a dry flat prairie; when we arrived at the hills we ascended them, from which we had a most sublime and beautiful prospect. On the right, we saw the mountains which we passed in the morning and the prairie in their rear; like distant clouds, the mountains at the Prairie La Cross; on our left and under our feet, the valley between the two barren hills through which the Mississippi wound itself by numerous channels, forming many beautiful islands, as far as the eye could embrace the scene; and our boats under full sail, their flags streaming before the wind. It was altogether a prospect so variegated and romantic that a man may scarcely expect to enjoy such a one but twice or thrice in the course of his life.

In the spring of 1835, Capt. Orrin T. Smith began to engage in commerce on the Mississippi River. As he passed by Wapasha's Prairie, he decided that one day he would lay claim to it. Thus, on October 15, 1851, he set Erwin Johnson and two others on the sandbar to lay a claim. Prior to Erwin Johnson, James Reed, who was married to a relative of Wapasha, had arrived at the island as a government farmer and storekeeper for Wapasha's band. He had come in 1842 and constructed a house in 1844, the first in Wapasha's Prairie. Reed retained his appointment until the Treaty of Mendota was signed in 1851, which opened Wabasha's Prairie for settlement and forced the removal of the Native Americans.

The population of the treeless sandbar known as Wapasha's Prairie grew from the original two men in late 1851 to 300 by the end of 1852. This growth continued, and by 1856, some 3,000 souls were living in Winona. With this growth, government developed, and the Winona City Charter was approved in March 1857. Martin Wheeler Sargeant was elected Winona's first mayor.

This new community expanded outward from the levee, as steamboats were the primary means of transportation. In 1856, over 1,300 steamboats had stopped at the levee to unload supplies, refuel with wood, and leave the latest news. By 1855, commerce had been well established, and numerous buildings had been erected.

Most of the early settlers were American Yankees from New England, but they also included Germans, all looking for new opportunities. Some of these settlers provided new avenues of commerce while others provided the labor. They also brought their culture, which translated into new industries and leisure time activities.

Almost from the beginning, there was an interest in westward expansion. Railroads had reached the Mississippi but not beyond; therefore, a railroad going west from Winona was considered important. Early in 1854, a railroad company was formed and authorized to build a rail line westward from Winona to the Dakota Territory via St. Peter.

Henry D. Huff was one of the important residents in early Winona. He had purchased a good share of the land from the original owners and named the new community. Huff was the first resident to have a large mansion, known as the Chateau on the Frontier, built on the highest point on the prairie. It was from this beginning that a vibrant community developed as the gateway to the west.

Early in 1857, when Congress designated lands to be used for the building of the railroads, two railroads chose Winona as their terminus. With the arrival of the railroad in La Crosse in 1858, the railroad had made its first approach toward Minnesota. However, with the terminus in La Crosse, all products going to Winona had to be shipped by steamboat. The railroad was proposed to connect La Crosse with Winona, but crossing the Mississippi River was a problem until a bridge was completed at Winona on November 25, 1871, after nine months of construction. At the time the bridge was built it was the longest in the world, at 363 feet.

However, for all other traffic to reach Winona, a ferry was required. Ferry service was sporadic until May 1865, when Samuel D. Van Gorder started a ferry between Wisconsin and Winona. In 1868, Van Gorder had a road constructed across the Wisconsin bottomlands to a ferry landing on the river. He also constructed a floating dock at the foot of Walnut Street. Van Gorder operated his ferry service until 1880, when the City of Winona took it over.

In 1883, the city made improvements to the road across the bottomlands. Later, in 1886, the Winona City Council had a 1,500-foot long wooden bridge built across the slough from the ferry landing to Latsch Island. The bridge was completed in March 1887, and at its south end, it met up with a cable ferry. The ferry service continued until the high steel bridge was constructed over the main channel of the river in 1892. The high steel bridge approach terminated at Main Street with two 90-degree turns before reaching the high span. The high bridge then crossed the main channel to Latsch Island, where it connected with the old ferry bridge. This new bridge, a toll bridge, was inaugurated on June 18, 1892.

In 1912, the old wooden ferry bridge was replaced with a new bridge made of 72-foot arched concrete and steel spans. Because of the right-angled turns and 17-foot roadway, the high bridge turned out to be a transportation hazard, and numerous accidents occurred. Work began on the construction of a new high bridge in the late summer of 1940. Compared to the old high bridge, this new one went straight across from approach to approach and had a 27-foot roadway and a four-and-a-half-foot sidewalk for foot traffic. Following the dedication of the new bridge on November 21, 1942, crews began the work of dismantling the old high bridge, and by the first of June 1943, all that remained of the old steel high bridge was a memory.

A number of entrepreneurial citizens also engaged in a variety of transportation businesses needed in a thriving community, including passenger and freight-hauling services. Late in 1883, the Winona Street Railway was inaugurated with horse-drawn trolley cars, and about 10 years later, these were replaced by electric trolley cars. The streetcar business had reached its peak around 1920, but due to the automobile, trended downward. In 1938, the streetcars were replaced by a bus with a gasoline engine.

Winona had its share of community leaders, including those who started various businesses that provided jobs and products needed by its citizens. These leaders also provided for many of the cultural and entertainment venues and housing opportunities that improved the lives of many of their employees as well as the general citizenry.

Over the years of Winona's existence, numerous conflicts and war occurred in which Winona's citizenry has taken part. Soon after the founding of the city, the Civil War began, and Winona was the first to provide volunteers to defend the Union. As later conflicts drew the United States into war, once again Winona stepped up to provide its citizens as soldiers to support the cause. Even in peacetime, Winona provided for the military with the National Guard and the Civilian Conservation Corps. Today, many of these heroes rest in the city's two cemeteries.

For a city to thrive, it must provide for the well-being of its citizens. Winona has done its part to this end. Early on, doctors, nurses, dentists, and druggists have lived in Winona, providing for the sick and injured. Most early medical care occurred in the home, but eventually, hospitals were started. Some of them, however, were too small. The first of these hospitals were started as only a place to die. Cemeteries were also important, and several small ones were found scattered around the community. It was not until around 1862 that permanent resting places for the citizens of Winona were formed.

Early in its history, education was deemed to be important to the Winona citizenry, and educational opportunities were provided for. Small, private schools were started in homes and later in other facilities. A board of education was formed in Winona in 1861 that governed the city's public schools. The first school building was erected early in 1863, with others to follow.

Winona was also the site of the first school devoted to teacher training west of the Mississippi River. Dr. John D. Ford provided the argument to the community that it would be in Winona's best interests to provide money and a place for the state's first normal school for teacher education. Convinced, the community provided the necessary monies, and a building was constructed to establish the state's first normal school.

Churches in Winona start with the beginnings of the community. The clergy and others in religious service were in Winona early in its history to serve its people. Early on, churches were established and places of worship built. Sunday schools were organized, some of which evolved into parochial schools affiliated with the host church. The religious community also brought a hospital to the city along with two colleges and a host of church-related buildings.

Arts and entertainment were always important to the community. The community "captains" often provided some venues for the arts and entertainment while community entrepreneurs provided others. Entertainment was provided early in the history of the community with local talent and traveling shows. The early German population had brought their musical culture with them and quickly organized a singing society, as did the Yankees form New England. Later, groups organized their own societies along with many other civic organizations and playhouses.

After World War II, the community leaders were determined to modernize Winona's main business district. With funding available from the federal government, Winona embarked on a program of urban renewal with the mantra, "Down with the old and in with the new." A number of old, but historic, buildings were razed and replaced with "something better." Urban renewal started in 1963 with the razing of the old post office, which was replaced with a cement box block in Central Park. This caused the removal of the Princess Wenonah statue and fountain from Central Park, sending the princess on a long trip around the city.

One

The Early Years

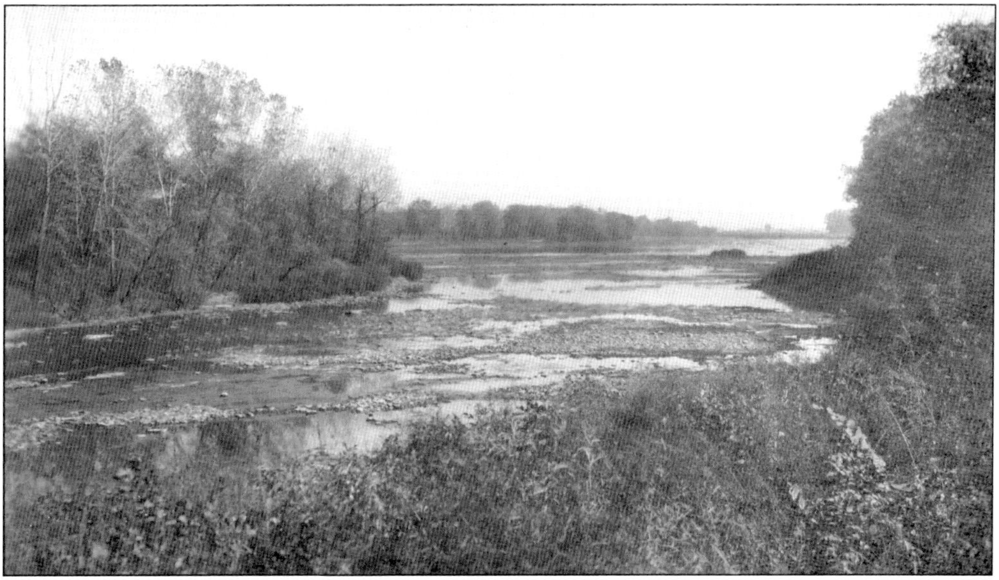

The early Mississippi River had numerous channels, many of which were filled with sediment that made river travel difficult.

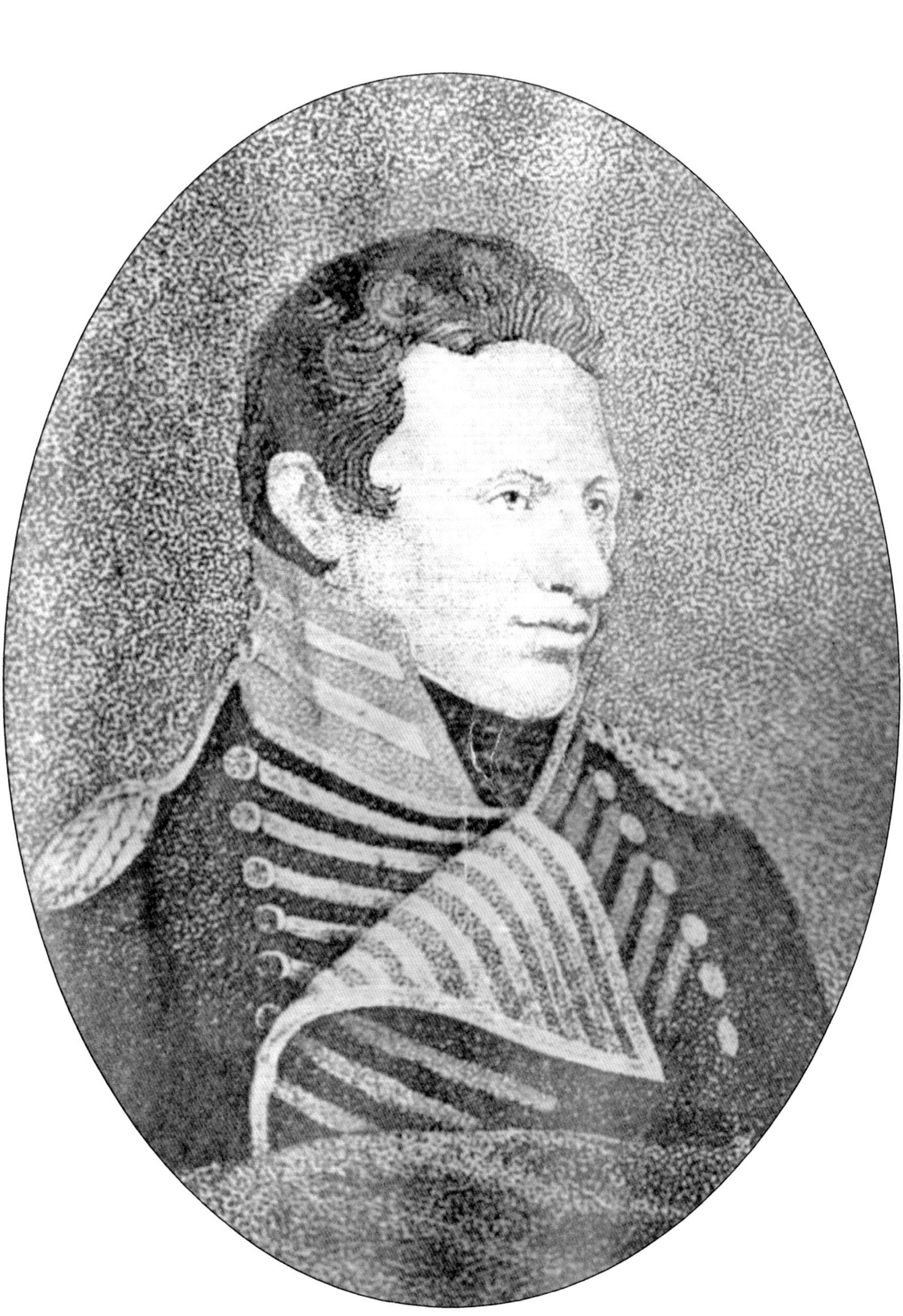

Zebulon M. Pike (1779–1813) was one of the first explorers to actually record his stop on September 14, 1805, at what later became Winona. Pike was born in New Jersey, and his father was a military officer who served in the Revolutionary War. Pike began his military career at age 15, and by 26, he had been sent to explore the upper reaches of the Mississippi River and to make contact with the native people. He later explored the Rocky Mountains and was killed as he led an attack into Canada in 1813. (Upham.)

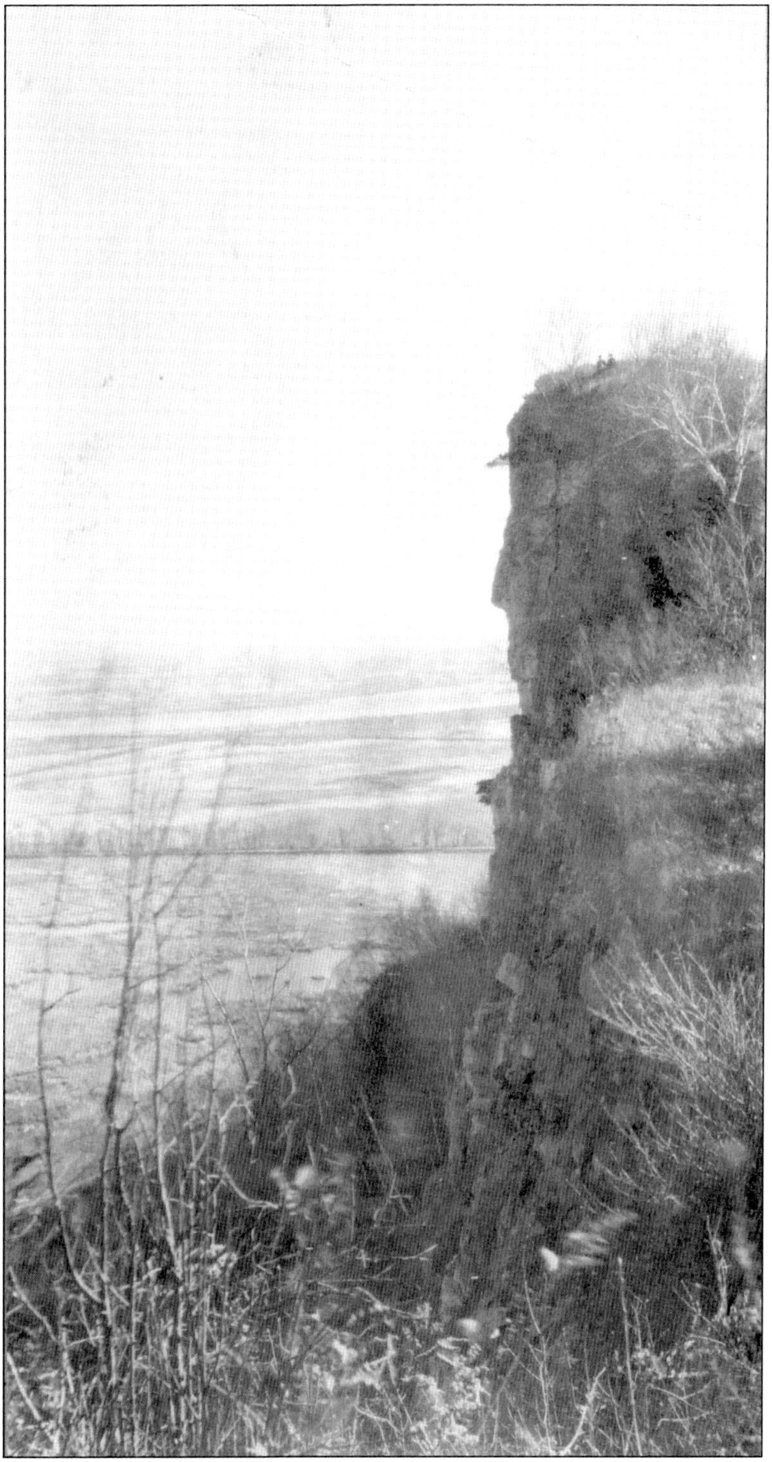

This photograph of the Mississippi River Valley shows the view from the top of the bluffs above Wapasha's Prairie soon after it was settled. This may be similar to the view Zebulon Pike saw when visiting the region.

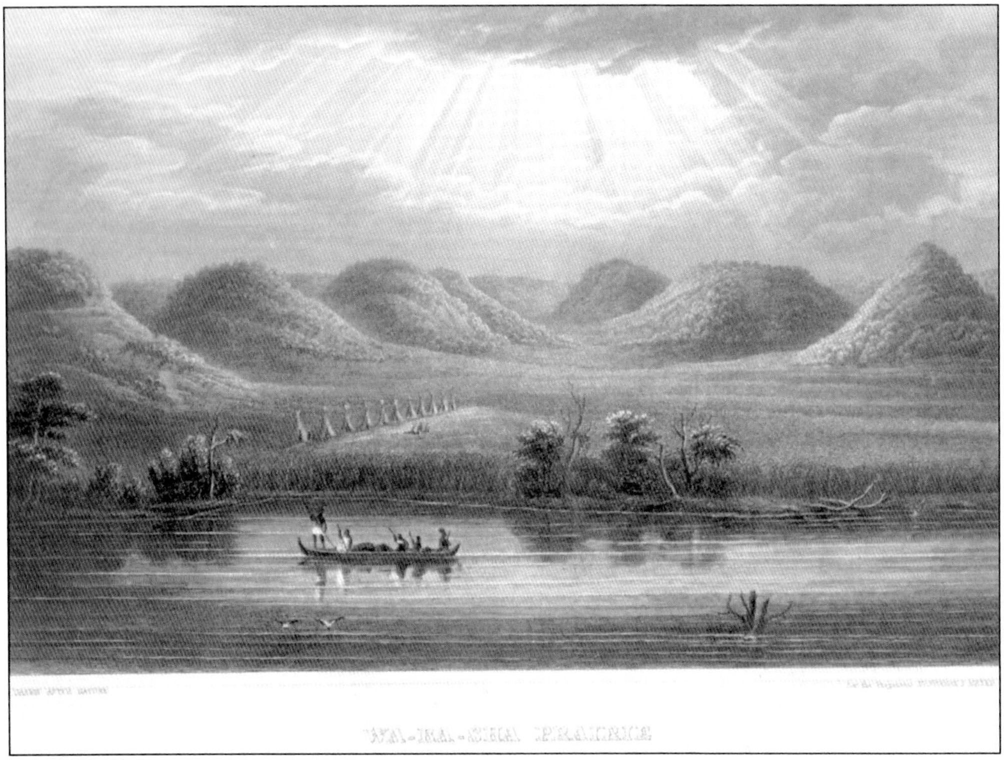

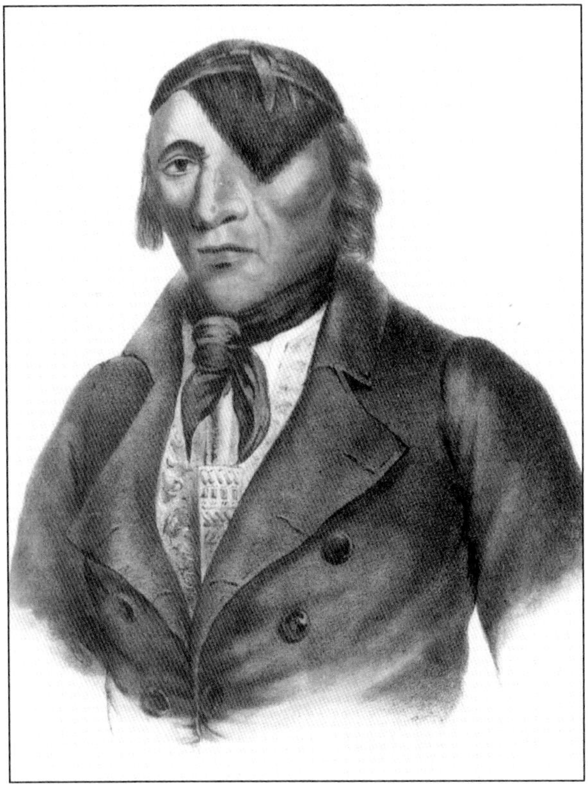

This engraving shows Wapasha's Prairie and the village of Keoxah, or "the Homestead," along the banks of the Mississippi River at the mouth of Burns Valley. The natives are traveling on the river by pushing their canoe along with poles. (Meyer.)

Wapasha II (1786–1836) moved his band to Wing Prairie in the spring of 1817. The large rock formation that looked like his father's red cap may have influenced the selection of the site. Wapasha I had supported the British during the Revolutionary War and was awarded a red cap for his service. Wapasha II had supported the British during the War of 1812. He was born near the mouth of the Upper Iowa River and had assumed the role of chieftain in 1806. The band suffered from a smallpox epidemic, and Wapasha II died in Prairie du Chien while seeking help. (Minnesota Historical Society.)

James Allen Reed (1794–1873) was a government farmer and custodian of supplies for the Wapasha Band. He was born in Kentucky and served in the military at Fort Crawford in Prairie du Chien. Reed was married three times to Indian women and outlived them all. In 1844, he built a log cabin on the sandbar called Wapasha's Prairie by the edge of the river. Lafayette Bunnell, who was living nearby in Homer, assisted him. This cabin was located at the foot of Center Street in present-day Winona. The cabin was finished with sawn lumber, which Reed later used in his home in Trempealeau, Wisconsin.

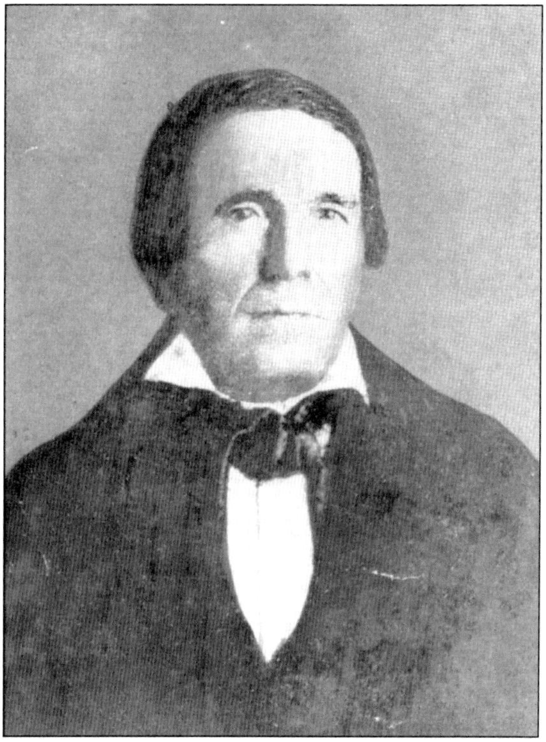

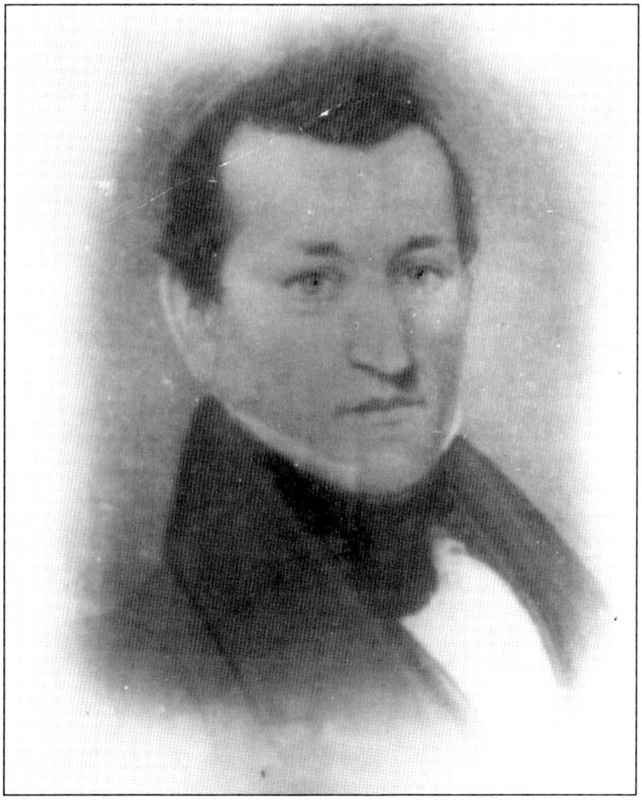

Capt. Orrin T. Smith (1806–1881) plied the Mississippi in his steamboat between Galena, Illinois, and Fort Snelling to supply the fort. Smith was born in New York and moved west with his parents in 1812. In 1823, he moved to Galena, Illinois, where he engaged in lead mining and smelting. In 1835, Smith purchased his first steamboat and engaged in river commerce. With the Treaty of Mendota being signed, he dropped off Erwin Johnson and two others to claim Wapasha Prairie with the intention of building a city.

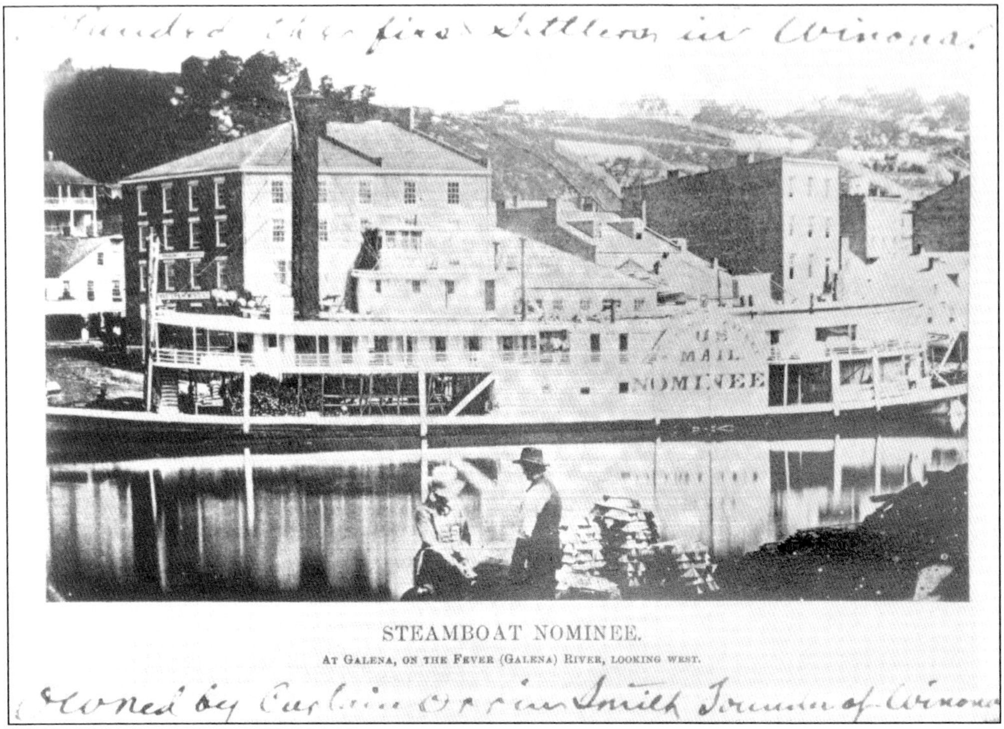

In this photograph, Capt. Orrin Smith's steamboat can be seen tied up at its homeport of Galena, Illinois. The *Nominee* was a packet boat and carried mail and supplies on the Mississippi River as far north as Fort Snelling, which was located at the mouth of the Minnesota River.

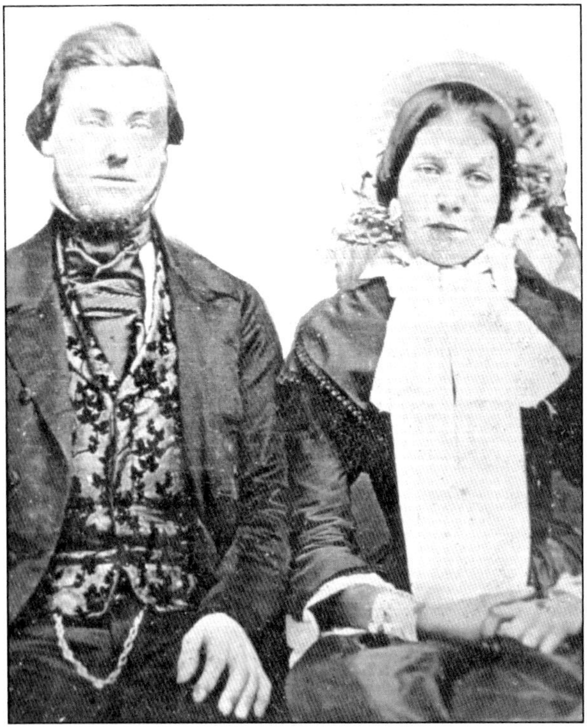

This photograph shows Erwin H. Johnson (1829–1867) with his wife, Abigail (Evans) Johnson. Erwin Johnson was the first resident of Wapasha's Prairie. He was born in Canada and employed by Orrin Smith as a ship's carpenter. Captain Smith had an agreement with Erwin Johnson and two other men to drop them off on Wapasha's Prairie at 10:00 p.m. on October 15, 1851, in order to claim the island. A claim shanty was built near the foot of present-day Mankato Avenue, and it was defended against competitors, including Willard Bunnell of nearby Homer. A few more hardy men joined Johnson, and in 1852, he had John Ball survey and plat the town. More settlers came in, including Abigail Evans, whom Johnson married in 1853. In 1856, Johnson purchased a steamboat and later took up farming.

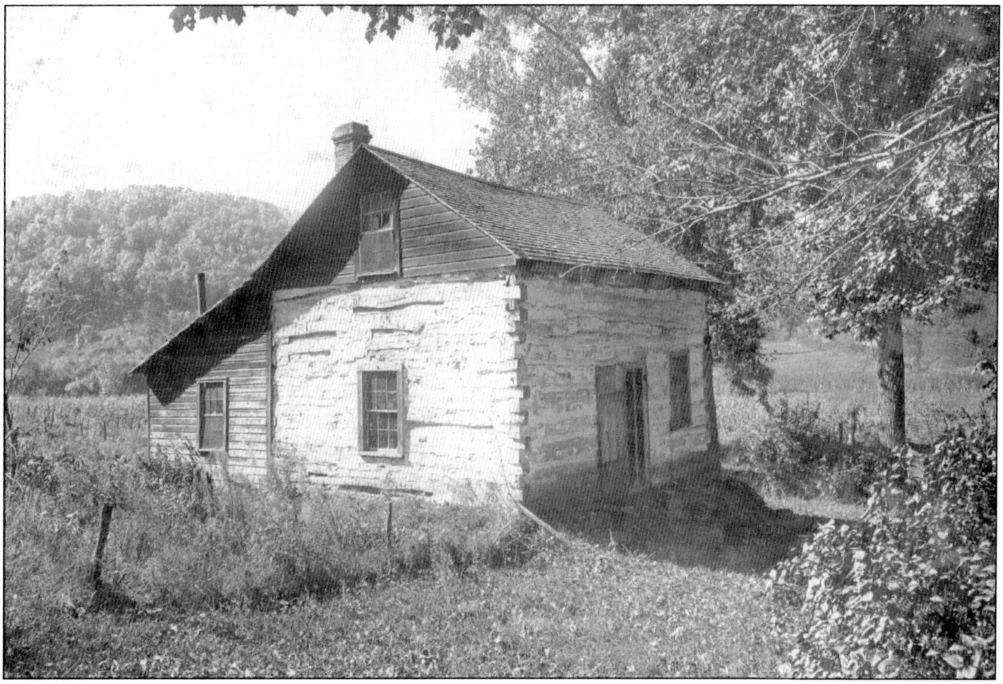

After the Treaty of Mendota was ratified and the Indians were exiled to western Minnesota, many settlers flooded the area to homestead and build cabins similar to this one, which was found in Cedar Valley.

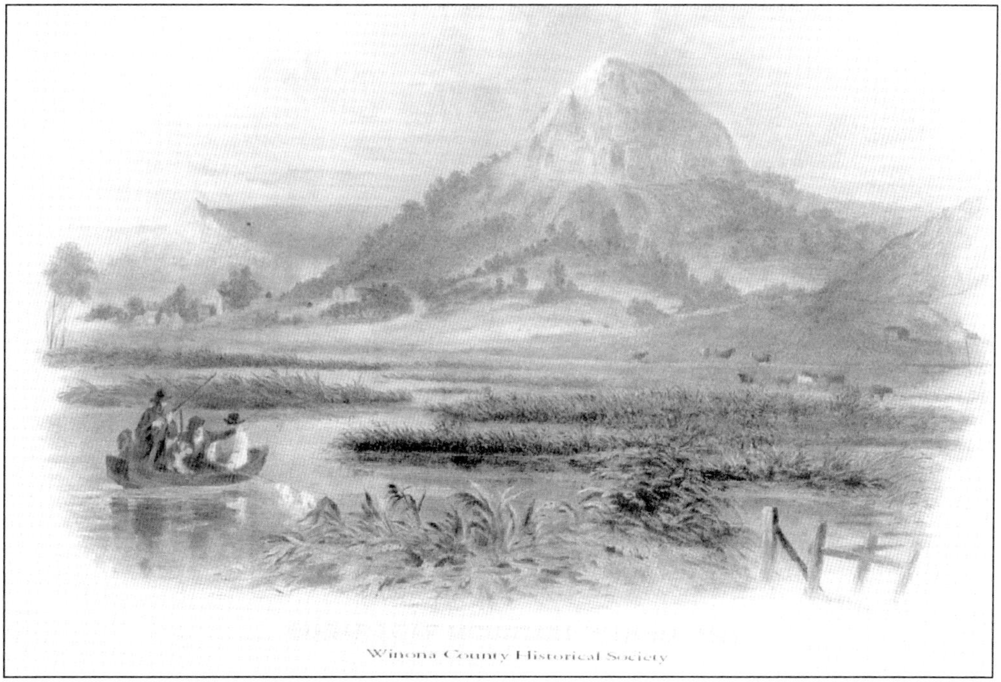

Wapasha's Cap, the large rock formation near the southeastern end of Wapasha's Prairie, was named for the red cap Wapasha I had received from the British for his service. Keoxah had been abandoned, and the white settlers occupied the land, building houses and fences. (Momberg.)

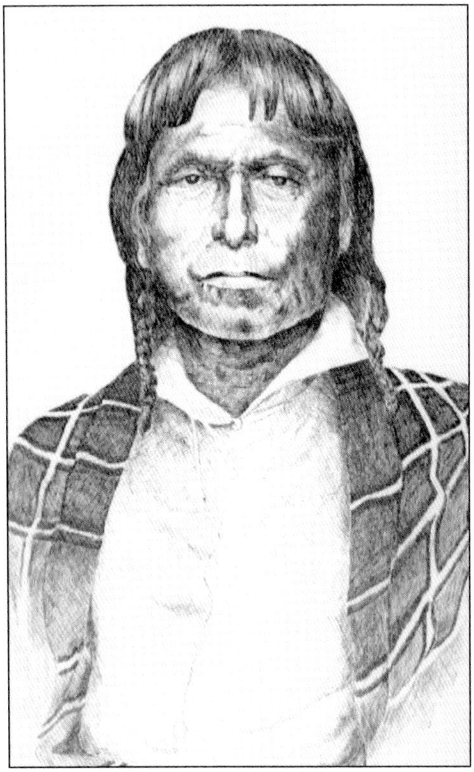

Wapasha III (1816–1876) was born just before the band had moved to Wapasha's Prairie. He assumed the role of chieftain when his father died in 1836. He had a hand in negotiating away the lands east of the Mississippi River, and in 1851, he negotiated away the lands west of the river. Late in 1853, Wapasha III and most of his band were exiled to western Minnesota, and after the Dakota War of 1862—which Wapasha III opposed—he and his band were sent to the Santee Reservation in Nebraska, where he died.

Small families of Native Americans used a typical Winnebago hut, which remained behind after the forced exodus to western Minnesota, and could be found in secluded spots in the countryside.

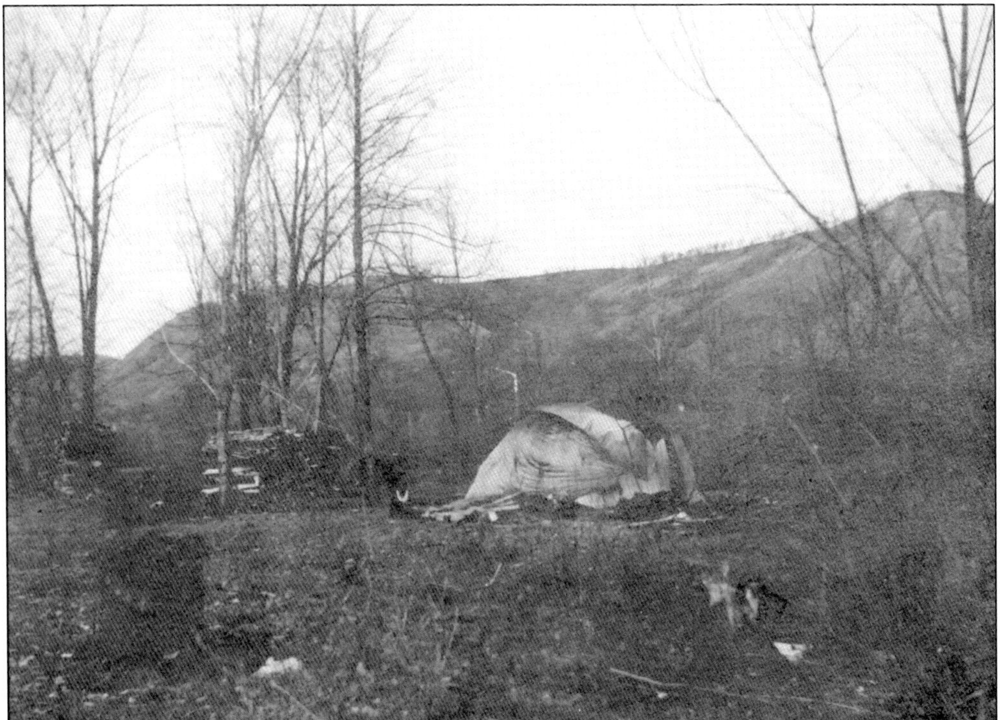

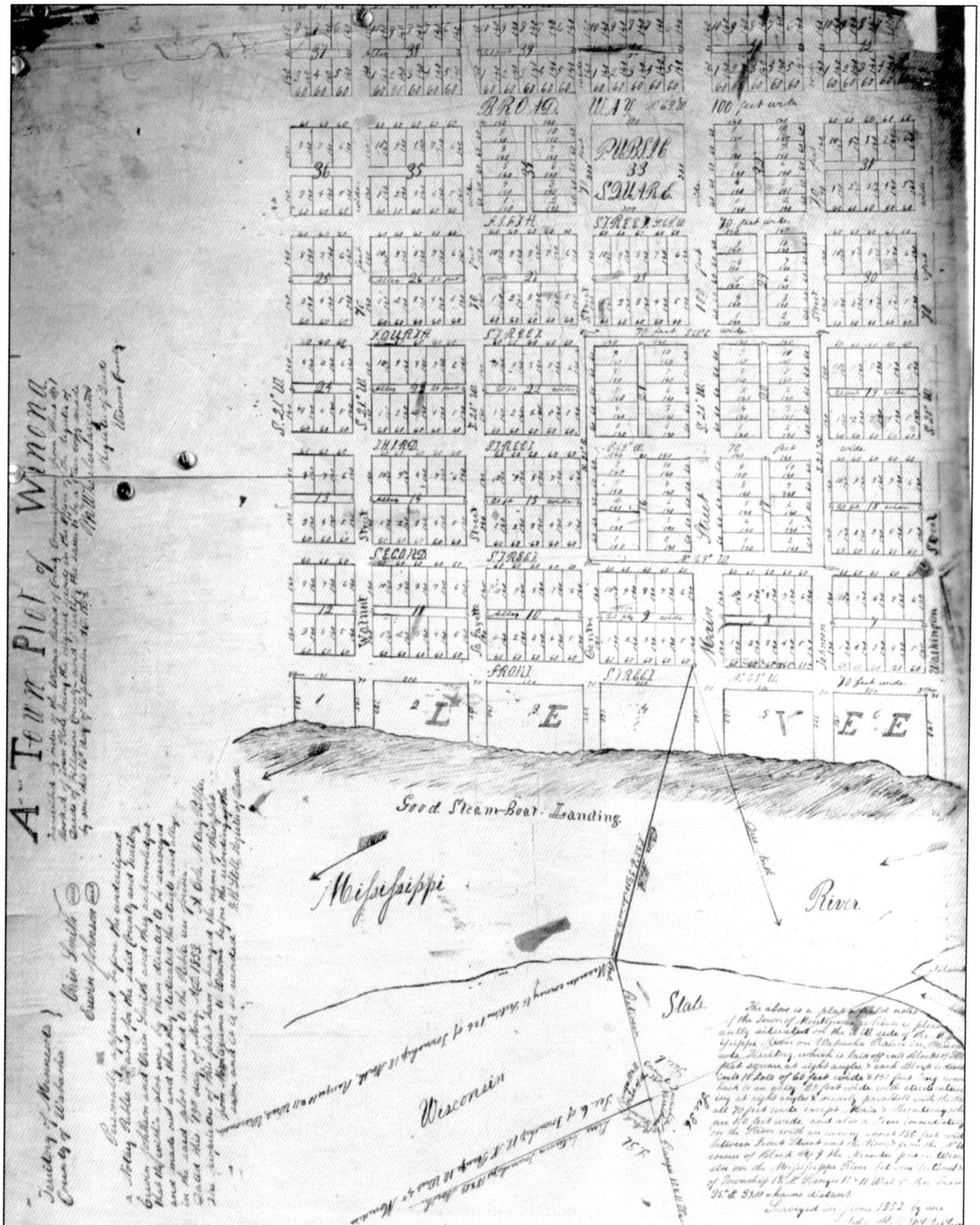

John Ball surveyed the town plat of Winona in June 1852 for Orrin Smith, Erwin Johnson, and Henry Huff. It was registered on September 16, 1854, in Fillmore County, Minnesota Territory, because Winona County had not yet been created. Since no government surveys had been made on the west side of the river, a point of reference was established across the river in Wisconsin. The city was bounded to the south along Wabasha Street, west to Washington Street, east to Walnut Street, and north to the river. A block strip along the riverfront was designated as a public levee, and a block near the south was designated as a public square.

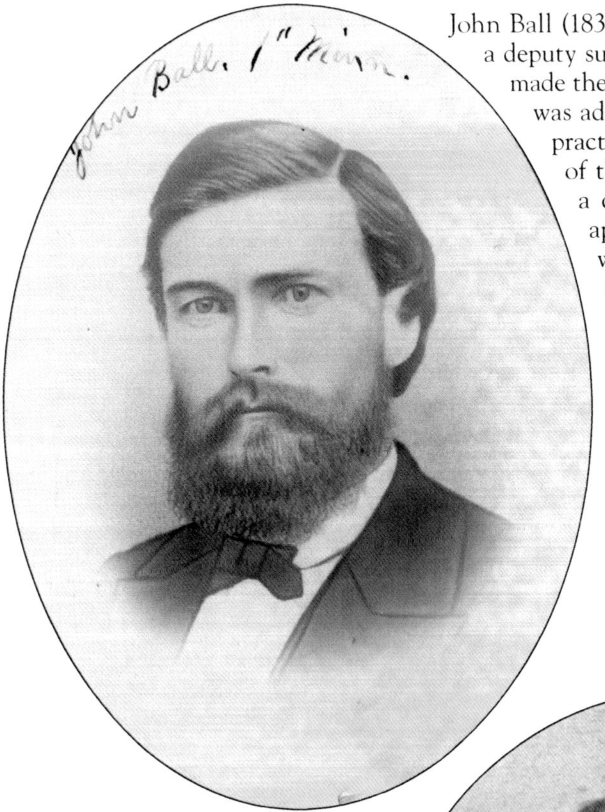

John Ball (1835–1875) was born in New York, was a deputy surveyor for the US government, and made the original plat for Winona in 1852. He was admitted to the bar in 1860, but never practiced law. He enlisted in Company K of the 1st Minnesota and soon earned a commission. In May 1863, he was appointed captain of Company F and was wounded at Bristow Station. After the war, he returned to Winona and married Emma Lewton. He started a land abstract business, but his health declined due to his wounds, and he died at the age of 40 at the home of his parents in New York.

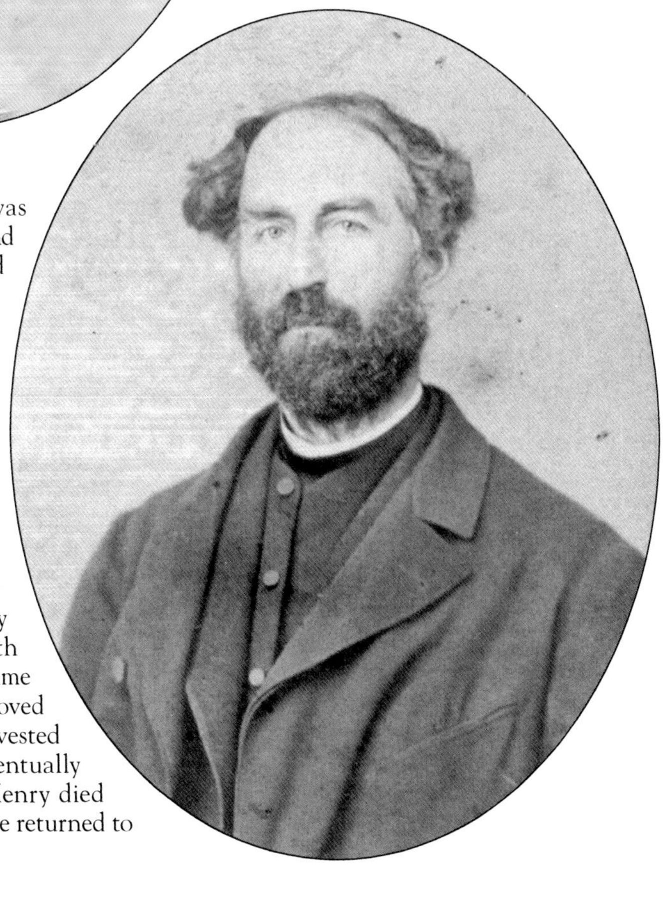

Henry D. Huff (1815–1889) was born in Horsehead, New York, and married Harriet Carpenter around 1830. Before arriving at Wapasha's Prairie in 1853, the couple had lived in Kenosha, Wisconsin. Huff came to Winona as an agent of Orrin Smith and purchased a good share of Edwin Hamilton's claims and interests as well as both Orrin Smith and Erwin Johnson's claims. He came to the area with the idea of developing it into a major trade region. He had his property platted and recorded with Smith and Johnson and suggested the name "Winona." Henry and his wife moved to Chicago in 1872, where he invested in apartments, which were eventually destroyed in the Great Fire. Henry died in Chicago and his remains were returned to Winona for internment.

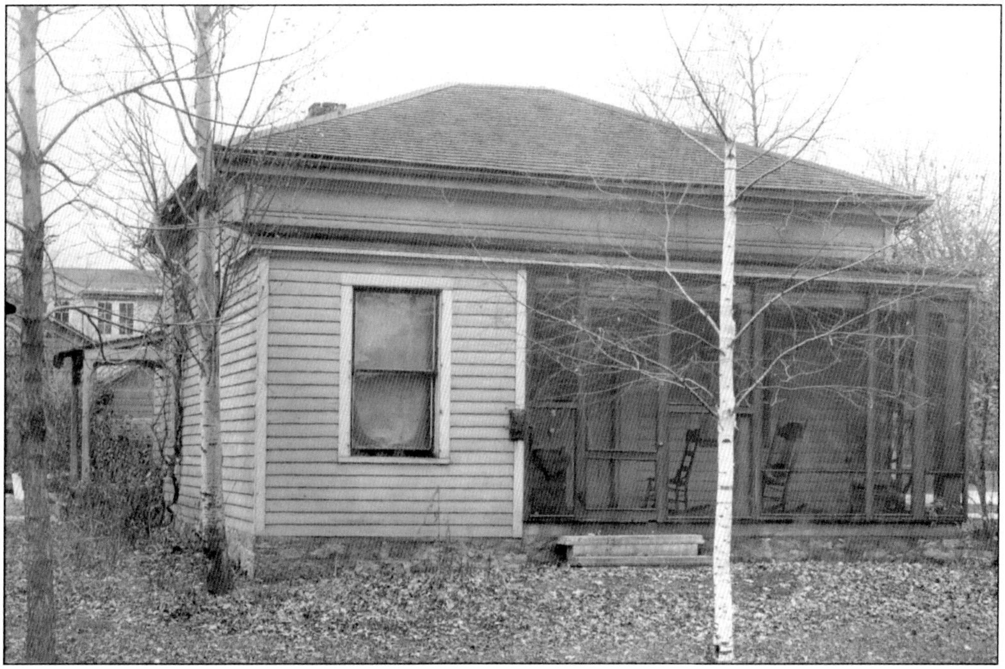

Henry Huff built his first house in Winona in 1853 at the southwest corner of Huff and Fourth Streets. This house remained where it was built until Robert Waldera moved it to 5328 Sixth Street in Goodview, Minnesota, in 1958.

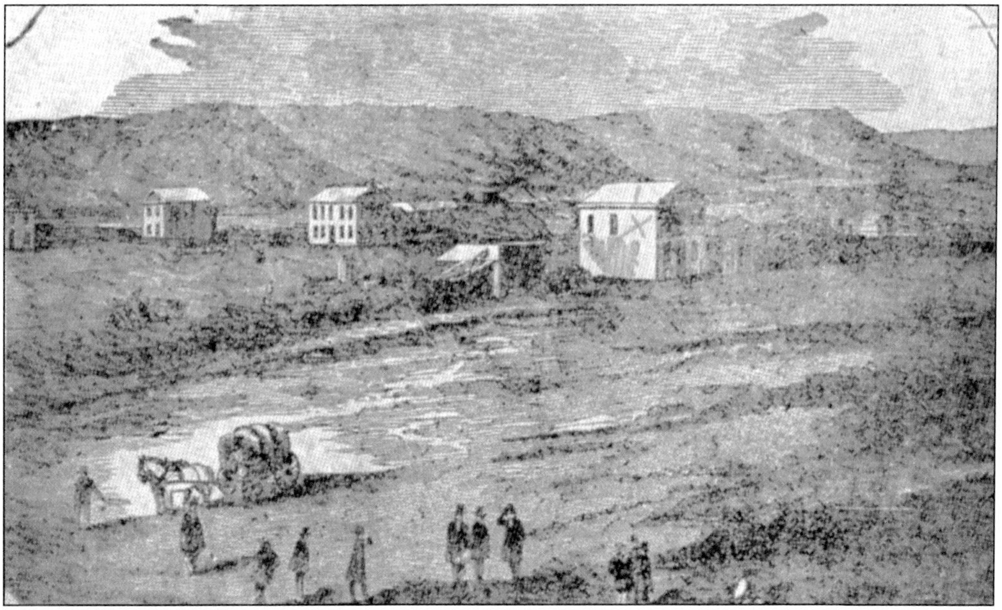

This 1853 view of the city from the levee at the foot of Lafayette Street shows when the town consisted of a half-dozen buildings, more or less. In the foreground at Front and Center Streets is the Viets' House, built by Byron Viets, which was the first hotel on the prairie. Next in line going south on Center Street is the Minnesota House, which was constructed by A.B. Smith in 1853. Further to the south along Center Street is the Edward Ely residence to the right and the first newspaper office, the *Winona Argus*, to the right.

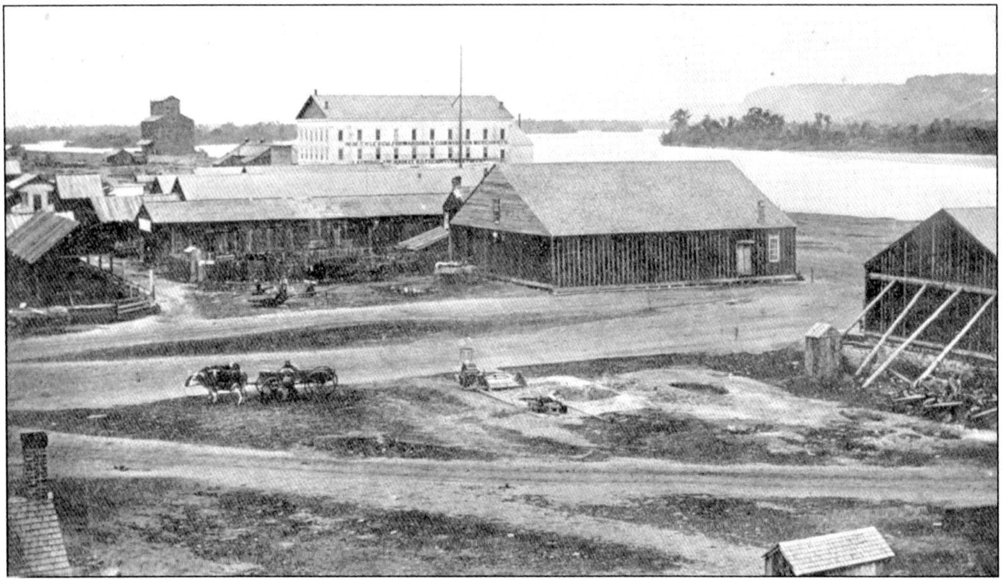

This 1856 view shows the Winona Levee looking toward the levee along Lafayette Street. The large building in the background was the home of the first bank in Winona, which eventually became the First National Bank.

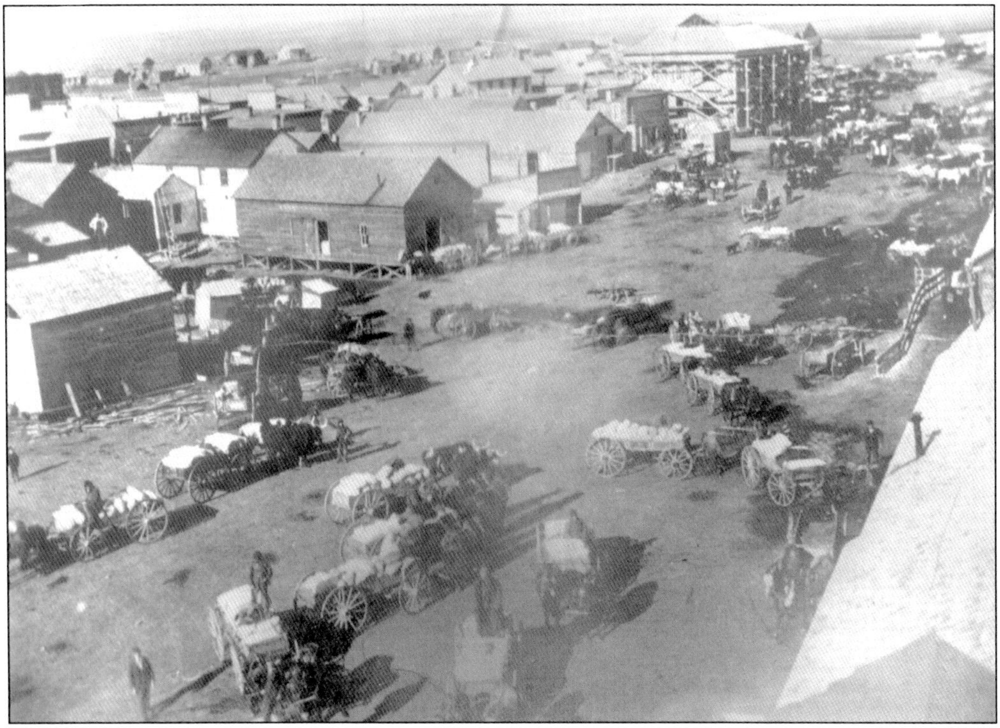

The levee is seen in this photograph looking upriver from Main Street. The large, white building in the background is Sanborn's Warehouse, which had a public hall on the top floor. The building was constructed by George Sanborn in 1855 and occupied by Joseph and Marshall Ehle, who were forwarding and commissioning agents. The third floor of Sanborn's Warehouse was being used by the newly formed German Dramatic Society.

Two

A New Community is Formed

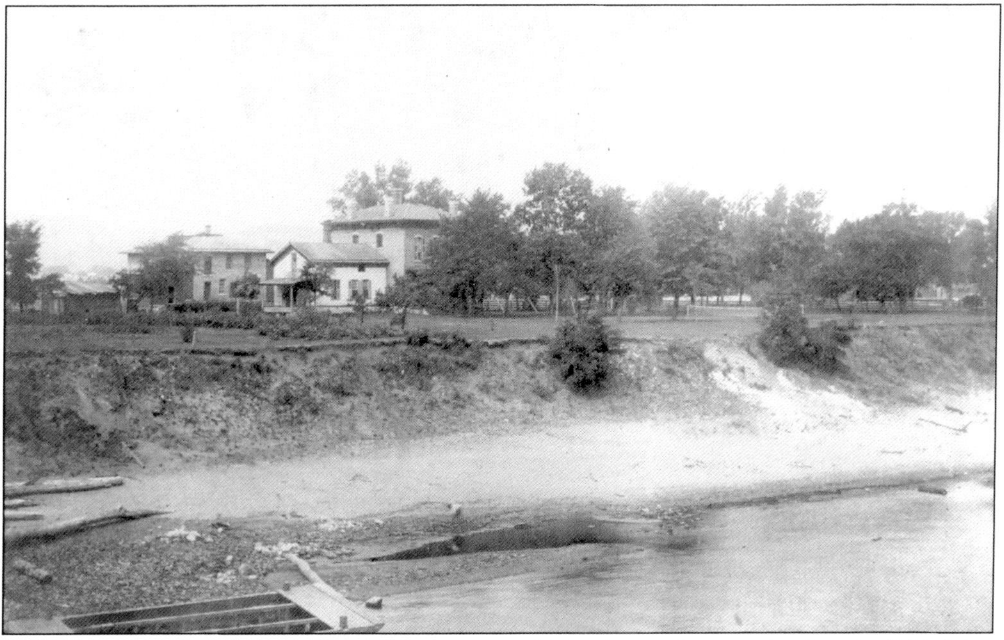

The sandbar known as Wapasha's Prairie appeared like this at the water's edge. In 1854, John Keyes (1819–1876) and his family settled at the far eastern end of the platted community and built a story-and-a-half house. Keyes was an early lawyer who had practiced law with Martin Wheeler Sargeant. Later, a larger house was attached, other homes were built, and trees were planted. (de Groot.)

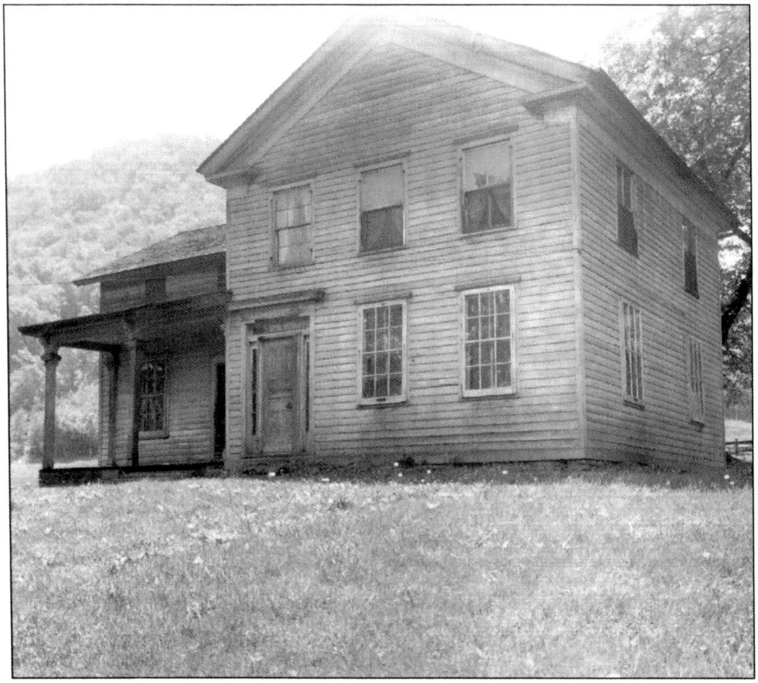

George Washington Clark, one of the earliest settlers to Wapasha's Prairie, settled along the southwest side of Lake Winona. He built his house along present-day Clark's Lane in 1856, and the wing to the left was added later. Due to its decay, the house was razed in the 1970s.

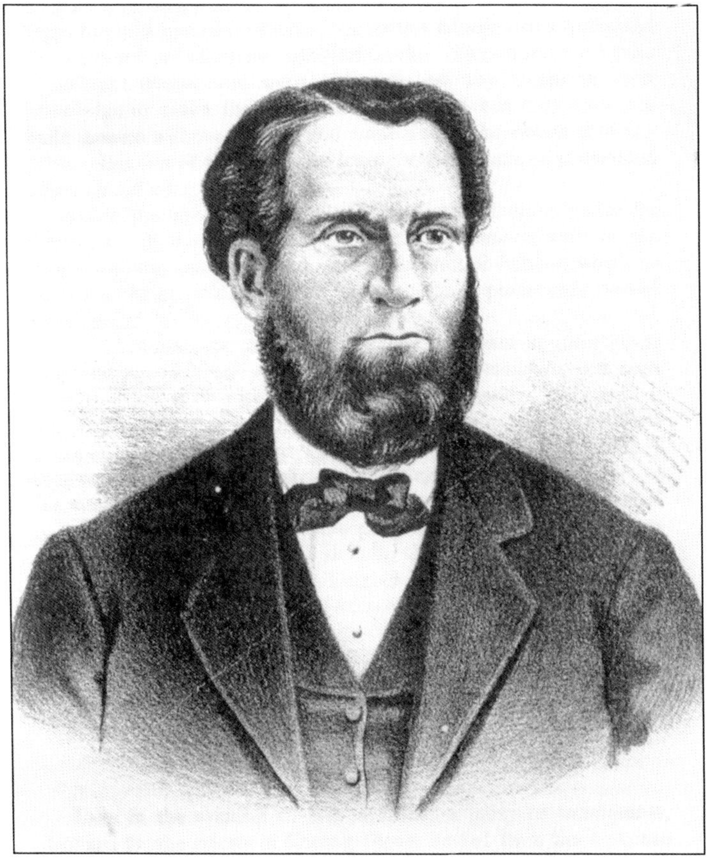

George Washington Clark (1827–1897) was born in New York and in 1851 moved to La Crosse, Wisconsin. Clark, Edwin Hamilton, and Silas Stevens traveled on board the *Excelsior* to Wapasha's Prairie in November 1851, where they found Johnson and Nash. Clark staked his claim at lot number six, west of the other five. However, the following spring, his claim was taken over by John Evens, a late arrival. Clark withdrew from that claim and claimed land across the slough and along the bluffs. Clark was married to Jennie Lockwood, and the couple had seven children.

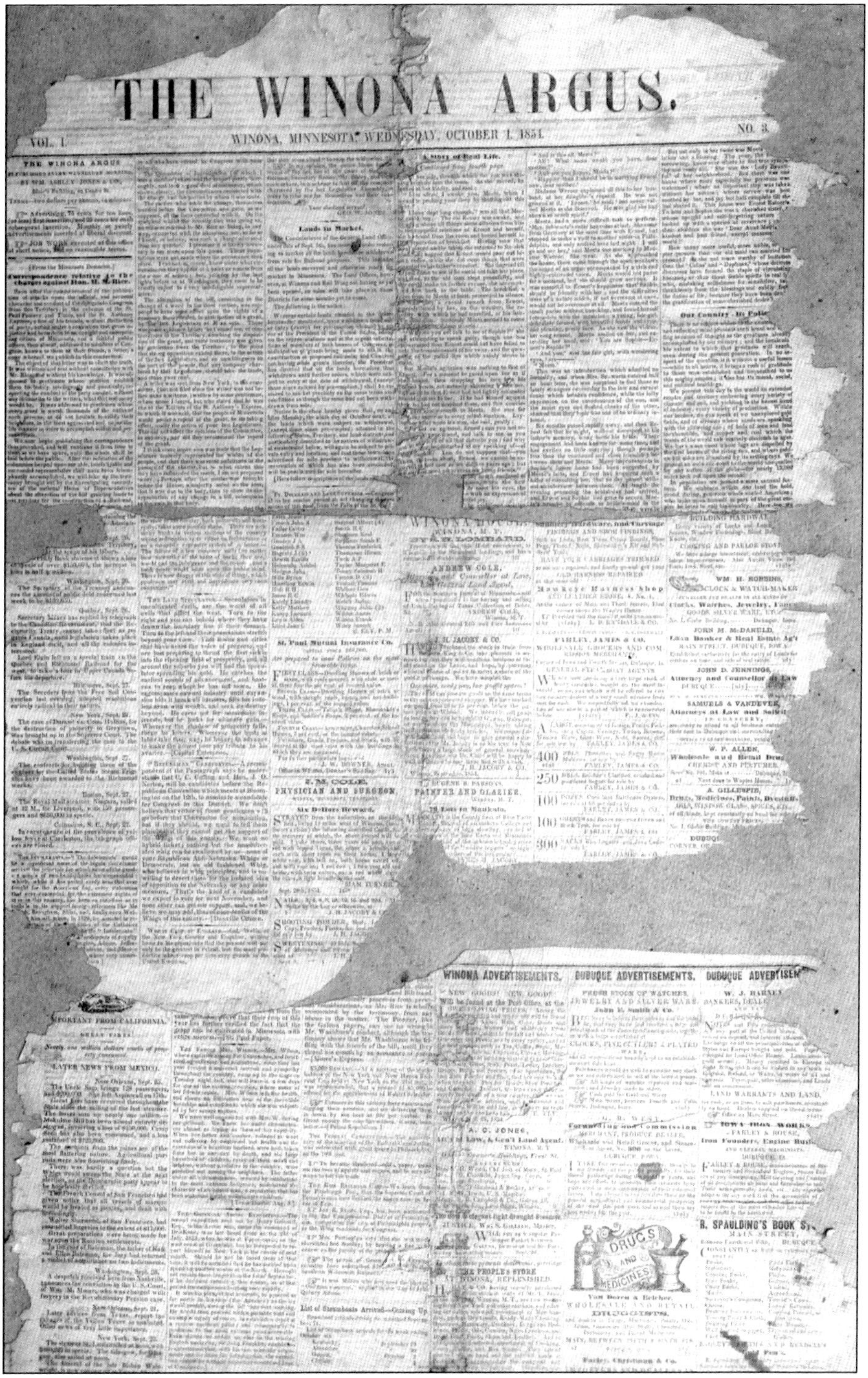

THE WINONA ARGUS.

VOL. I. WINONA, MINNESOTA, WEDNESDAY, OCTOBER 1, 1854. NO. 3.

WINONA ADVERTISEMENTS. DUBUQUE ADVERTISEMENTS.

The *Winona Argus*, volume one, number three, was published on Wednesday, October 1, 1854. William Ashley Jones, a government surveyor and banker, started the *Argus*. The first issue was printed on September 20, 1854. It was published every Wednesday morning until September 3, 1857. The paper was a four-page, six-column sheet with Democratic political leanings.

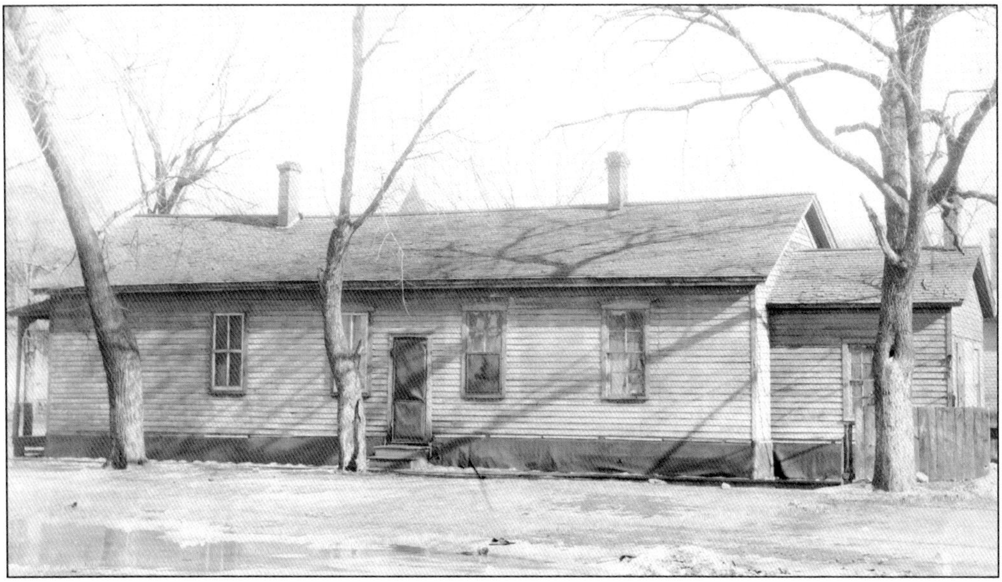

The First Presbyterian Church was originally located in this rude frame building that had been erected in 1856 on East Fourth Street between Lafayette and Walnut Streets. The Presbyterian Society occupied it until 1866, when it was sold to the Unitarian Society, which in turn sold it to Verrazano Simpson. A real estate broker and developer, Simpson had the former church converted into a dwelling.

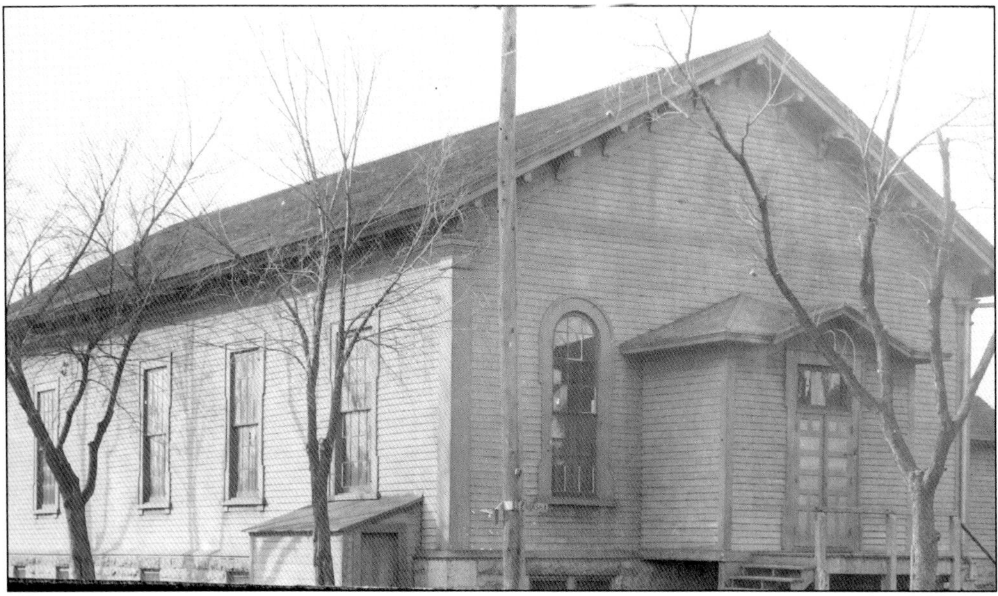

Dr. John Quigley dedicated the Methodist Episcopal Church on November 16, 1856. The church was located on the west side of Lafayette Street between Fifth and Broadway. The congregation later sold its original church after it built a new one. The building was moved to the southwest corner of Wabasha and High Forest Streets and was used as a hall by the Polish Dramatic Society and by the Czech Radecky Society. It was razed in 1937 when the Radecky Society was dissolved.

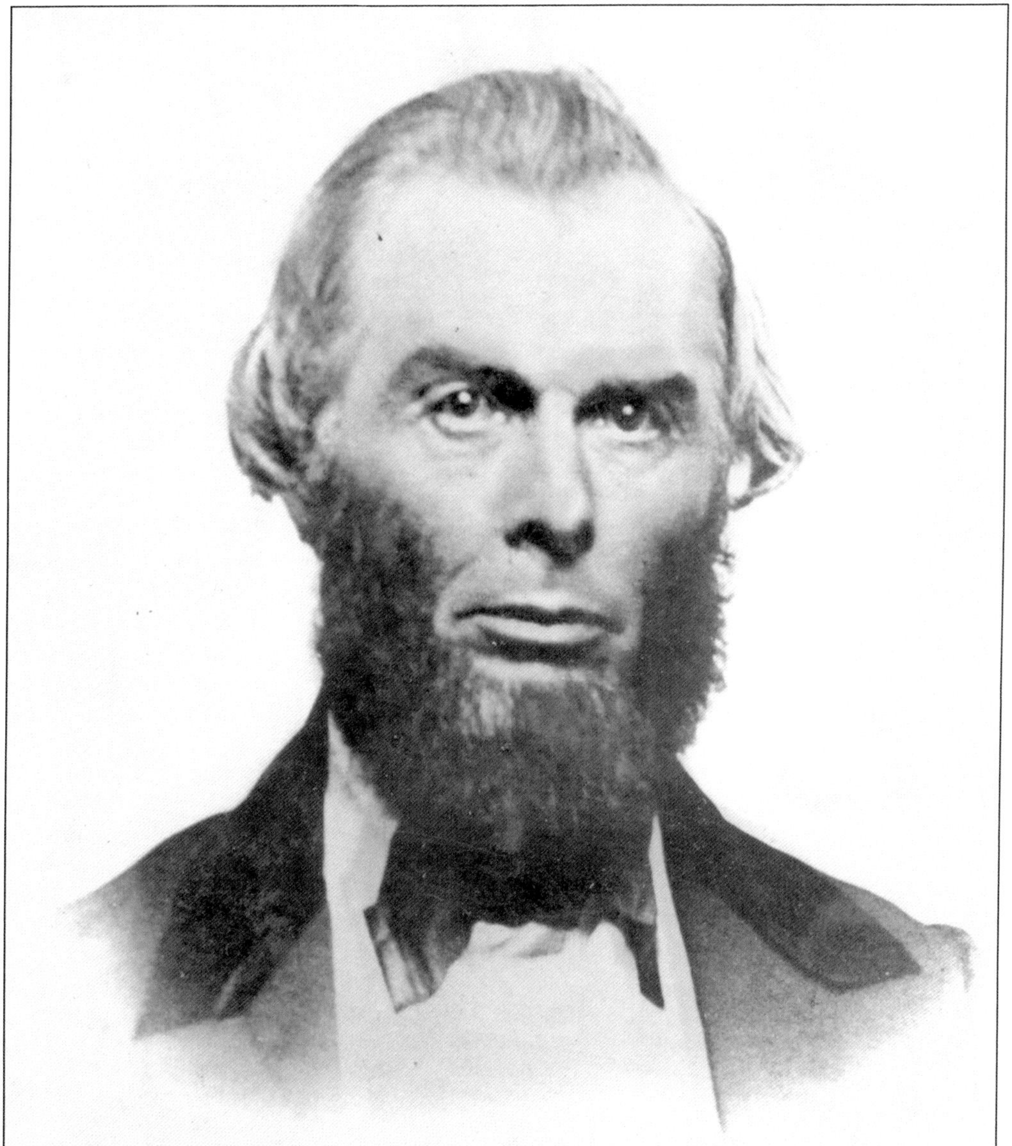

Rev. Hiram S. Hamilton (1811–1871) was born in Massachusetts and moved to Michigan with his family at the age of 18. He studied for the ministry in Ohio and moved to New York prior to 1850. Later, due to poor health, he came to Wapasha's Prairie in 1852 with his wife and two sons. Soon after he arrived to the prairie, he obtained Caleb Nash's claim in a slightly questionable manner. Elder Hamilton was the first member of the clergy to arrive on the prairie and was involved in the organization of the Congregational Church in Winona, of which he was the first preacher. Elder Hamilton sold his property to Henry Huff and left Winona soon after the financial crash of 1857. He moved to Chicago and later back to Michigan, where he died of lung disease.

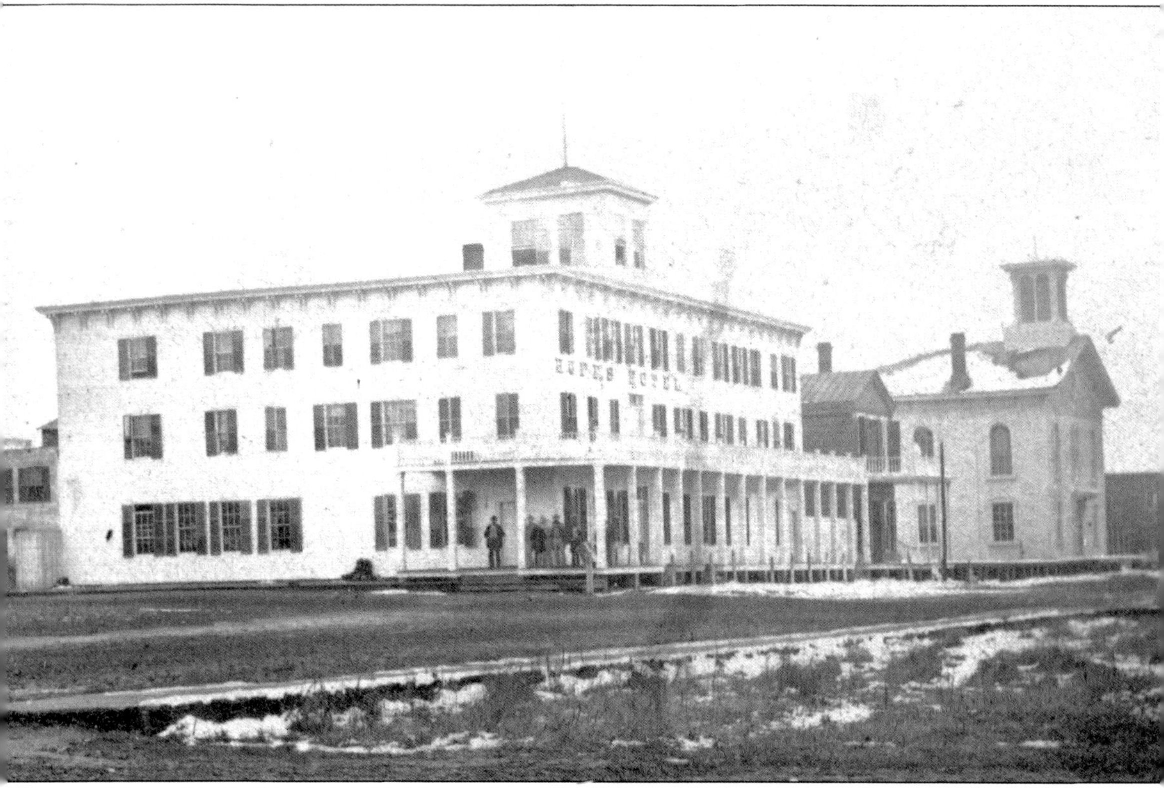

Henry D. Huff built Huff's Hotel, the leading hotel in Winona for 35 years, in 1855 at the southwest corner of Johnson and Third Streets. The hotel was constructed at a cost of $34,000 with 84 sleeping apartments and could accommodate up to 300 guests. The hotel was owned and operated by Francis M. Cockrell, Leroy R. Hawthorne, and Ezekiel D. Williams until 1861, when Hawthorne sold his share to Cockrell and Williams. After Williams was killed in an explosion in 1872, Cockrell became the sole owner. The hotel was closed in 1889 and cut into quarters. Each quarter was moved so another larger hotel could be built on its location. The large building with a cupola by the hotel was the first courthouse.

Register ledgers from Huff's Hotel were donated to the Winona County Historical Society by the Winona Public Library in 1962. The collection of 41 volumes dates from June 5, 1856, to May 1899 and was in the possession of the public library for years. Alberta Seiz, Winona librarian, and Merrill O. Holland, chairman of the Winona County Historical Society curator's committee, are pictured examining one of the volumes.

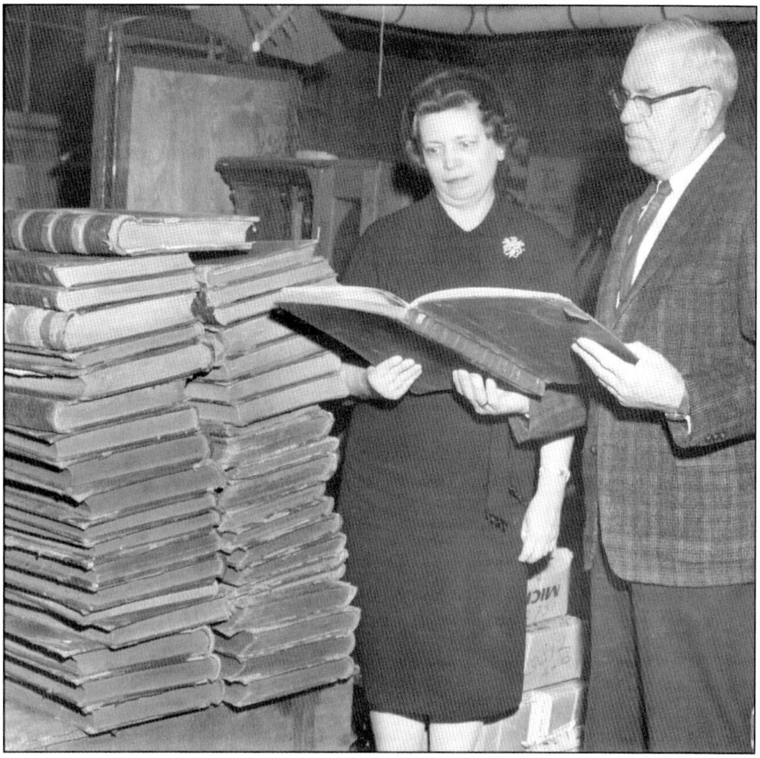

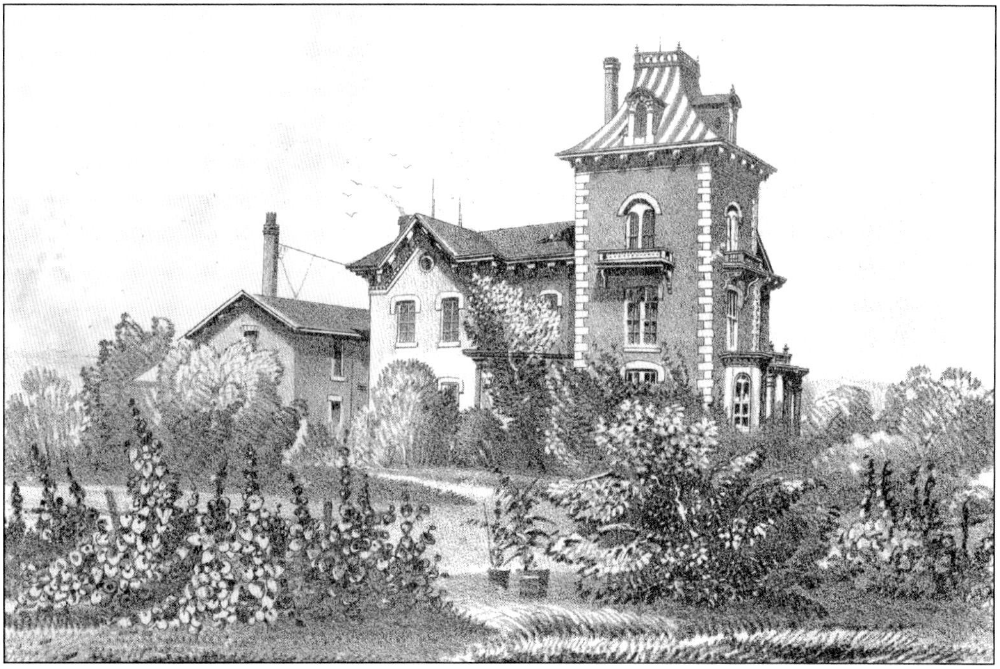

Henry Huff's Chateau on the Frontier was constructed in 1858 of local brick, stone, and wood; however, many special pieces were imported from back east. The mansion was built on the highest piece of land in Winona at that time. The widow's walk at the top of the tower allowed Huff to watch river traffic and Indian attacks.

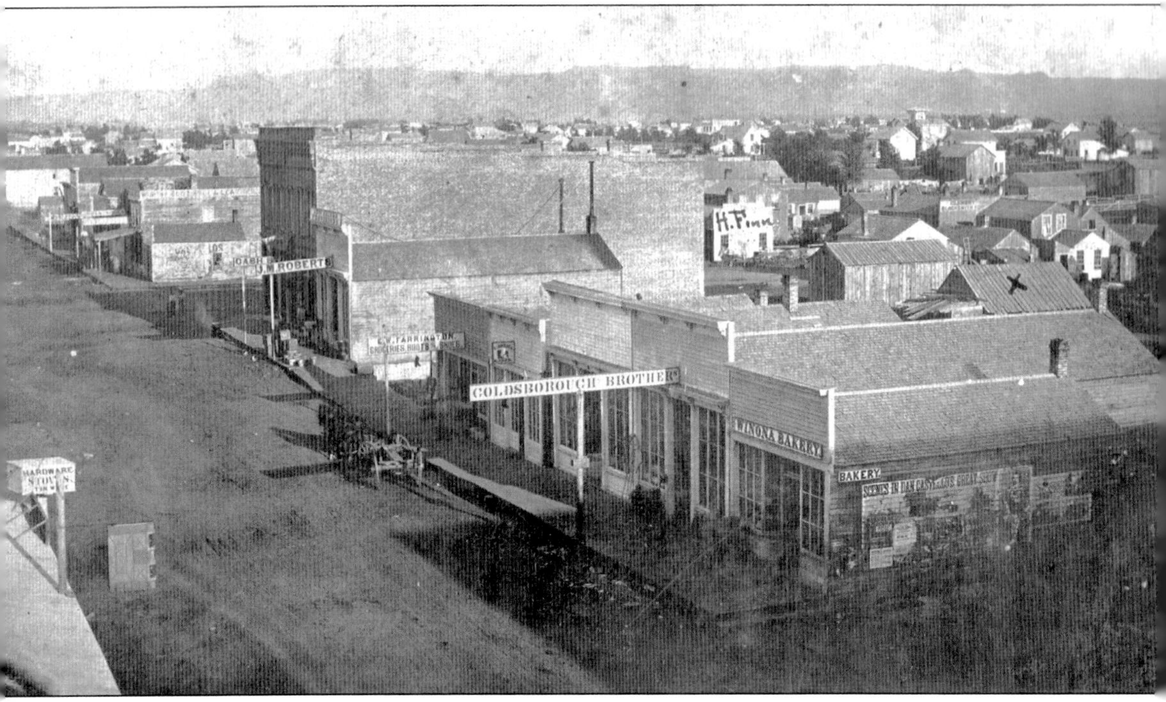

This 1858 photograph of Winona looks east along Second Street from Center to Lafayette Streets, showing some businesses along the south side of the street, including Robert Clapperton's Winona Bakery; Charles and Henry Goldsborough, dealers in provisions; James E. Mitten, boot maker; Orlando M. Farrington's hardware store; Joseph M. Roberts's grocery store; and Ralph Cavenaugh, boot maker. The sign on the north side of the street is the location of Royal D. Cone's hardware store. The "X" mark on the shed to the right is the site where the fire of 1862 started.

Three

Crossing the Great River

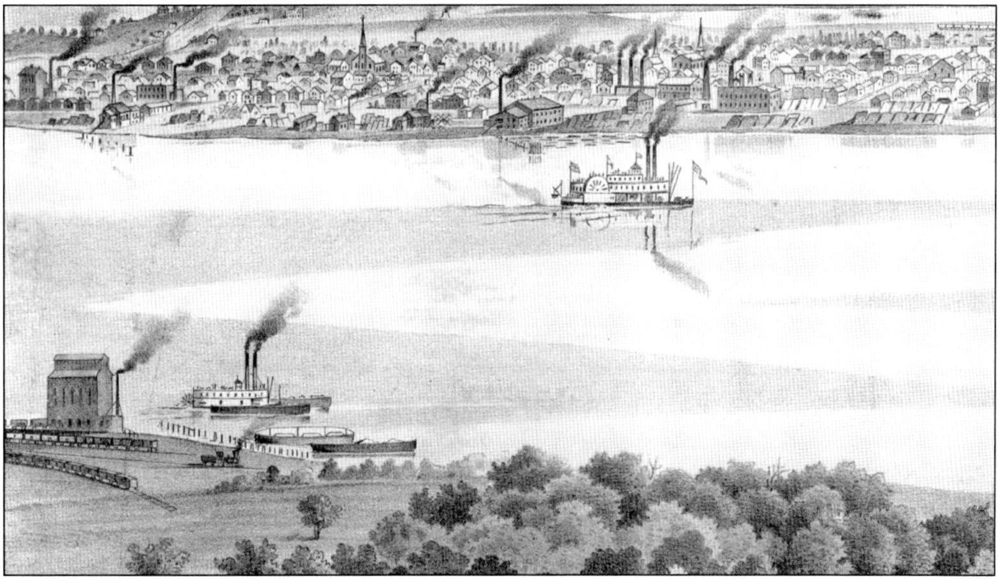

As Winona grew, the Mississippi River became a barrier for conducting commerce, as all goods had to be transferred across it before moving by railroad eastward. Likewise, all goods coming to Winona by railroad must be transferred to boats before getting to Winona. In the foreground is the Green Bay & Minnesota Railway's elevator and railroad siding. (Ellsbury.)

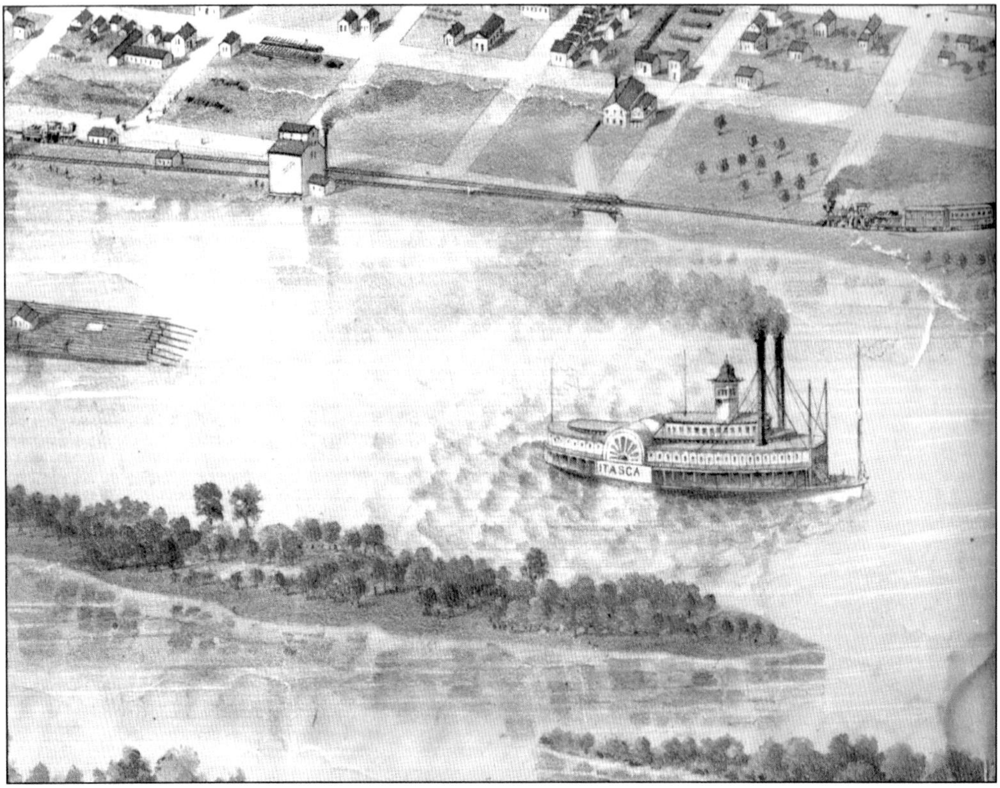

In the early years, the Mississippi River was a barrier and limited access to Winona to travel by boat. (Ruger.)

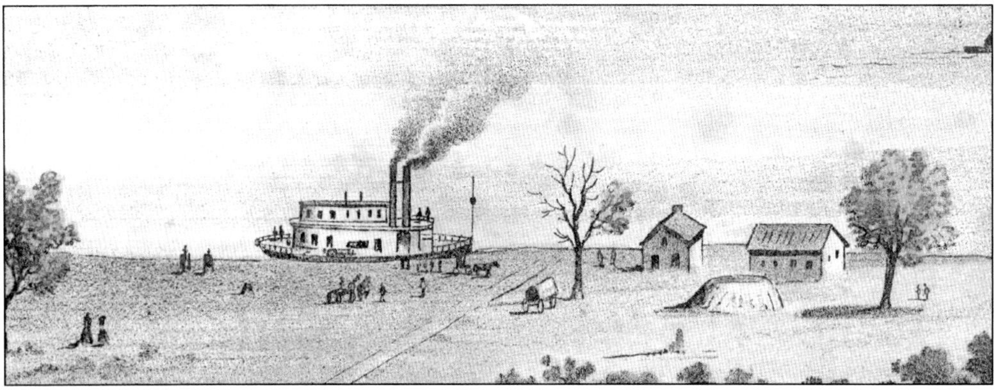

In order to cross the Mississippi River, a ferry service was established in the early 1850s. However, the service was sporadic until 1865, when Samuel D. Van Gorder started a ferry service from Wisconsin to Winona. (Andreas.)

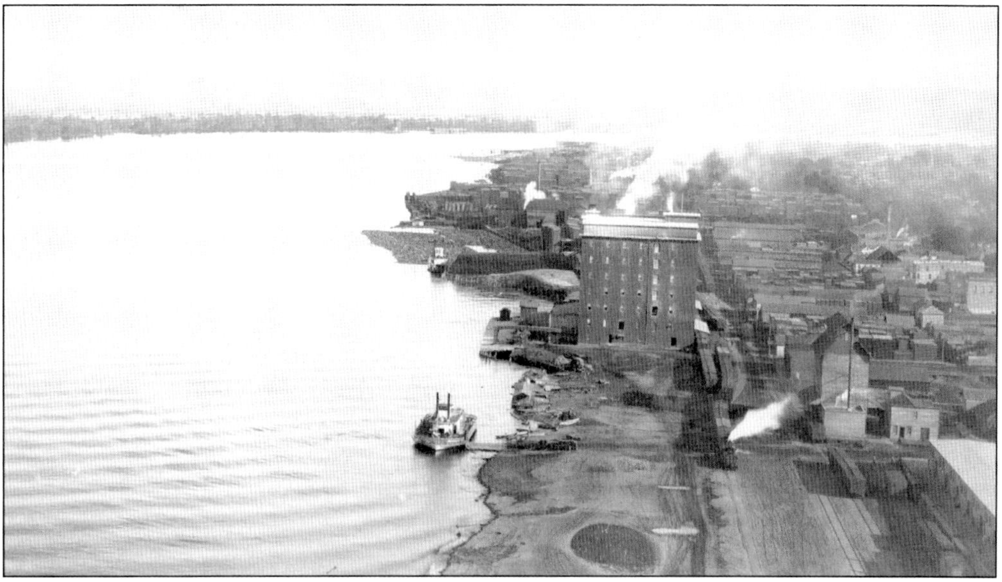

Samuel D. Van Gorder's ferryboat, the *Van Gorder*, would stop along the levee at his floating dock at the foot of Walnut Street. The large building along the river is the Winona Milling Company's steam-powered flourmill, which began operations in 1880 and was said to be the largest in the United States at the time. The rail tracks belong to the Winona & St. Peter Railroad Company. (Tenney.)

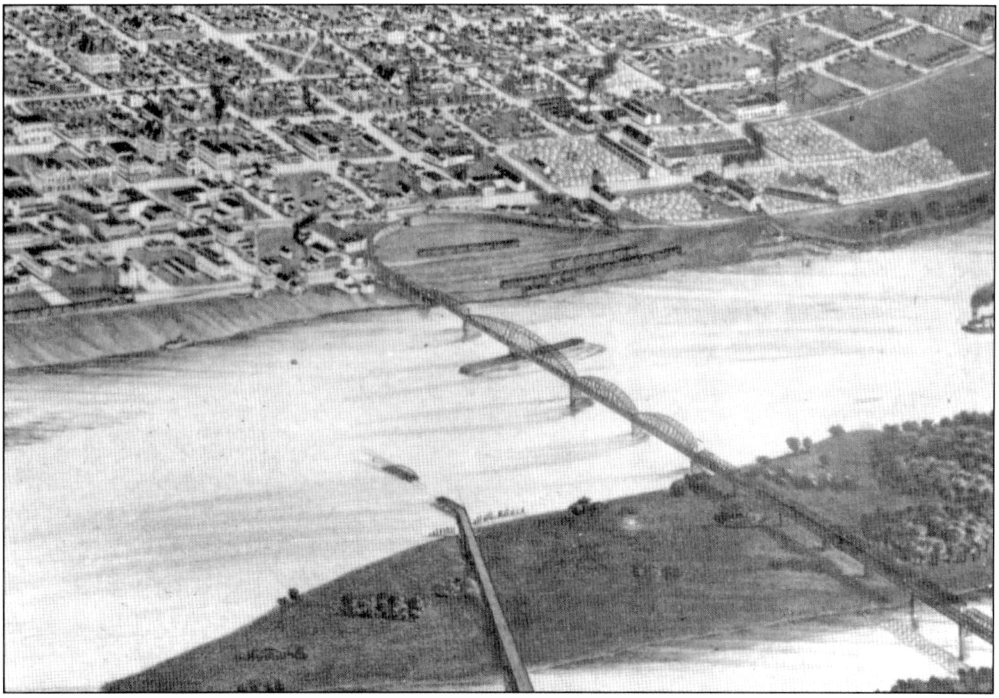

The Winona & St. Peter Railroad had the first railroad swing bridge built across the Mississippi in the region in 1872. At 363 feet, it was said to be the longest of its kind in the world at the time of its construction. The Wisconsin end of Van Gorder's ferry is also shown, with a roadway and bridges constructed across the bottomland to Latsch Island. (Andreas.)

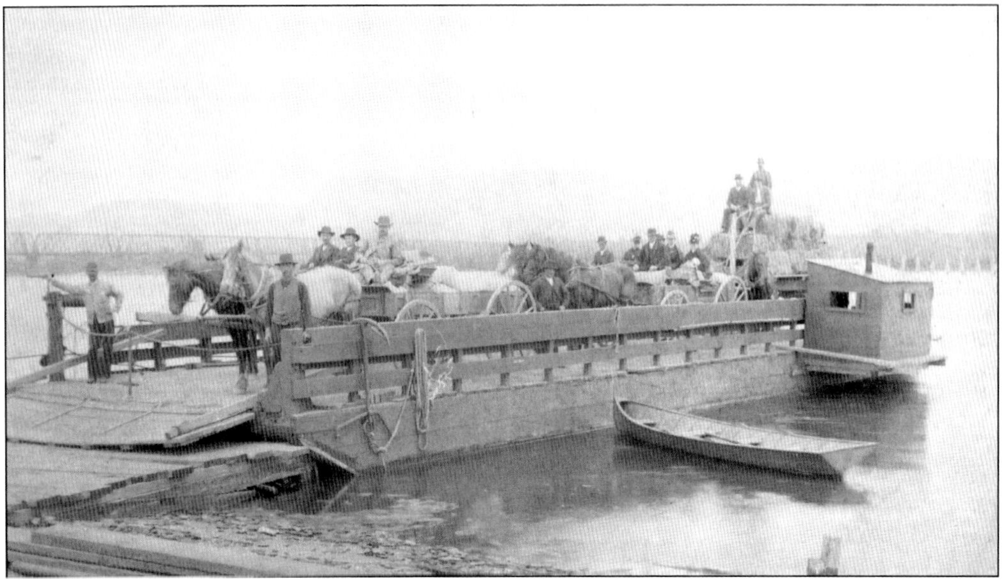

This cable ferry was operated by the City of Winona between March 17, 1887, and July 4, 1892, when the steel high bridge went into operation.

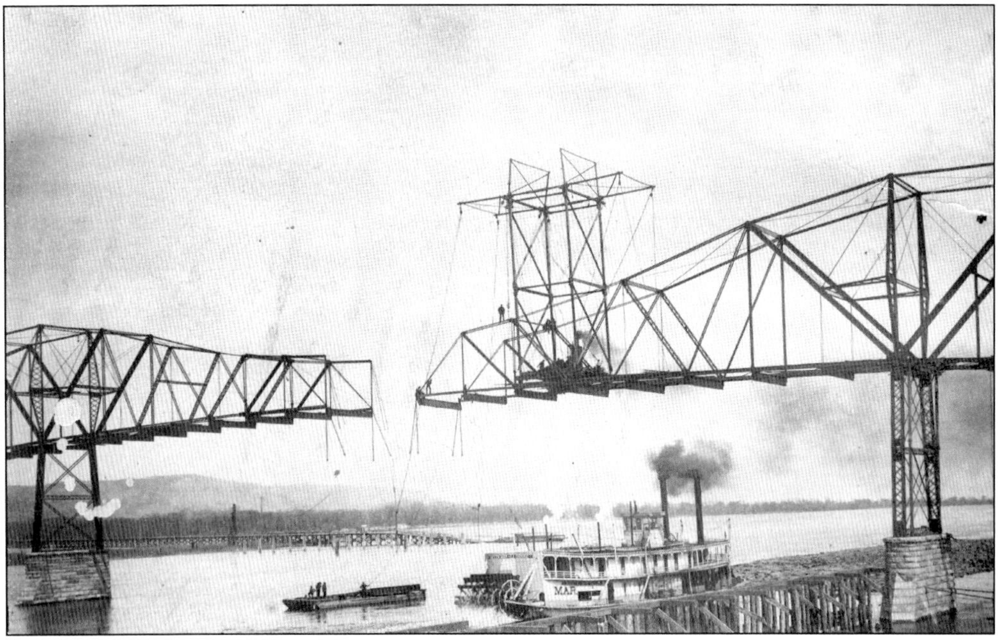

The steel High Wagon Bridge, pictured under construction in 1891 by the Chicago Bridge and Iron Company, was completed in June 1892 at a cost of $100,000. It first operated as a toll bridge with charges from 5¢ to 25¢. The paddleboat seen in the construction zone was the steamer *Helen Mar* out of the port of La Crosse.

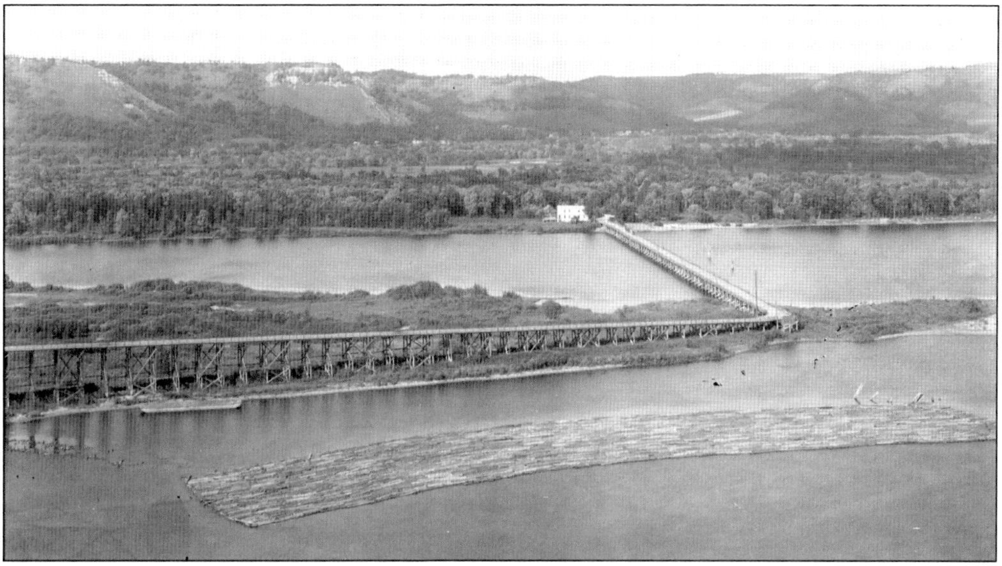

The old ferry bridge went from the old stone house to the steel High Wagon Bridge over the main channel. The original portion of the bridge, seen in the background, was used to take wagons to the Latsch Island ferry landing. The remainder was built as an approach to the High Wagon Bridge. The old Stone House, a former stagecoach stop, is seen in the foreground with a log raft.

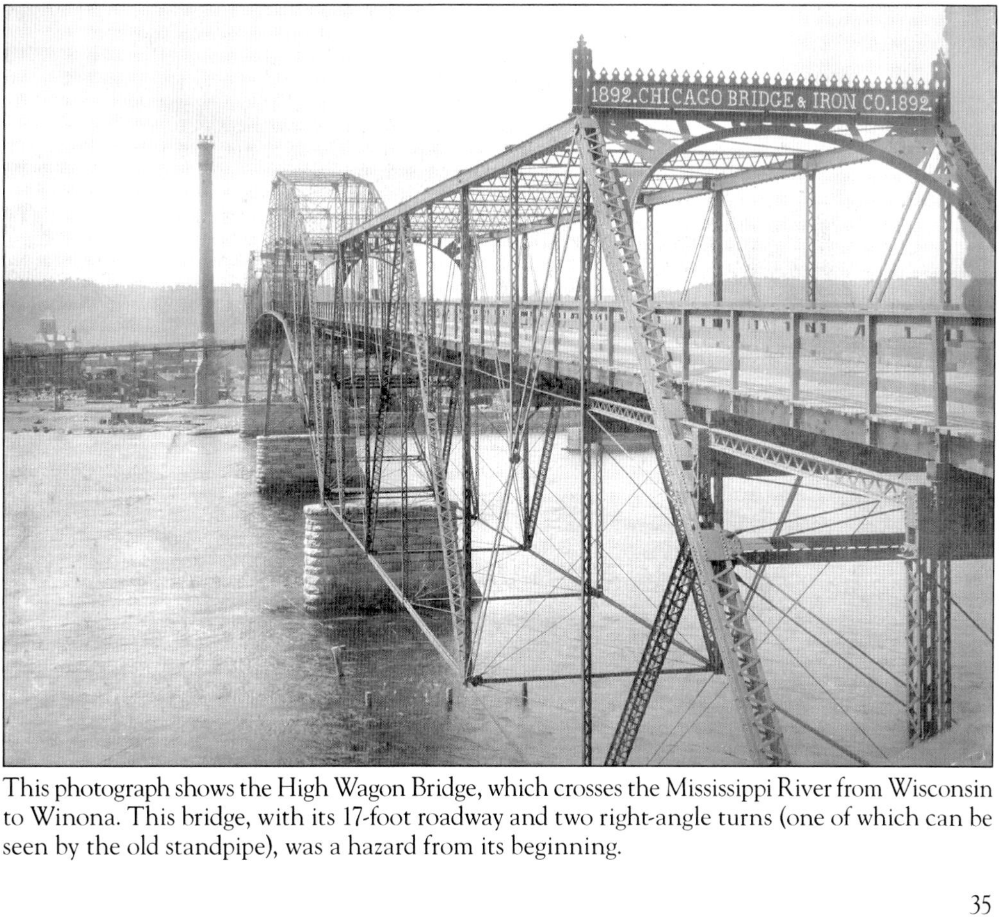

This photograph shows the High Wagon Bridge, which crosses the Mississippi River from Wisconsin to Winona. This bridge, with its 17-foot roadway and two right-angle turns (one of which can be seen by the old standpipe), was a hazard from its beginning.

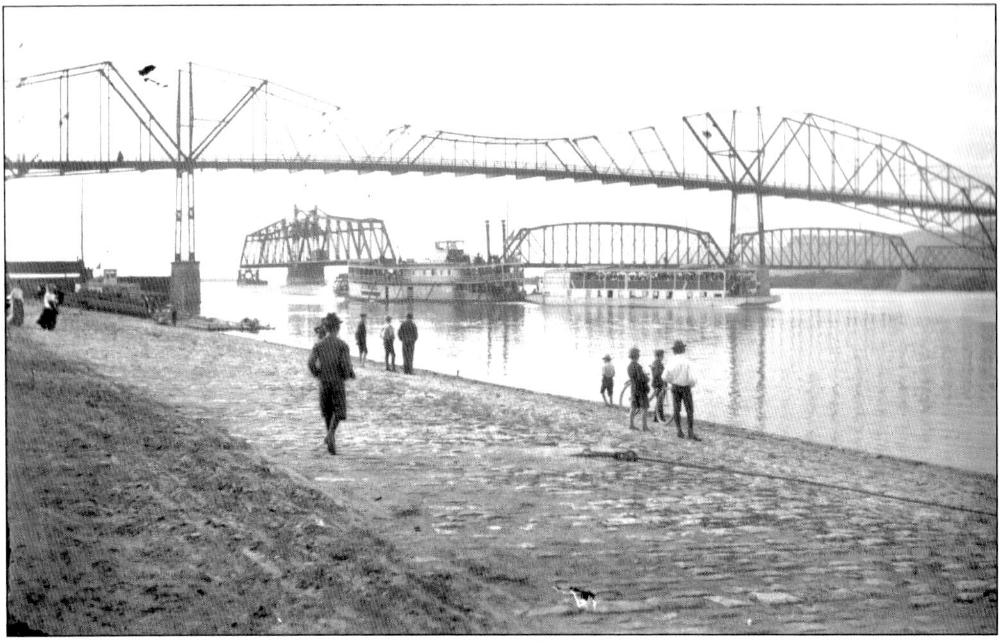

The J.J. Hill excursion paddleboat and barge, the *Twin Cities*, crosses by the swing bridge and under the High Wagon Bridge to stop at the Winona levee in August 1903, picking up excursion passengers for a moonlight ride.

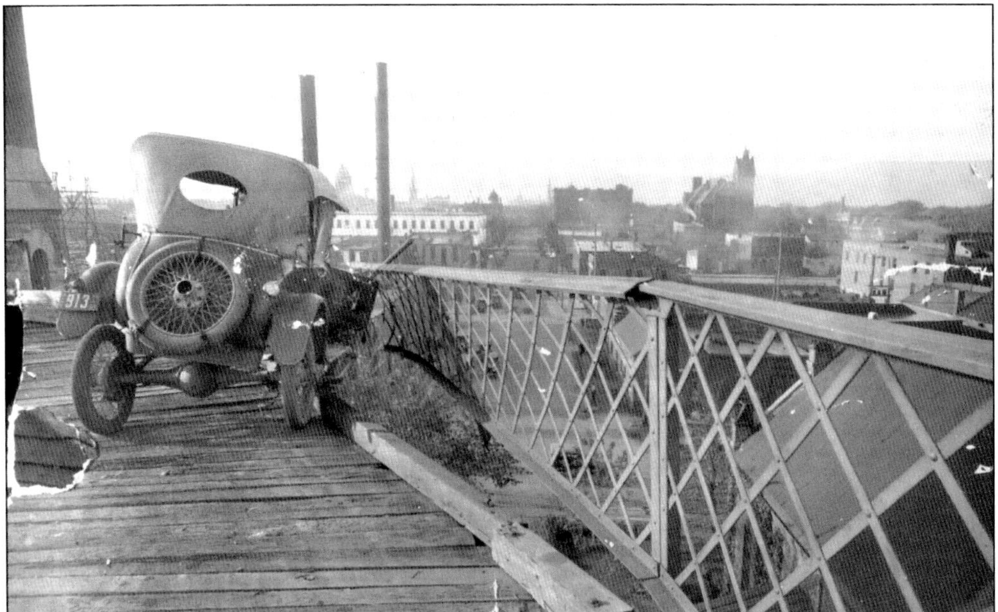

Numerous accidents occurred at the bridge's right-angled turns, such as this one in the wee hours of October 3, 1919, when John Barry, Stanley Olhoff, Percy Rollinger, and Dennis Lynch were out for a ride in Barry's cross-country Overland. Intoxicated, the four were crossing the bridge when Barry missed the turn and collided with the railing. Lynch and Rollinger slipped out of the right side of the car and fell 65 feet to the levee, where Lynch was killed and Rollinger survived by falling on top of Lynch. The other two men were dazed, but not injured.

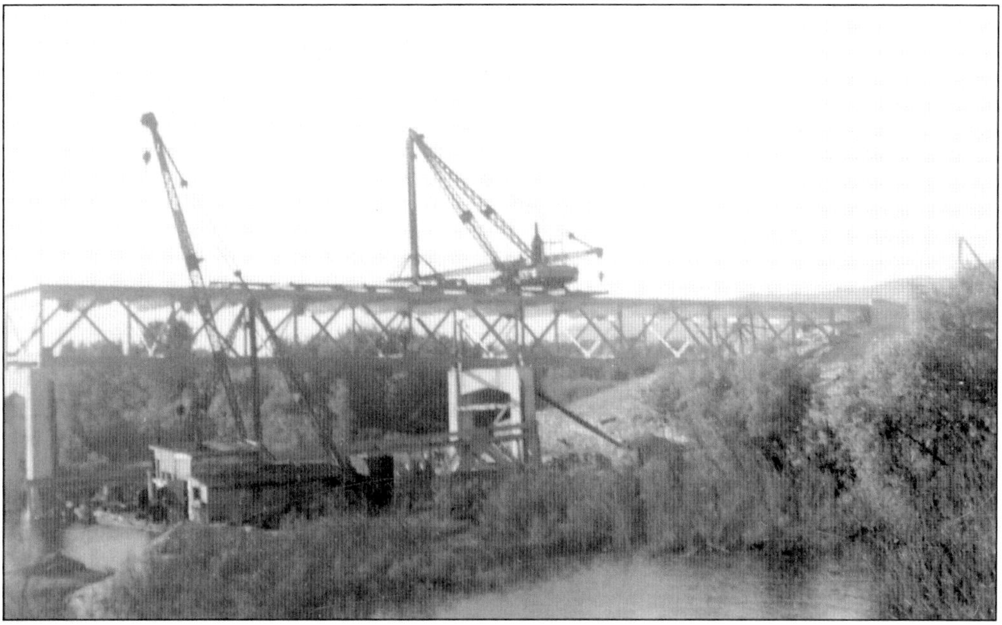

The Industrial Contracting Company of Minneapolis, Minnesota, constructed the new interstate bridge between Winona and Wisconsin. The steel beams for the bridge were fabricated in Gary, Indiana, and transported by barge to Winona via the Illinois River.

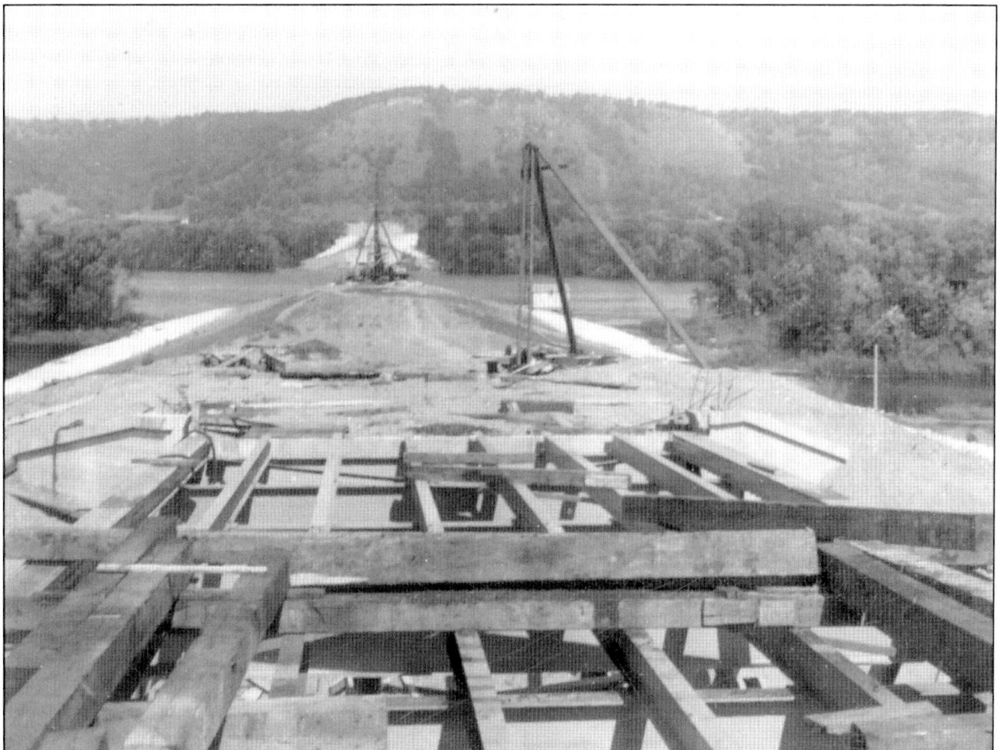

Looking north toward Wisconsin, this August 1941 photograph shows the construction of the deck of the new interstate bridge.

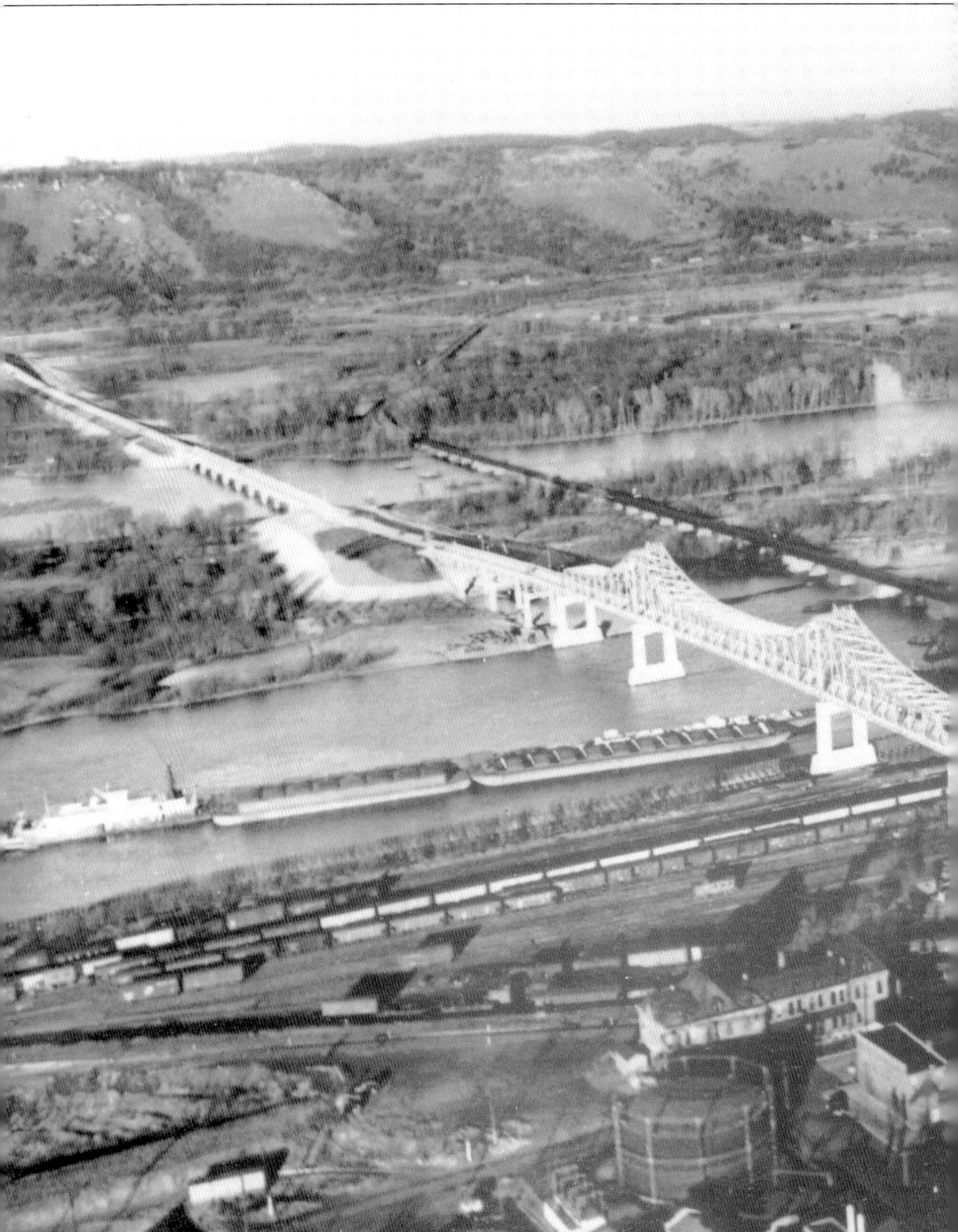

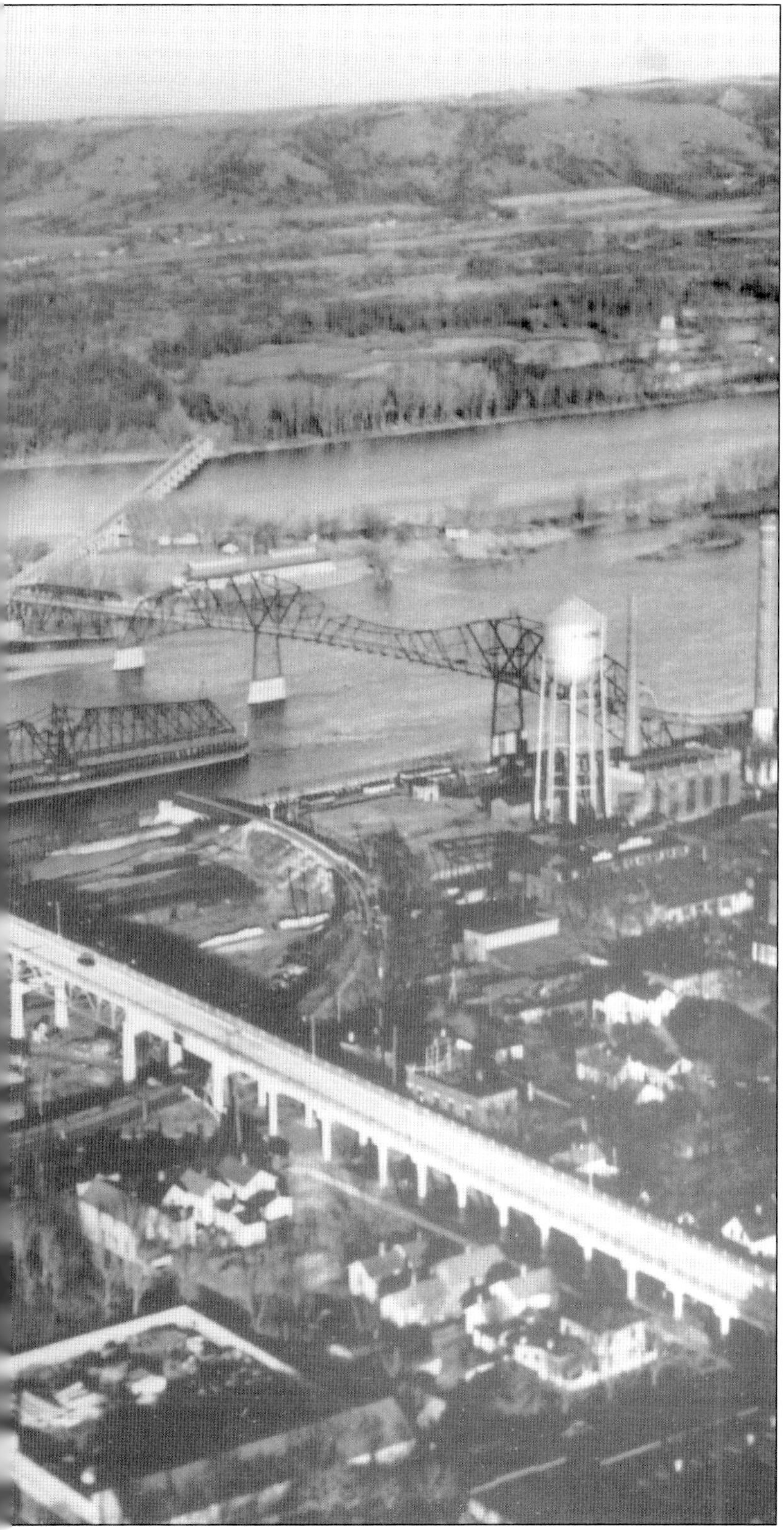

There were three bridges crossing the Mississippi River at Winona on November 20, 1942. The new $1.5 million cantilever bridge, seen to the left, was dedicated on November 21, 1942. The old steel High Wagon Bridge, seen to the right behind the water tower, was to be razed for scrap metal during the winter. In the middle was the Chicago and North Western Railway swing bridge, which was open to allow the Federal Barge Line's towboat, the *Mark Twain*, to pass through. Seen to the right of the water tower are the city's waterworks and the standpipe, a relic of a bygone era. Beneath and to the left of the new bridge, one can see the Chicago and North Western rail yards and, in the immediate foreground, the railroad's depot, the Northern States Power Company's gas and coke plant, and the Winona County Highway Department's yards.

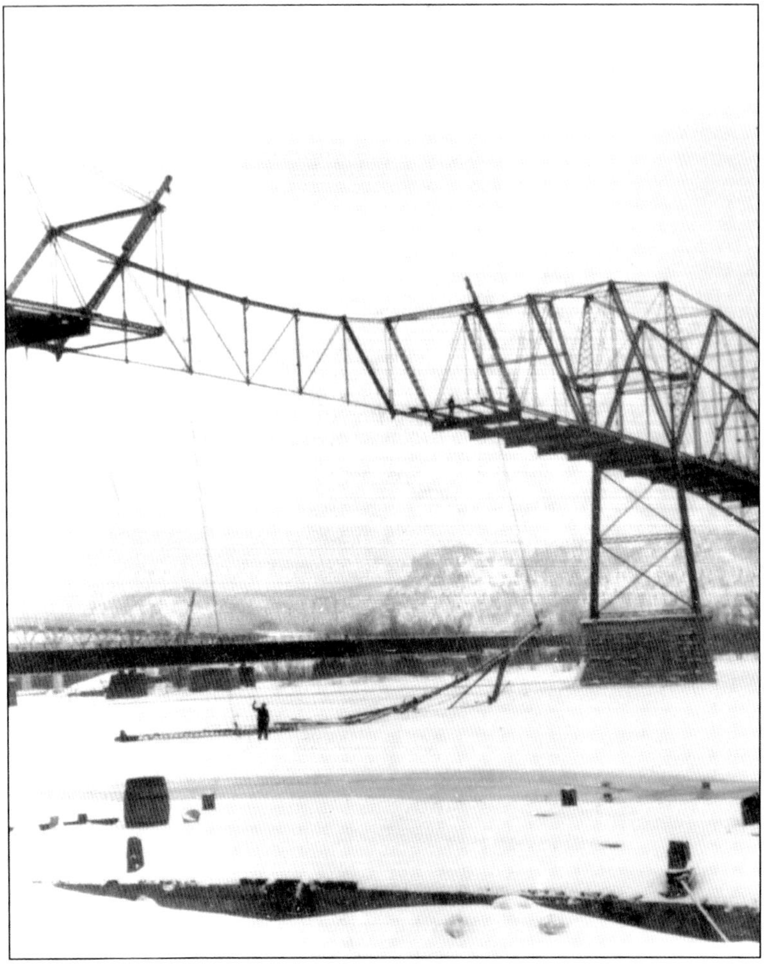

The M.E. Souther Company of St. Paul razed the old steel High Wagon Bridge during the winter of 1942–1943. Its steel went toward the war effort.

On December 17, 1989, the Burlington Swing Bridge, which had not been in use for about four years, was accidently set on fire by some boys. The fire destroyed the bridge, which was removed the following summer. The Chicago and North Western swing bridge had been removed 10 years earlier, leaving no railroad bridges into Winona.

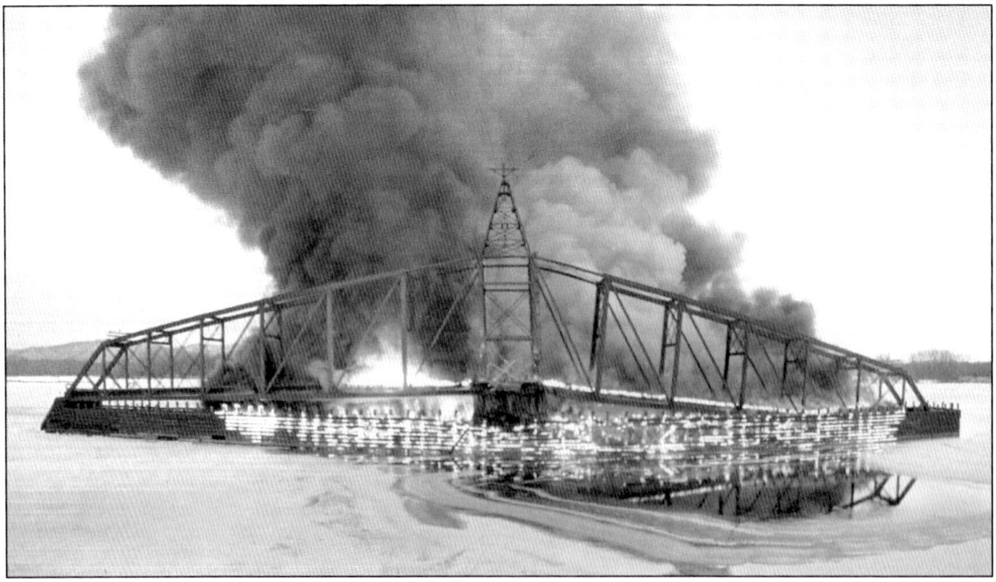

Four

Getting Around Town

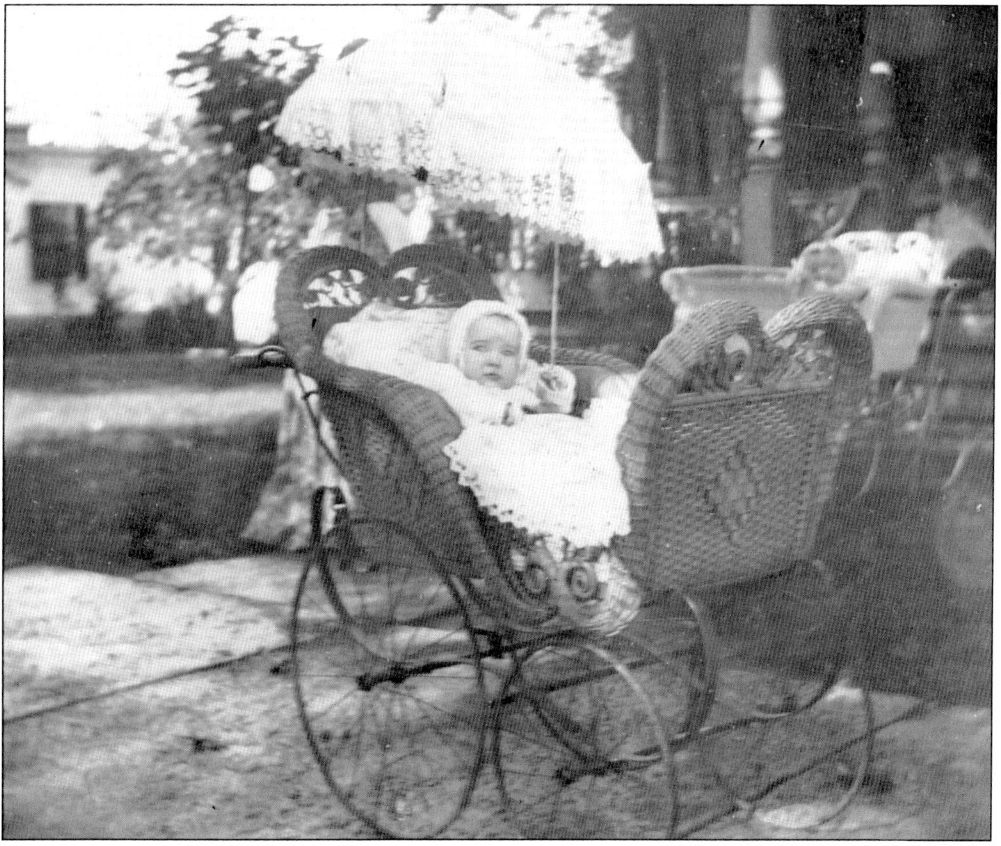

The Charles Boldt twins, Eben and Ralph, are going for a ride in their buggy. (Boldt.)

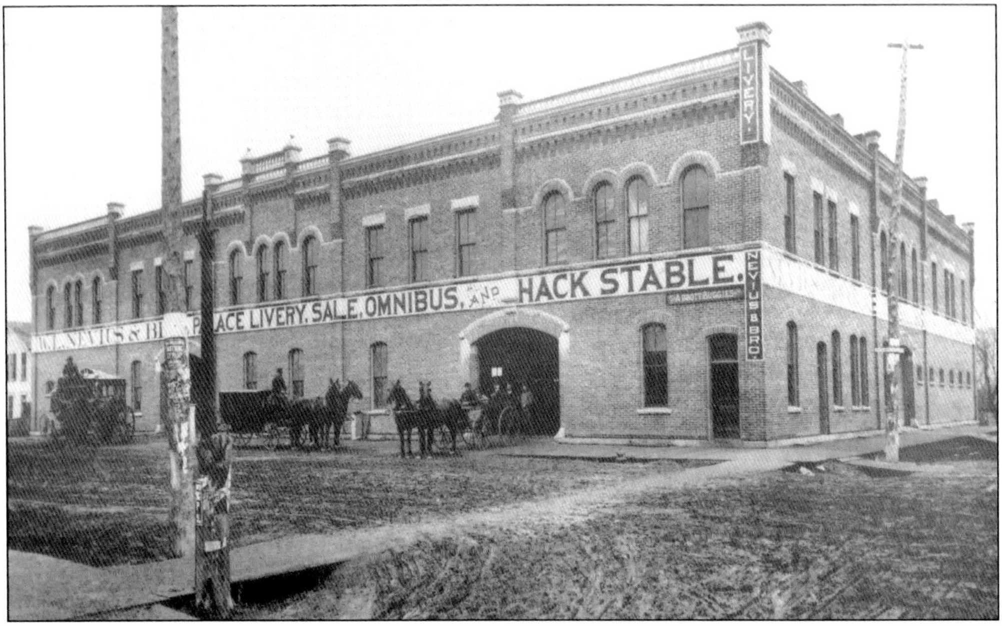

The livery stable, opened in 1865 by Charles L. Boardman at the southeast corner of Fourth and Johnson Streets, was purchased in 1872 by Emory G. Nevius. By 1909, it had been enlarged and could stable as many as 275 horses, which were used for taxi and transfer service for the community. The stable was converted to an auto garage around 1914.

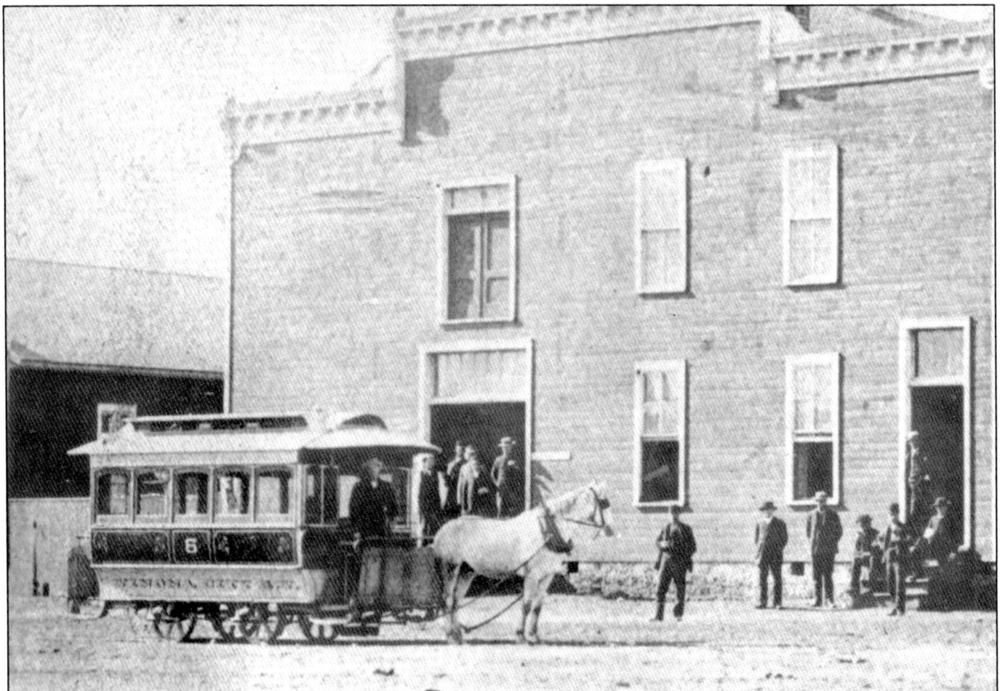

The Winona City Railway Company's car barn, located at East Third Street and Mankato Avenue, was built in late 1883. A smaller horse barn was located on the left. Horse car number six, shown in the foreground, is being pulled by the horse. (Tenney.)

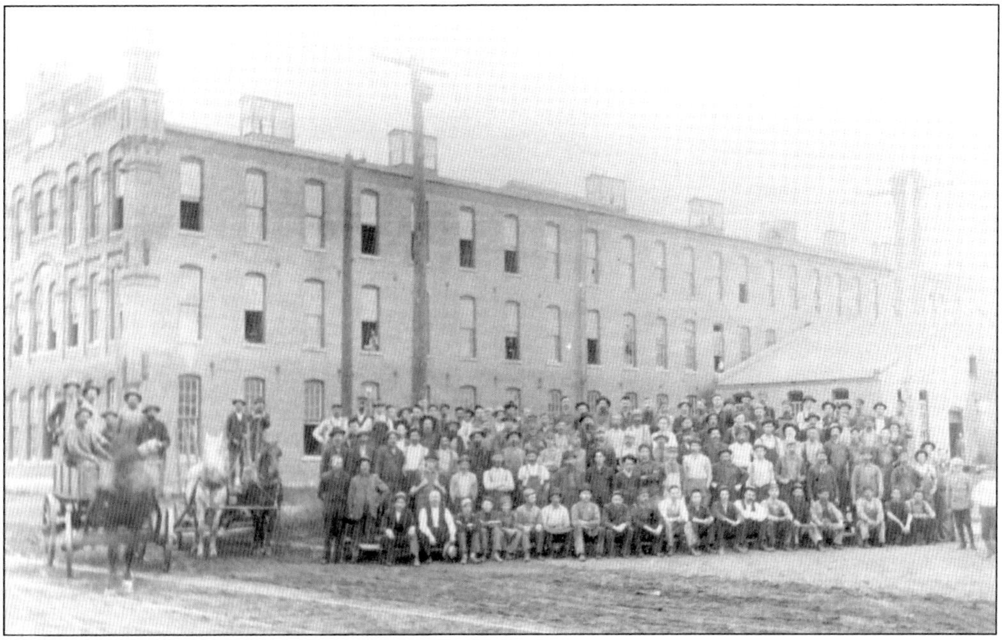

The Winona Wagon Company building was constructed in 1879 along West Fifth Street near the junction of the Chicago and North Western and Chicago, Milwaukee & St. Paul Railroads and began operations early in 1880. Its wagon, called the Rushford Wagon, was a very popular item and was sold around the country. When the street railway was built, it extended to the company's front door.

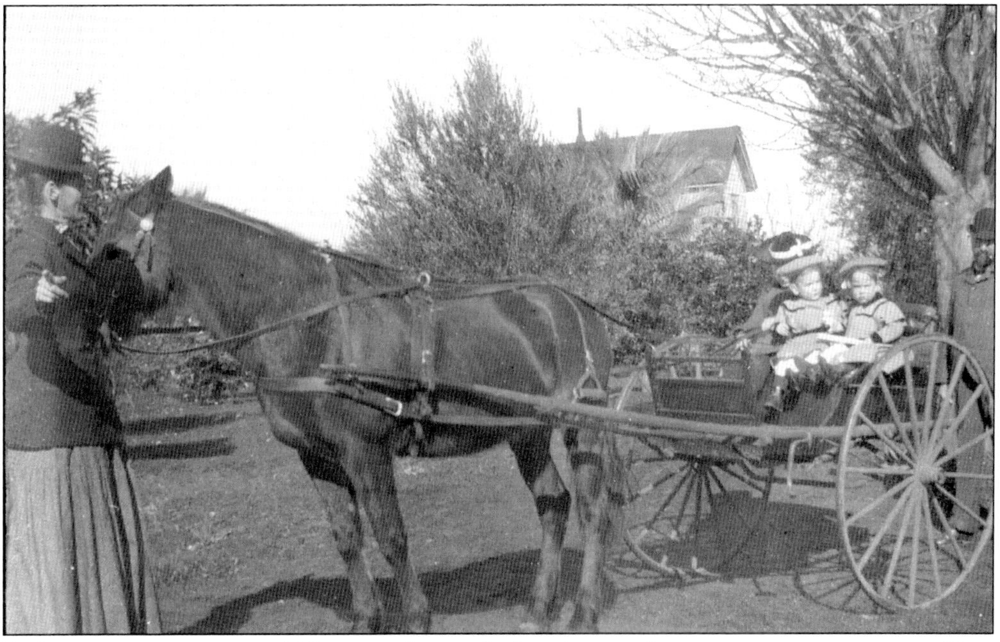

Early transportation around Winona often took place in one of two common conveyances. One, a two-wheeled cart pulled by a single horse, is pictured taking Ralph and Eben Boldt for a ride. Another common conveyance was the four-wheeled buggy, which can be seen on the following page. (Boldt.)

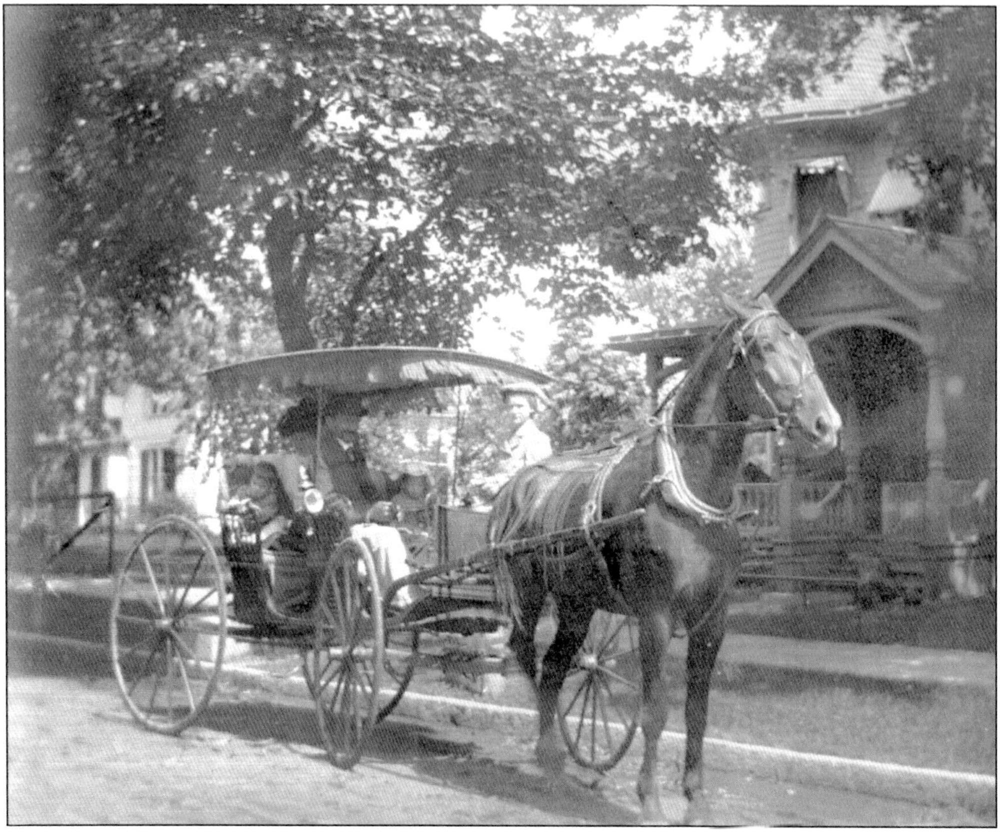

In 1902, during the early days of Winona's history, the horse and buggy was a common personal conveyance. Here is one owned by the Charles Boldt family in front of their home at 302 West Fourth Street, which is visible behind the horse's head. (Boldt.)

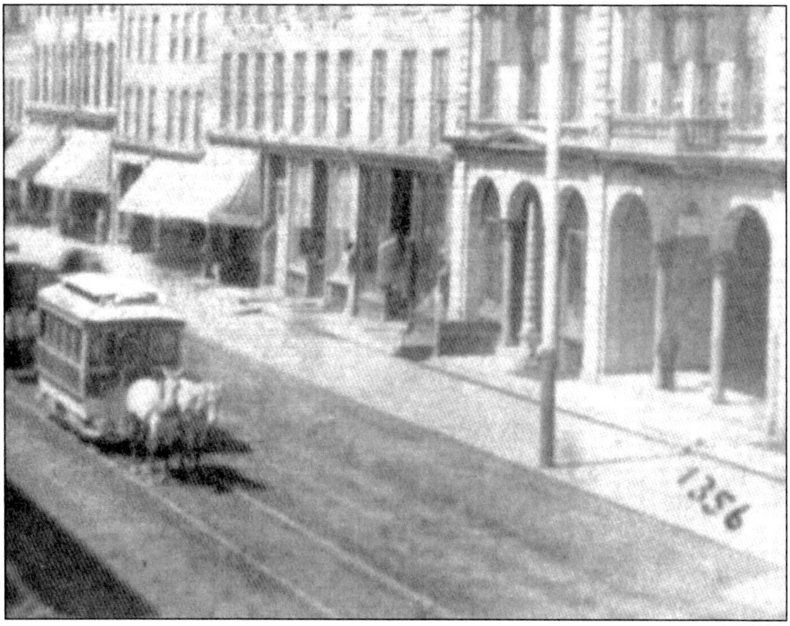

A horse-drawn streetcar is traveling east on Third Street in the downtown business district during the mid-1880s. Two horses were often used in the winter months when the tracks were covered with snow.

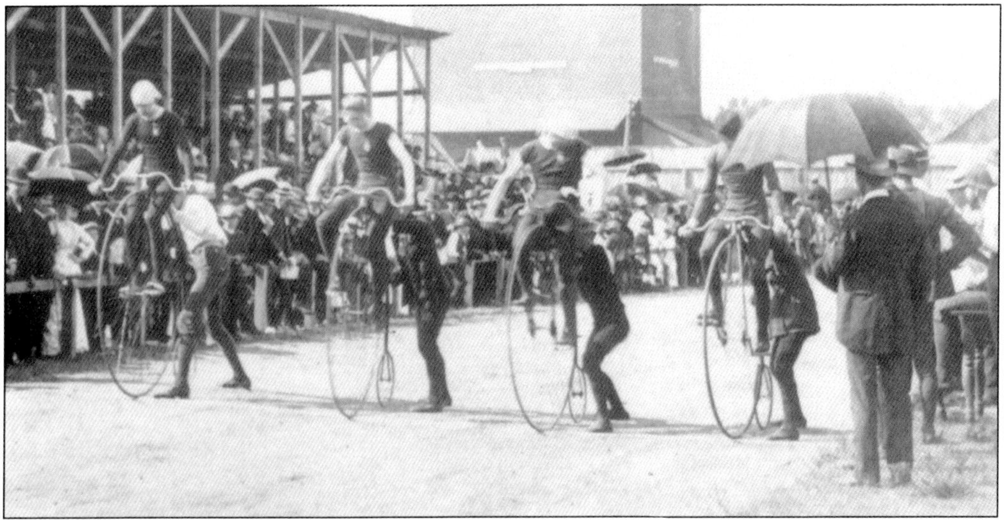

This velocipede race was at the Winona Bicycle Track, which was located behind the present-day West-End Recreation Center. The first appearance of the velocipede in Winona occurred in 1869, when John C. Slorah purchased one. (Tenney.)

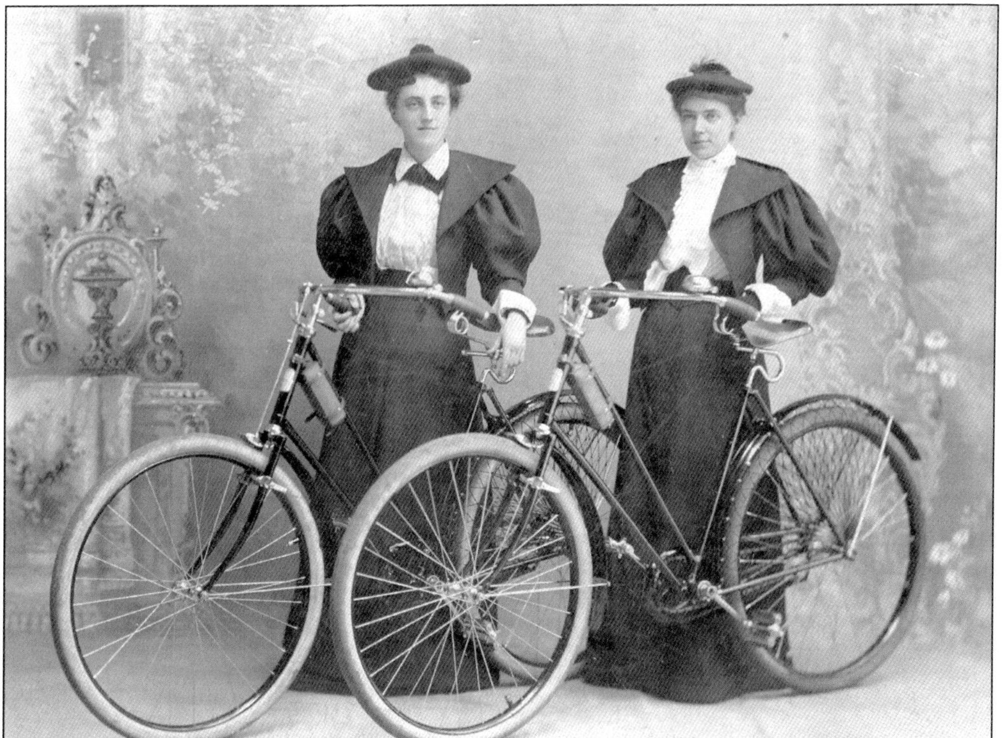

Jane Cornwell and Maude Carpenter are pictured with their so-called safety bicycles, which were said to be more suited for ladies than the large-wheeled velocipedes. Both of these ladies had taught at Winona Public Schools during the early 1900s.

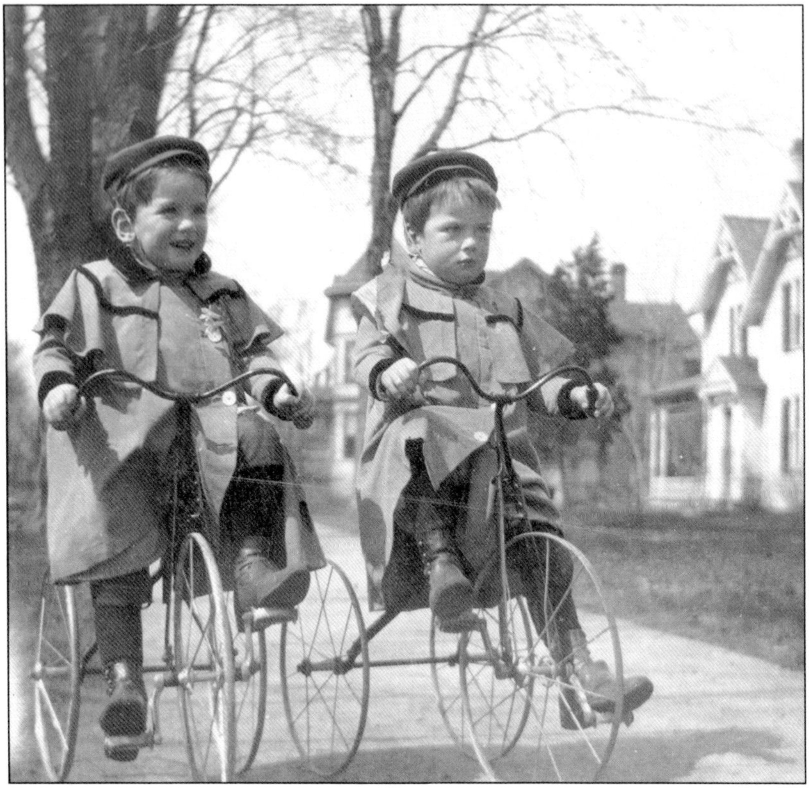

Charles Boldt's three-year-old twin boys, Ralph and Eben, are riding their tricycles near their home at Huff and West Fourth Streets during the spring of 1903. (Boldt.)

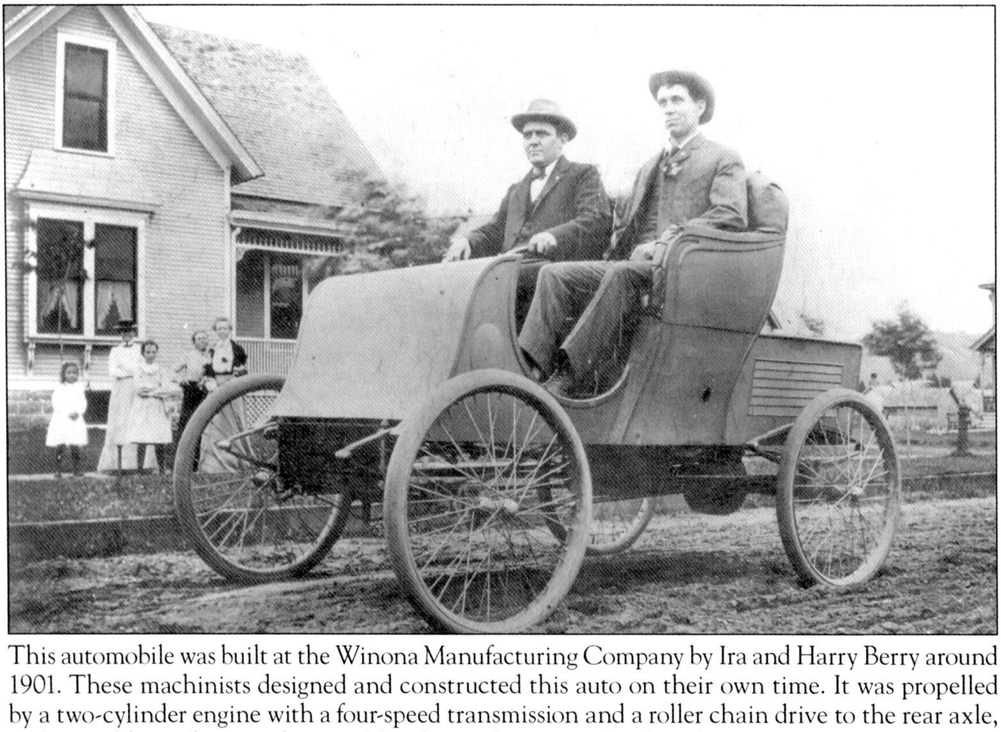

This automobile was built at the Winona Manufacturing Company by Ira and Harry Berry around 1901. These machinists designed and constructed this auto on their own time. It was propelled by a two-cylinder engine with a four-speed transmission and a roller chain drive to the rear axle, and it could travel at speeds up to 30 miles per hour on a level road.

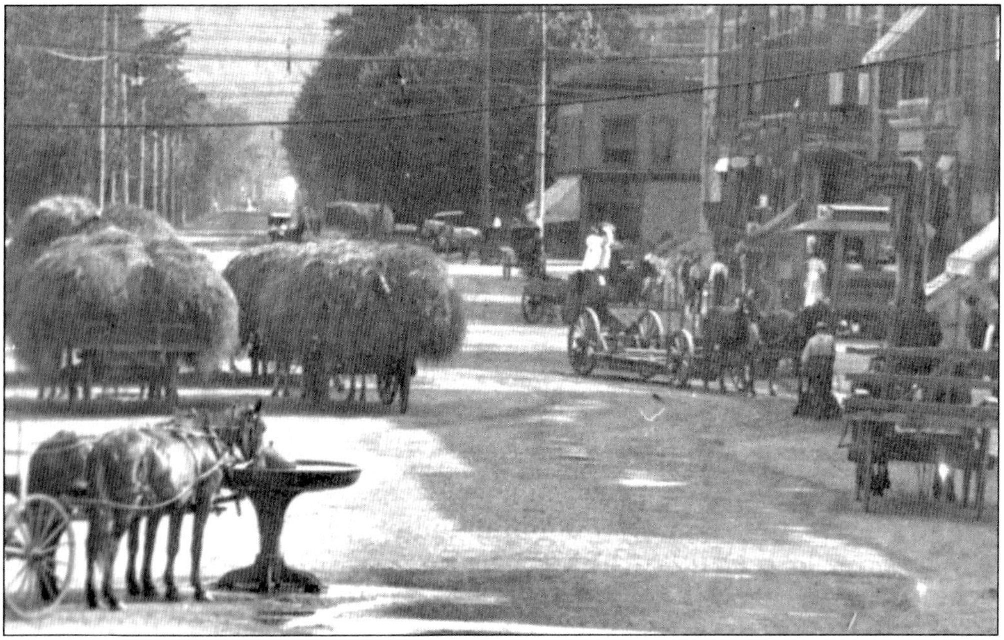

This c. 1900 photograph shows Main Street between West Second and Third Streets near the foot of the High Wagon Bridge. One can see an automobile in the background, which is almost obscured by the horse-drawn hay wagons.

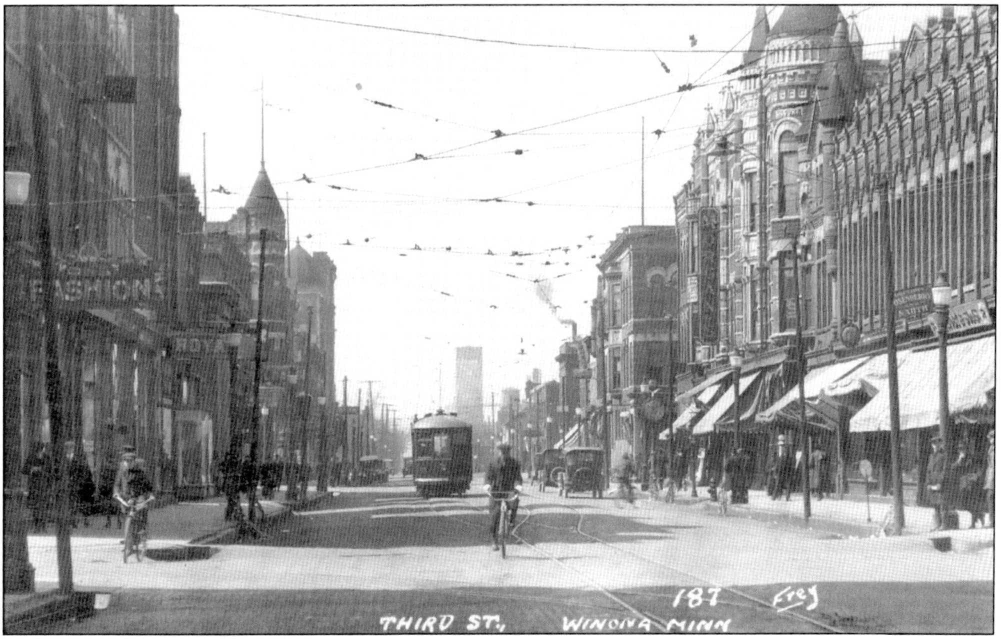

This photograph, looking west from Center Street, shows West Third Street in the early decades of the 20th century. The clock on the right is located at Morgan's Jewelry, and the streetcars are run by electric motors. Note the net of wires above the street and the line of tracks in the brick roadway that bend into two sets, allowing the streetcars to pass one another. Also note that there is a fair number of bicycles and automobiles, but there is an absence of horses and buggies on the street. The tall structures in the background are the elevators of the Winona Malting Company.

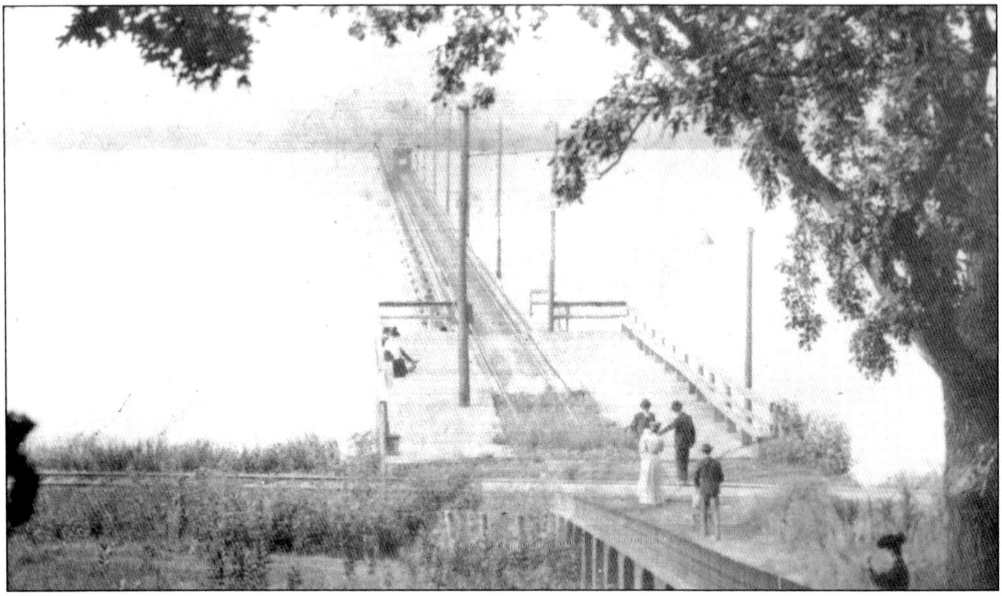

The Winona Railway and Light Company trestle bridge crossed Lake Winona. The loading platform in the foreground was located at the head of Dakota Street and is similar to the one at the opposite end near Woodlawn Cemetery. The bridge was built in early 1901 for the streetcars and operated for about 10 years before being closed. In May 1914, the city purchased the bridge and transformed it into a walking bridge. The bridge was condemned and razed by the city early in 1926 after parts of it had been removed as firewood.

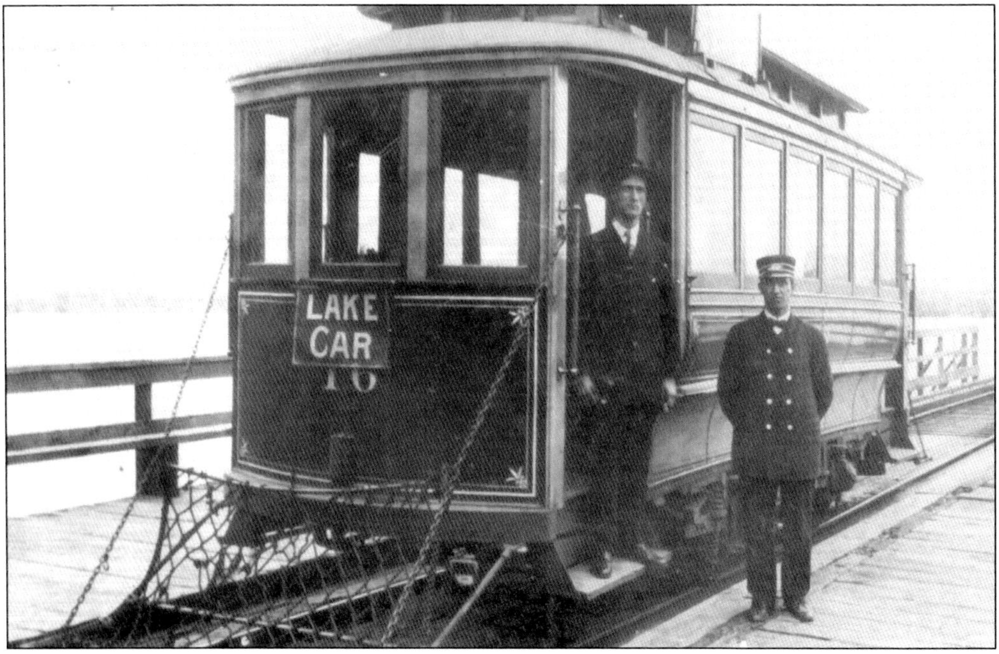

Theodore J. Miszke, a motorman on Winona's Number 16 streetcar, is pictured standing on the step of the car. The identity of the conductor standing on the platform is unknown. The photograph of the car on the bridge crossing Lake Winona was taken around 1908. Notice there is a net on the front of the car that was known as a "people-catcher."

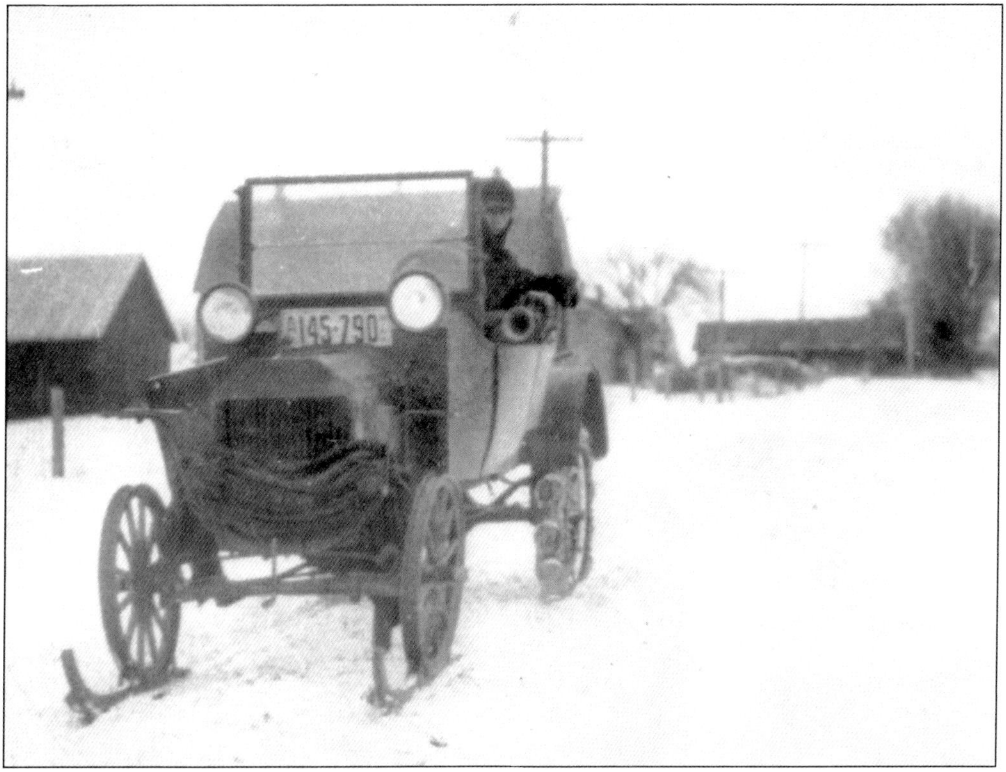

In 1925, Dr. Conrad Neumann customized this Ford Model T automobile for winter driving by attaching skis to the front wheels and chains to the rear drive wheels.

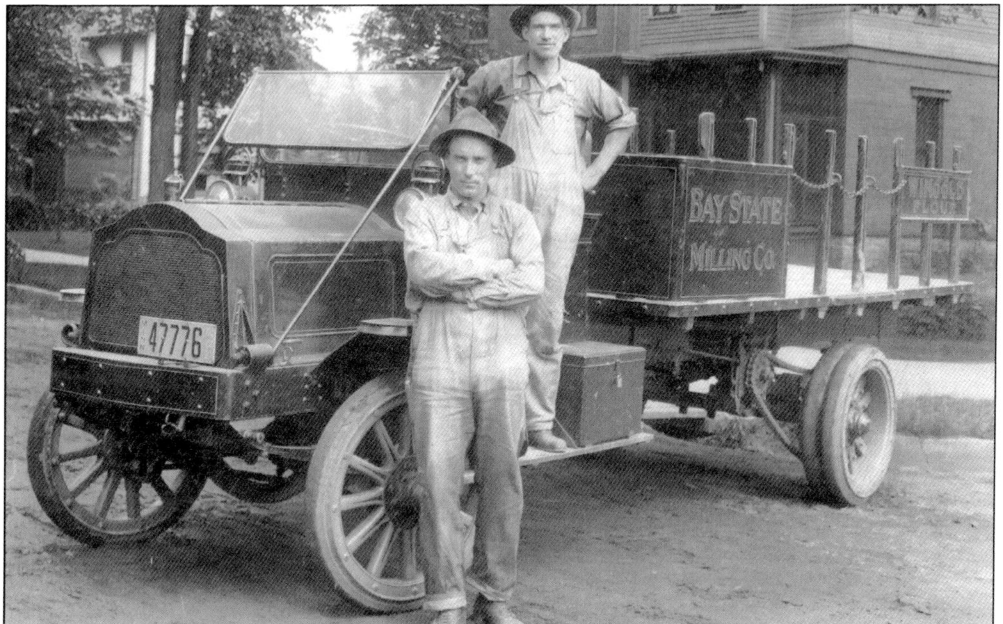

The Bay State Milling Company of Winona operated this Model T truck around 1920. The names of the two workmen seen with the truck are unknown.

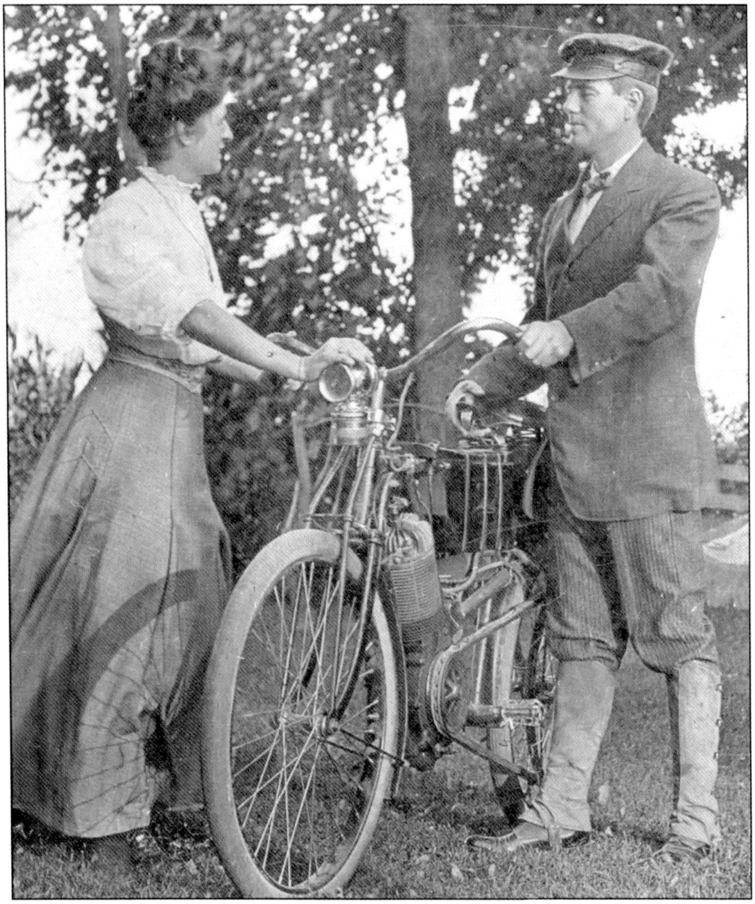

Around 1907, Earl Townsend and his future wife, Anna Hardwick, could be seen riding around town on Earl's new Harley Davidson motorcycle.

Jay C. Higgins, a dealer for the Dr. Ward's Medical Company during the second decade of the 20th century, is pictured in his automobile. He was the first direct-sales dealer in the area to convert from a horse-drawn buggy to a gasoline-operated automobile.

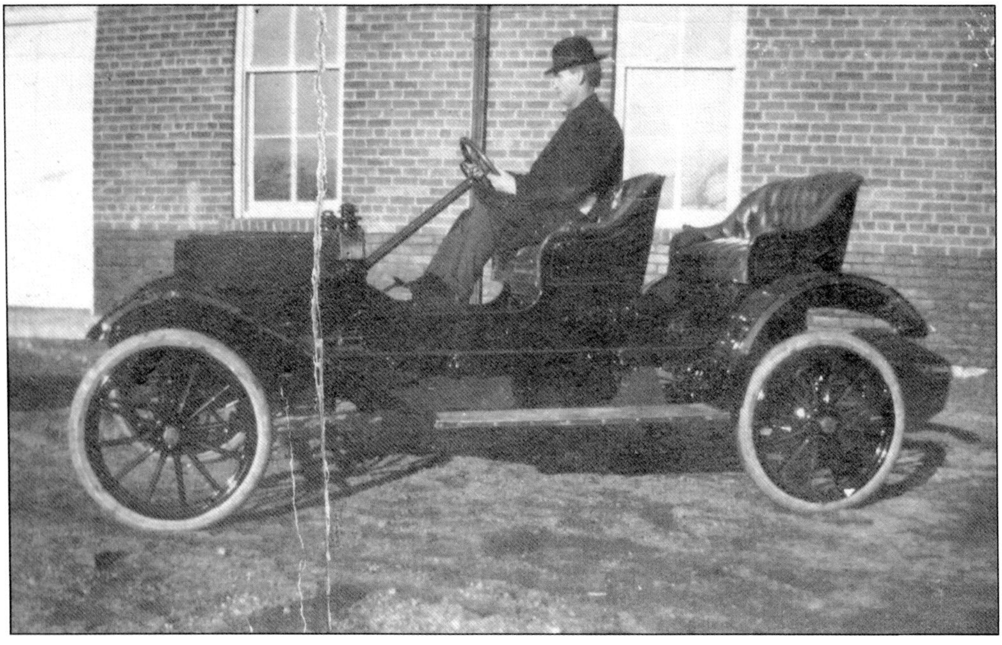

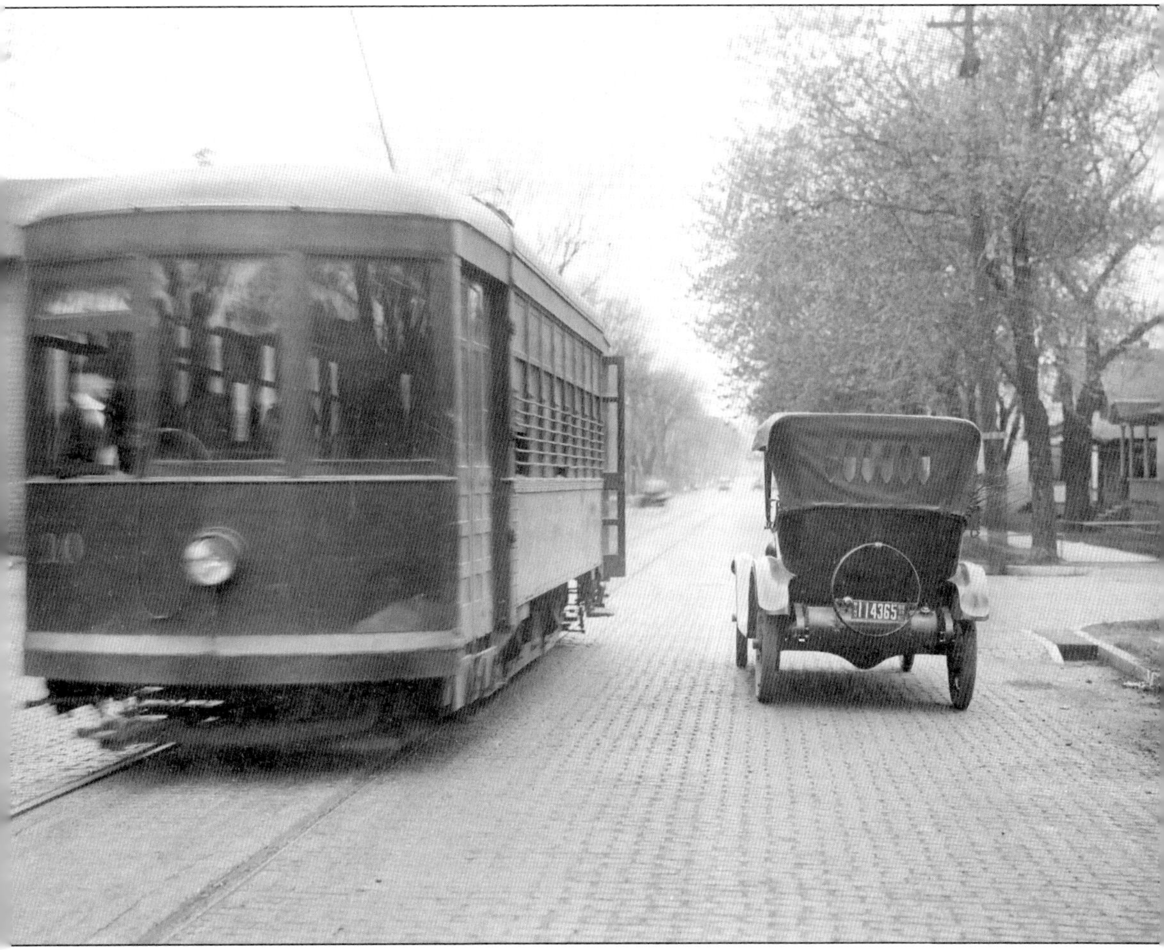

Electric streetcar Number 10 is pictured heading west on West Fifth Street at McBride Street and passing a Model T. Notice that the street was covered with brick pavers.

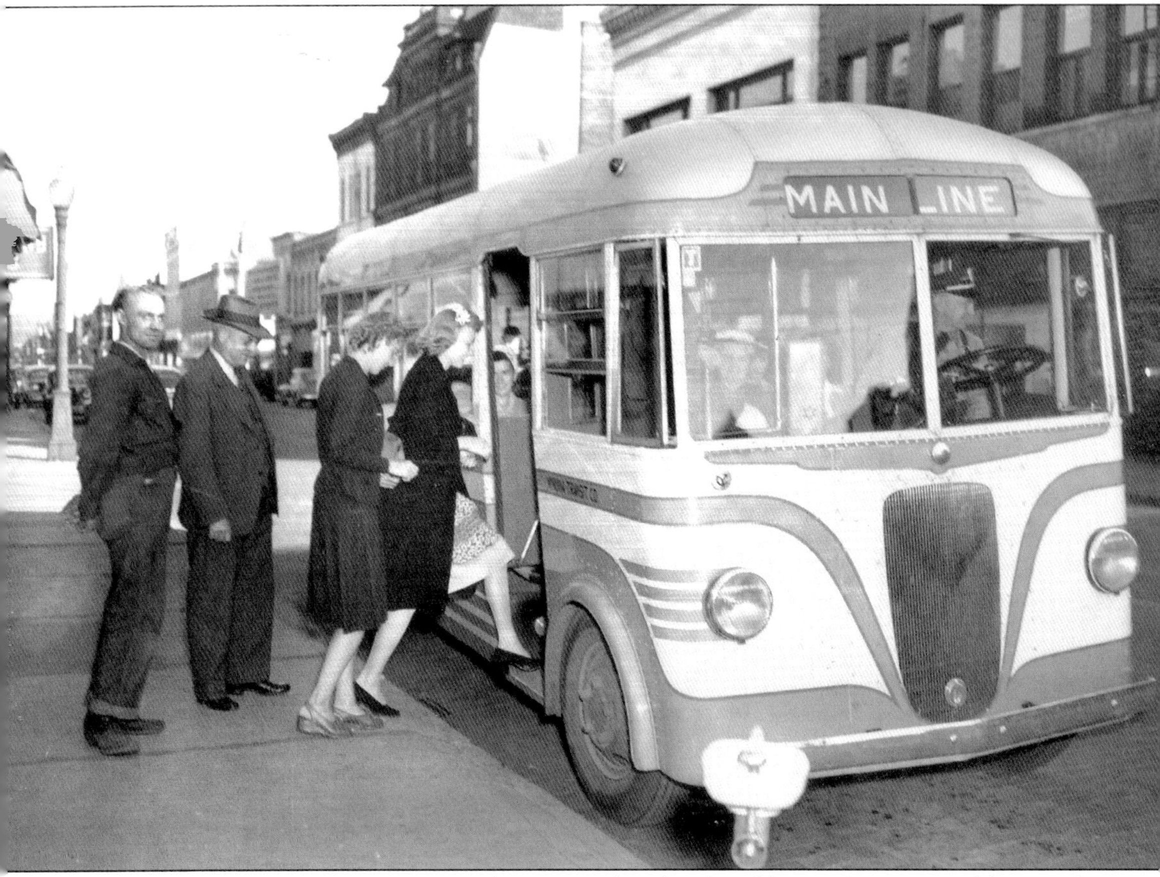

In 1938, the electric streetcars were discontinued and replaced by gasoline-powered buses. The tracks were soon removed, and the streetcars were discarded. Streetcar Number 10 ended up as a summer home in Lamoille and eventually found its way to the Minnesota Street Car Museum in Excelsior, Minnesota.

Five

Some Leaders of Industry and Commerce

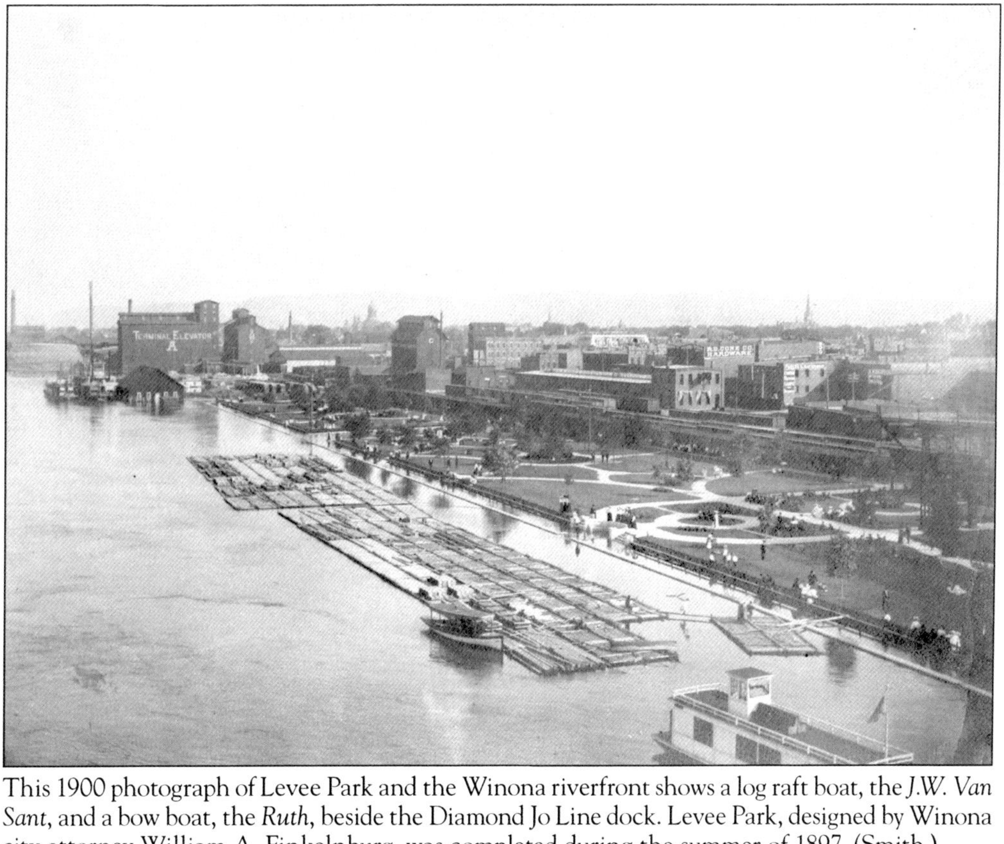

This 1900 photograph of Levee Park and the Winona riverfront shows a log raft boat, the *J.W. Van Sant*, and a bow boat, the *Ruth*, beside the Diamond Jo Line dock. Levee Park, designed by Winona city attorney William A. Finkelnburg, was completed during the summer of 1897. (Smith.)

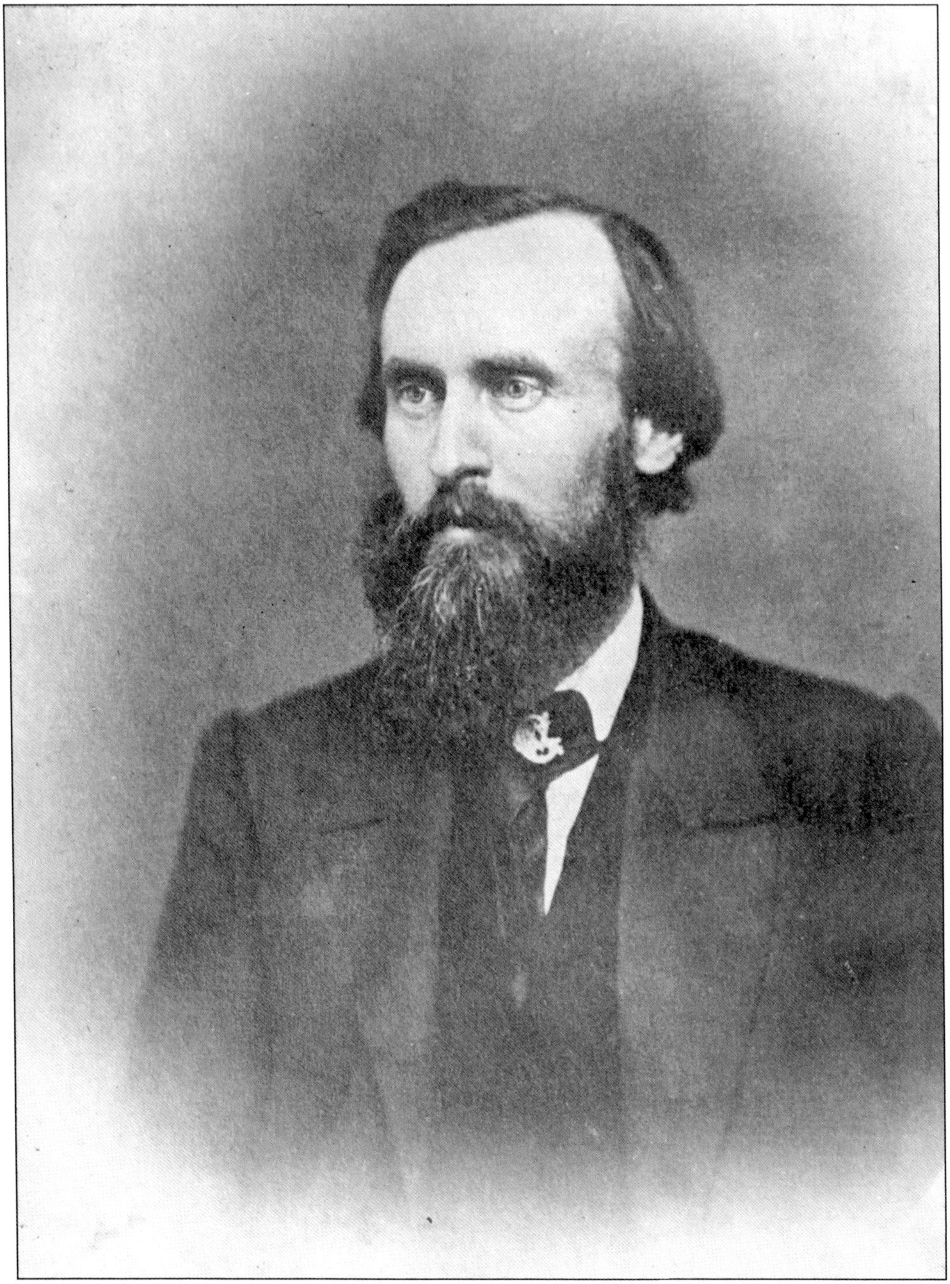

Martin Wheeler Sargeant (1822–1866) was born in Vermont. He arrived in Winona in 1853 as a surveyor, but soon set up a law practice and was the first lawyer on Wapasha's Prairie. As a land speculator, Sargeant had obtained many sections of land in Winona County, which he later sold. He was instrumental in the organization of Winona County and was appointed the first clerk for Winona County District Court. He was elected the county's first register of deeds and Winona's first mayor in 1857. He was also a member of the delegation of legislators to the territorial legislature from Winona County. In 1862, Sargeant was appointed paymaster of the US Army with the rank of major. He was forced to resign the position because of failing health. After he returned to Winona, his health improved, for a time. (de Groot.)

John O'Dea (1838–1921) was born in Ireland and came to America in 1855. He set foot in Winona around 1857 and was soon employed in the building of the Stockton Hill Road. He later operated a coal, lime, and cement business with offices on Market Street. This business continued until 1920, when it was closed. O'Dea purchased Sugar Loaf in 1878 and used it as a source for lime manufacture. He set up a limekiln at the base of the south slope with a road and railway from the kiln to the top. O'Dea quarried Sugar Loaf continuously until 1898, when he stopped operations due to a deceasing amount of good lime.

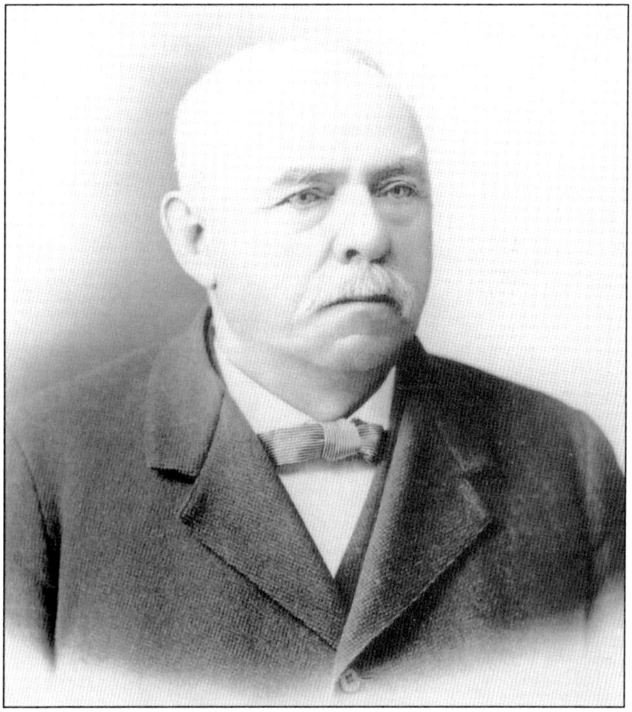

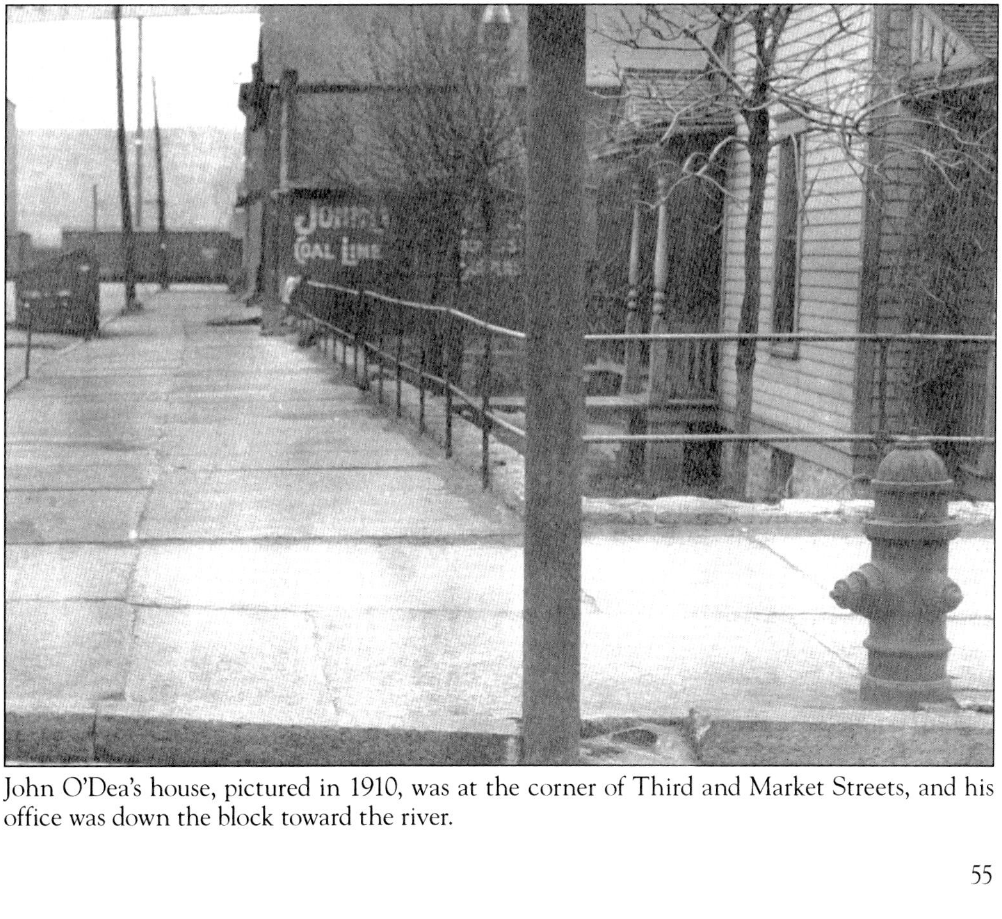

John O'Dea's house, pictured in 1910, was at the corner of Third and Market Streets, and his office was down the block toward the river.

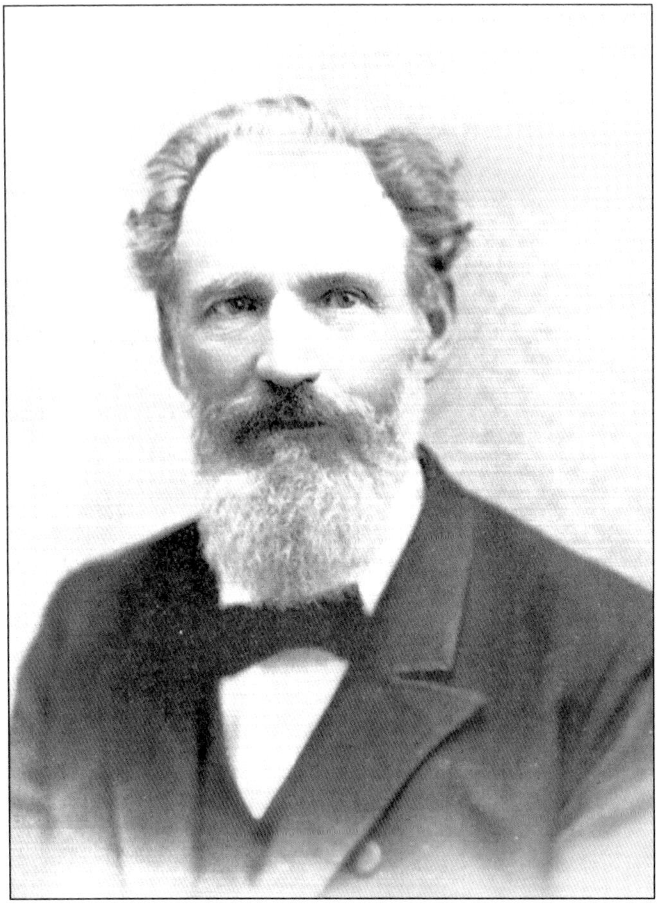

Samuel D. Van Gorder (1837–1901) was born in New York and arrived in Winona in 1856. Soon after he arrived, he helped build the first road out of Winona toward Sugar Loaf and the first bridge across Lake Winona. He later operated a sash and door factory, which was followed by a charter to operate a ferry service between Winona and Wisconsin. He operated the ferry until 1880, when he sold it to the City of Winona. While operating the ferry service, he was also engaged in the stone quarry business and provided stone for many river and community improvements, including the county courthouse. (Portrait and Biographical Record.)

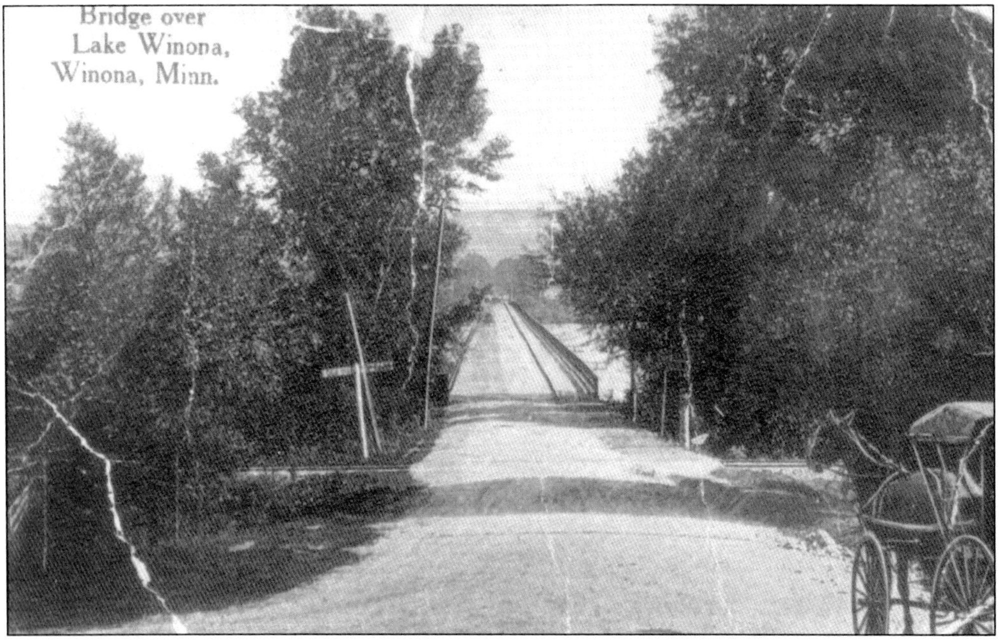

Samuel Van Gorder built this bridge, which was the first one to cross Lake Winona to Gilmore Valley, in 1861.

Bert A. Beyerstedt (1889–1938), a musical prodigy, was born in Winona and made his first appearance on stage at the age of three when he sang in a program at the Winona Opera House. By the age of eight, he was an experienced violinist, and as an adult toured the country playing in vaudeville with his brother Harry. Bert and Harry both worked together in the motion picture business and built two Winona theaters, the Dream in 1912 and the Apollo in 1926. After operating the Apollo for six months, they sold it to Louis Roesner.

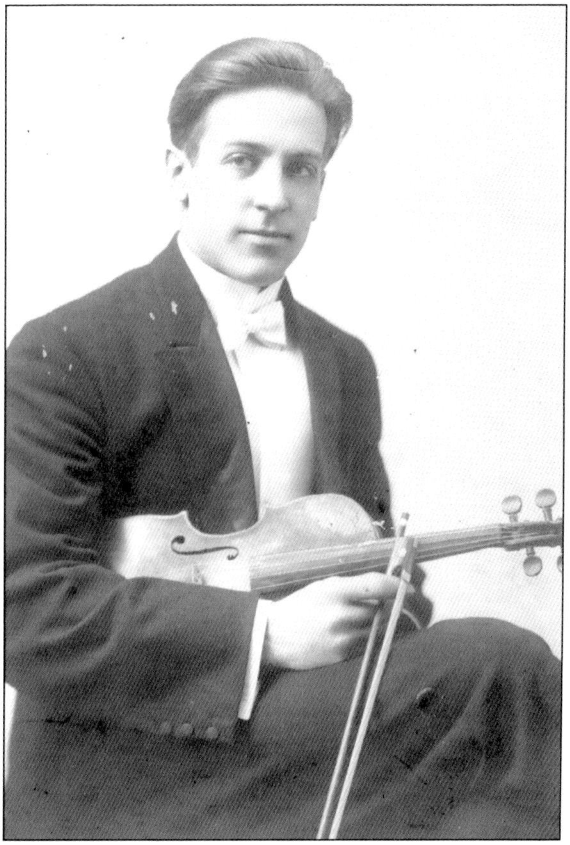

The State Theater, located next to the Armory Building, was built by Bert and Harry Beyerstedt and opened as the Apollo Theater in January 1926. One of the more exquisite theaters in the upper Midwest, it was built at a cost of $150,000. About six months after they opened the Apollo, the Beyerstedt brothers sold it to Louis Roesner, who renamed it the State Theater. At the time, Roesner owned several theaters in Winona.

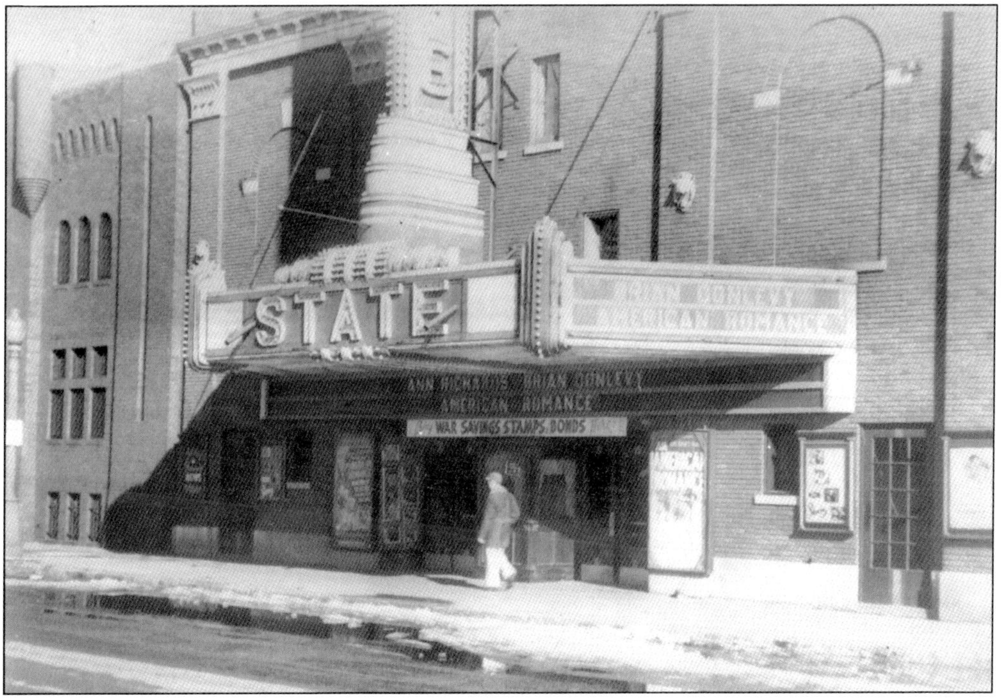

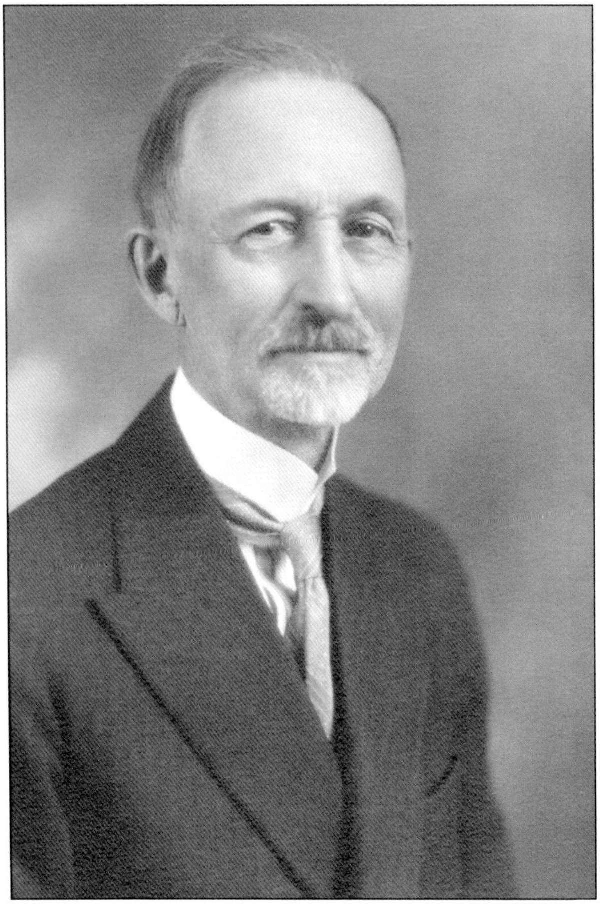

Clark E. Bailey (1856–1944), pictured here, and his brother Clinton were born in New York, where their father operated a dry goods store. Working for Bailey was Hannibal Choate, who later moved to Winona around 1861. In the early 1880s, the Bailey brothers also moved to Winona to work for Choate. In 1900, they opened a large dry goods store in a new building that had been built next to the Choate Building. This building had special amenities for the ladies who would shop there, including a ladies' waiting area. After Clinton's death in 1936, the store remained in the Bailey family until 1964, when it was closed.

A young woman is modeling a coat in the women's clothing department at Bailey and Bailey Department Store, which was located at 59–61 East Third Street.

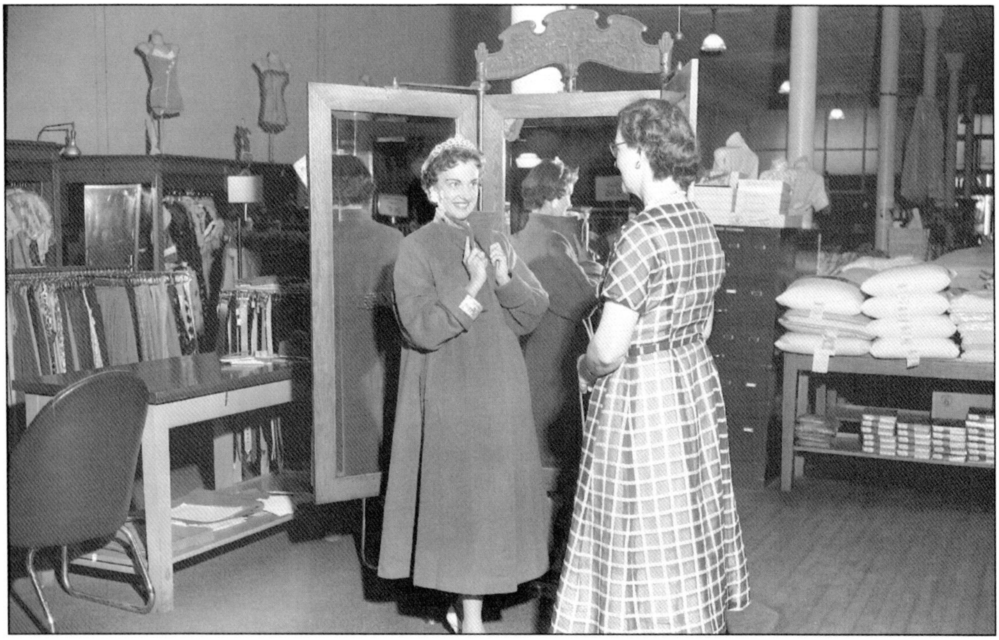

Emma Shelton (1865–1951) was a longtime beauty shop operator who specialized in chiropody, or foot care. She started her business by going door-to-door washing and styling hair. Once she opened her shop at 63 West Second Street, her clientele grew in numbers and variety. She was the first ladies' hairdresser to set up shop in Winona and the only African American woman in an independent position. Shelton's business flourished during the Depression, and she hired a number of high school girls to work for her doing odd jobs. She closed up her shop in the mid-1940s.

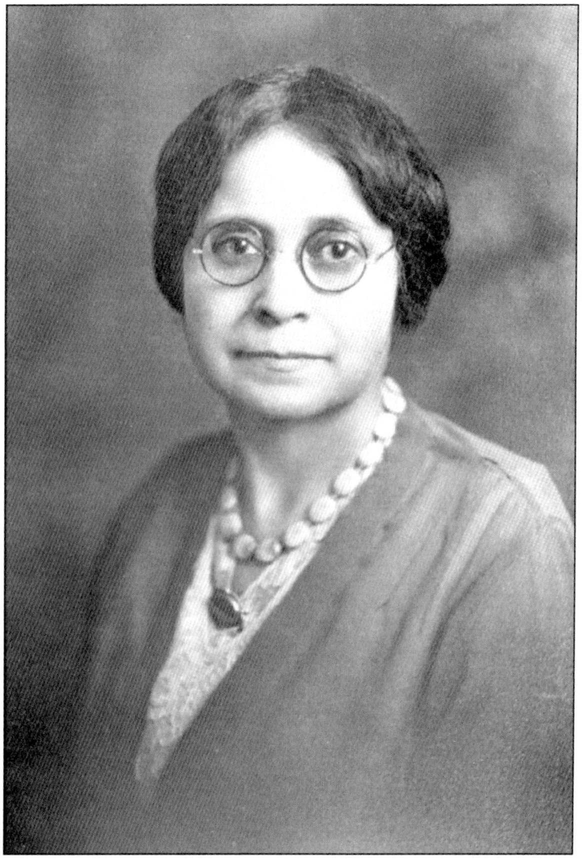

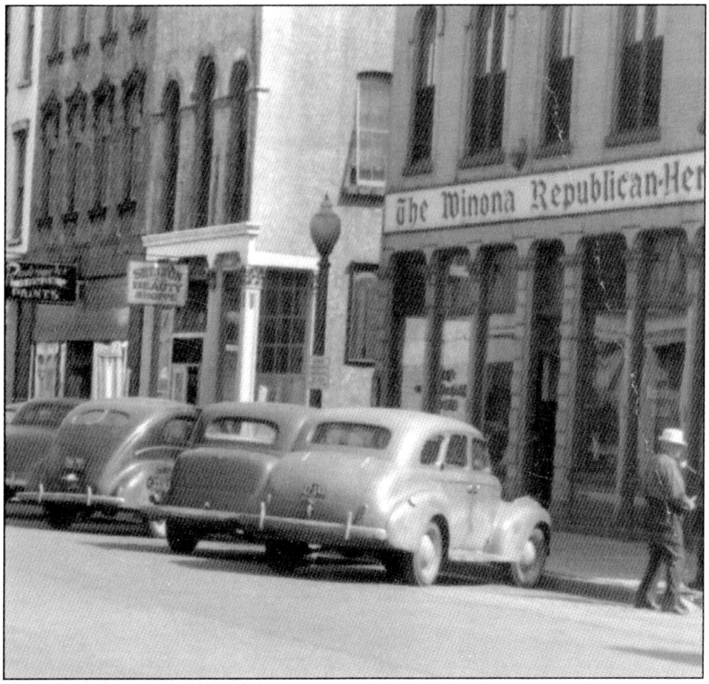

Shelton's shop was on the second floor of 63 West Second Street, just east of the *Winona Republican-Herald* newspaper office. Her sign is just visible in the center left of the photograph.

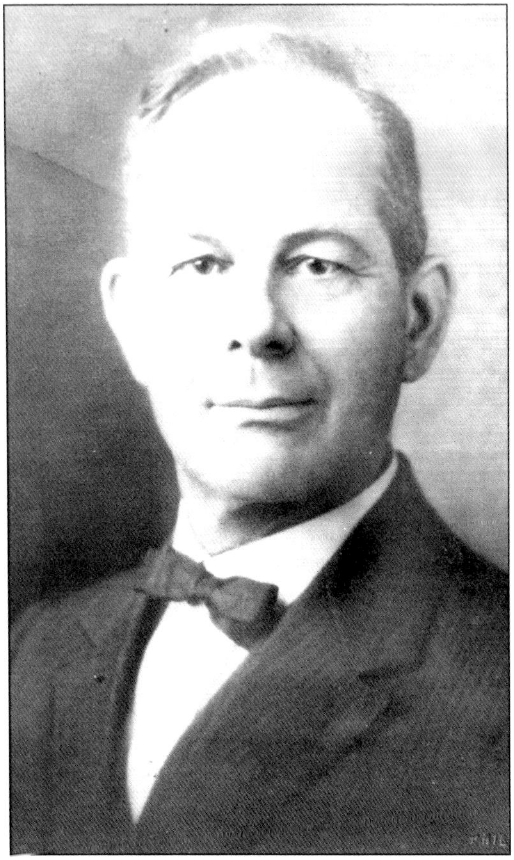

John A. Latsch (1860–1934) was born in Wisconsin and started working in his father's grocery business at the age of 14. He went into the wholesale grocery business with his father, and their company became one of the largest of its type in the upper Midwest, serving steamboats and area grocers. Latsch served as Winona's mayor from 1905–1907 and held many other civic positions. Although an excellent businessman, his true calling was philanthropy. He purchased land along the Mississippi River and donated it to the City of Winona and the states of Minnesota and Wisconsin to serve as parkland, recreational areas, and for conservation. His generosity also extended to hospitals, cemeteries, and other local establishments.

The Latsch Block, home of Latsch and Son Wholesale Grocery, was located on the north side of West Second and Center Streets. The property was originally the site of the James Reed cabin and, in 1853, the first hotel, the Minnesota House. These buildings were constructed around 1885 and purchased by the Latsch family in 1895.

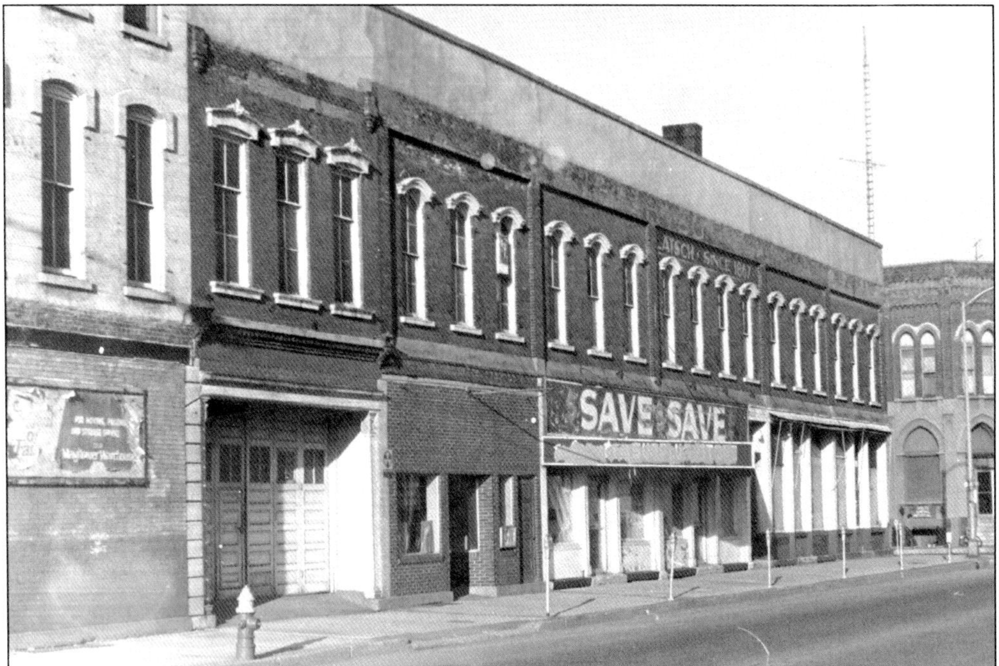

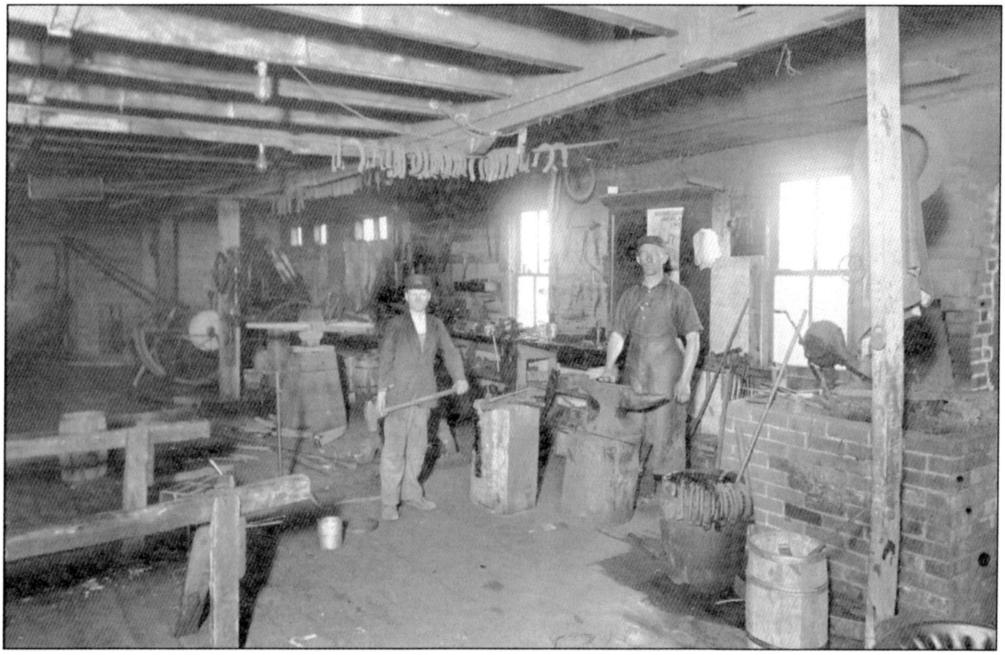

In 1895, the Wilhelm Benz blacksmith shop was located at Mankato Avenue and East Mark Street. It was opened in 1870 by Wilhelm Benz and continued under his son William until it was closed in 1951. The men in this photograph are probably Wilhelm (right) and his son William (left), who started in business with his father in 1893.

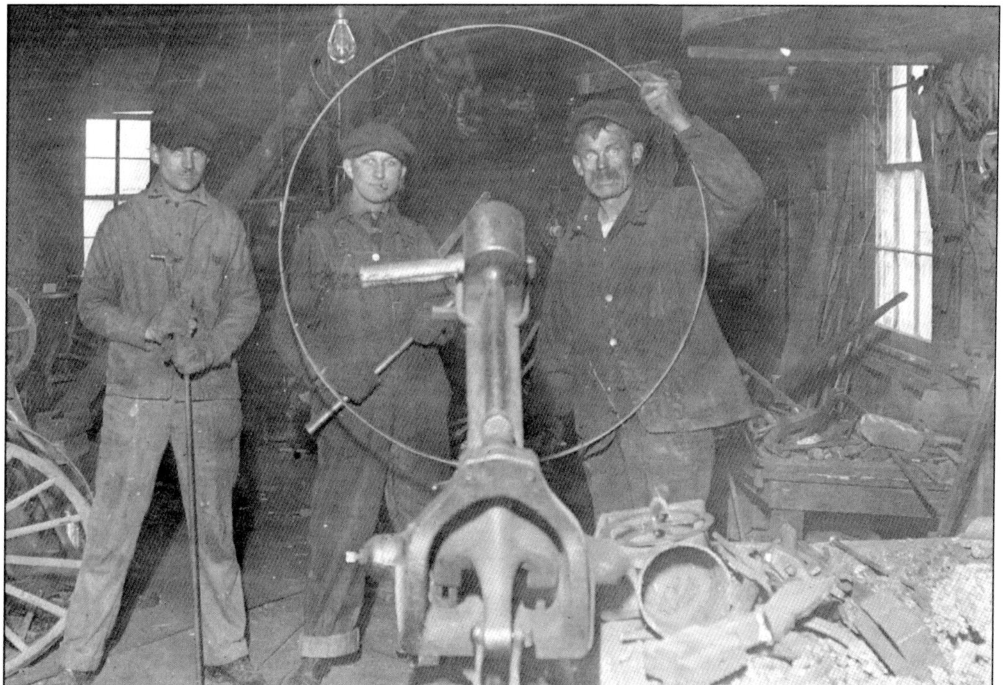

The William Benz blacksmith shop is seen in 1918, two years after Wilhelm died at the age of 73. William Benz (1871–1955) is probably the man to the right forming a wheel ring.

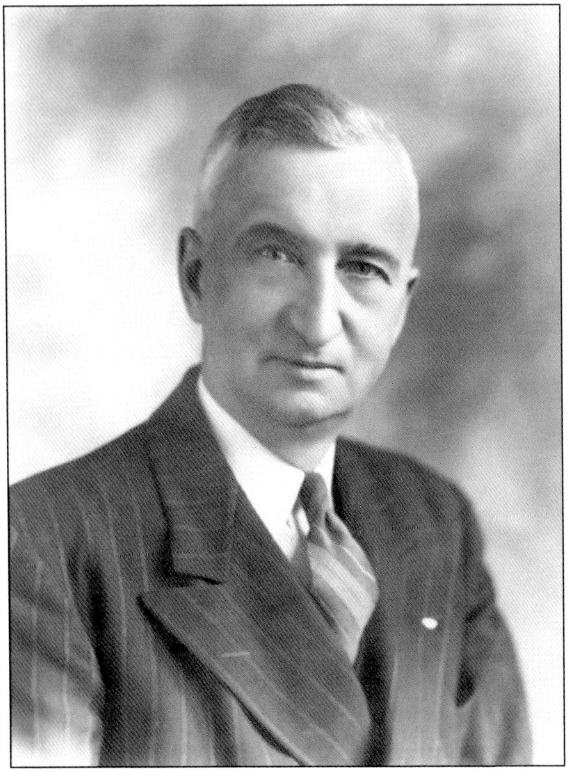

Clifford E. Williams (1891–1967) was the son of the founder of Williams Book and Stationery Store. The founder, George W. Williams (1866–1933), purchased the Alex McNie Bookstore in 1914 and expanded the business to include printing. The printing portion was sold off in 1929. After his father died, Clifford continued to run the business until he retired in 1952, at which time he turned it over to his daughter and son-in-law. They operated the business until 1996, when it was closed.

Located in the Morgan block at 52 West Third Street, Williams Book and Stationery was a mainstay for office supplies in downtown Winona for over 80 years. (Kelley.)

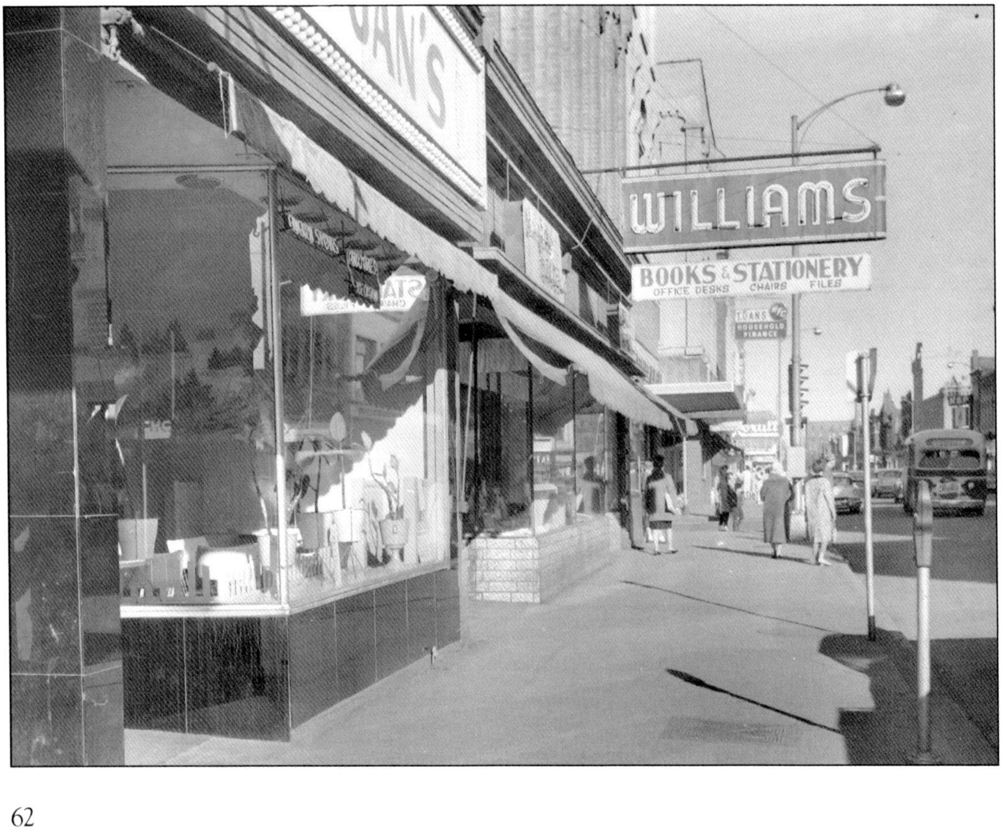

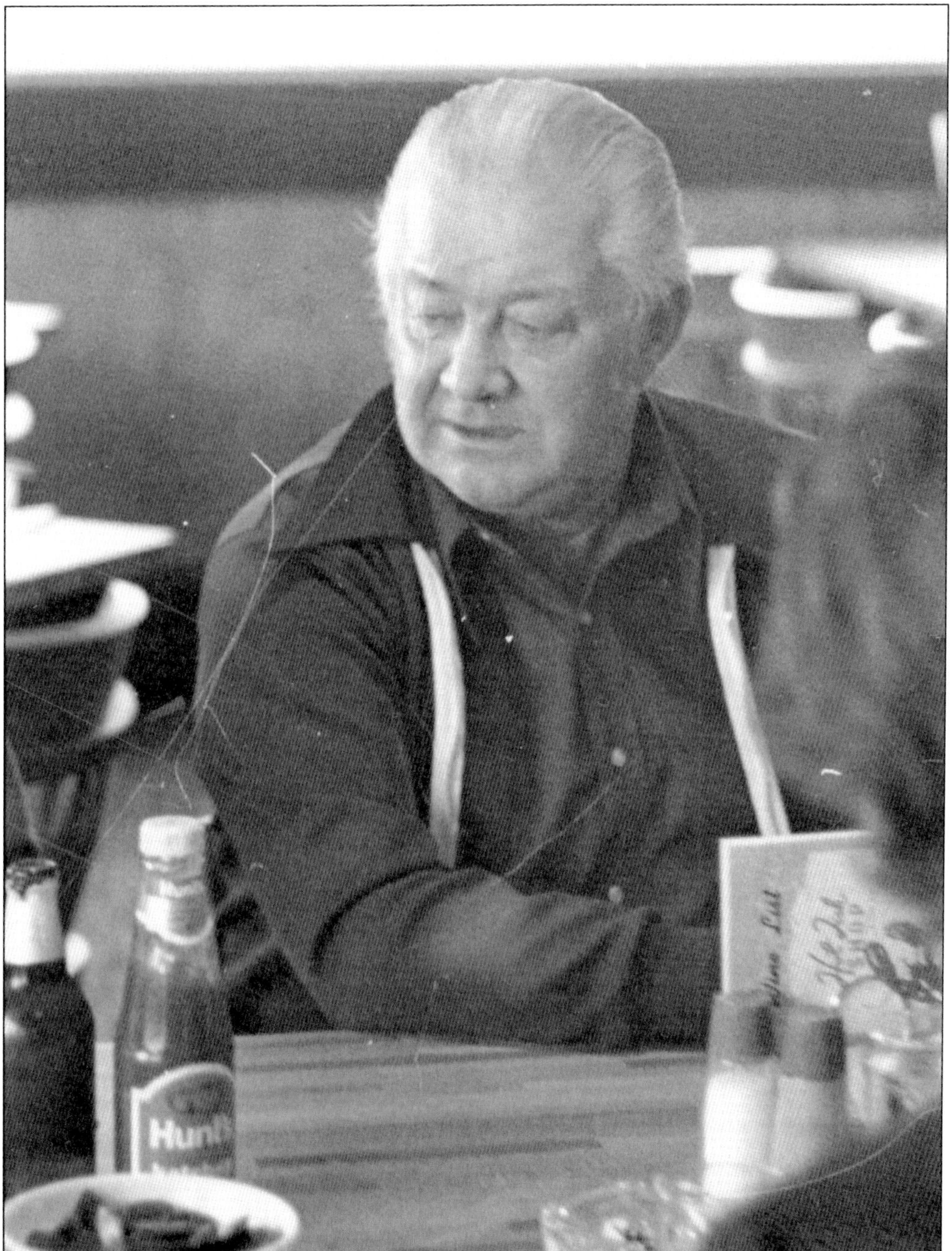

Lambert Kowalewski (1917–1987) was the son of Henry Kowalewski (1889–1966), founder of the Hot Fish Shop. Henry started the restaurant and fish market during Christmas 1931 at the corner of Mankato Avenue and East Wabasha Street. In 1935, after the school district purchased the property, the restaurant was moved to the corner of Highways 61 and 43. Lambert began working for his father in 1933, eventually taking over and expanding the business after his father's death. As a youth, Lambert was an excellent baseball player and served in the army as a cook during World War II.

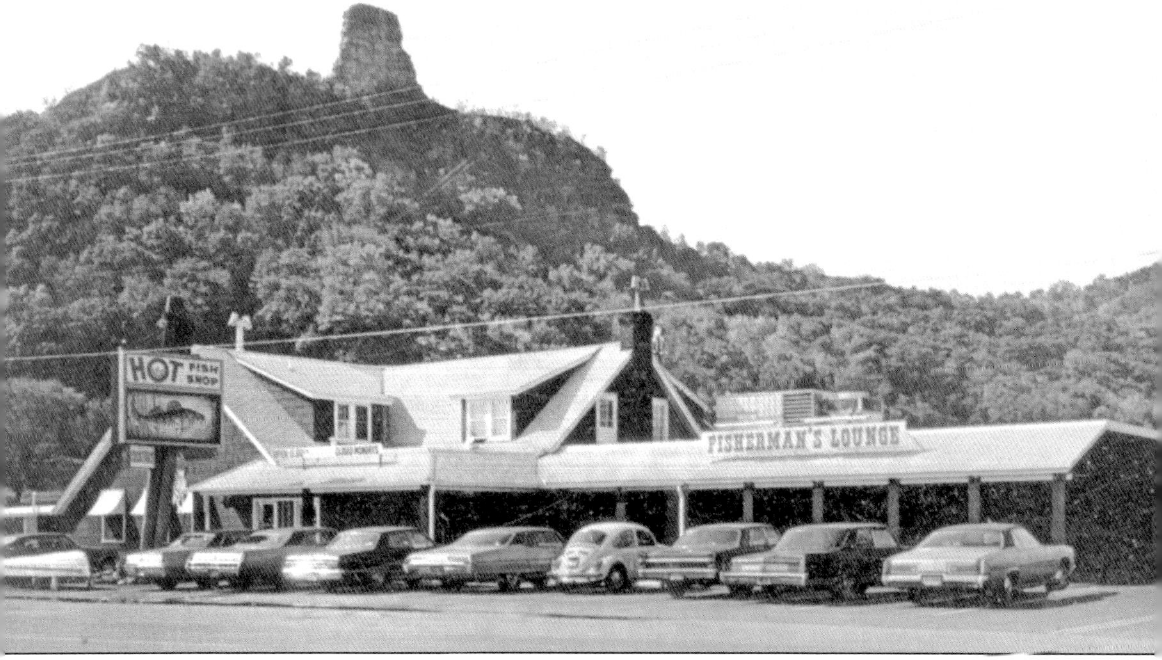

The Hot Fish Shop, under the shadow of Sugar Loaf, was located at the corner of Highways 61 and 43. It had an international reputation for fine dining and featured boneless walleyed pike, seasonal fish, and seafood. Later, the Fishermen's Lounge was attached and served favorite cocktails. Opened at this location on December 29, 1934, with all modern kitchen and ventilating equipment, the restaurant provided seating for 125 people at 14 tables as well as a long short-order counter. A gasoline filling station was located near the restaurant and was operated day and night. A tourist information bureau was also located in the shop to aid tourists entering the region. The shop changed its shape about four times before it was closed in 1999.

Six

Soldiers and Wars

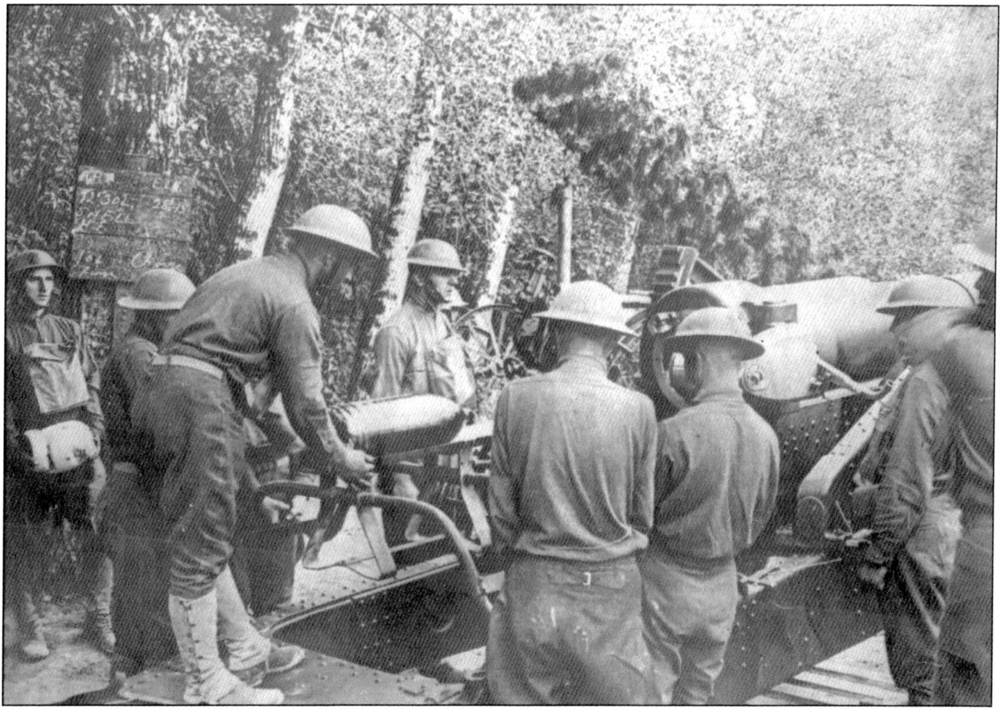

Shown is a US artillery unit somewhere in France during World War I. (Graham.)

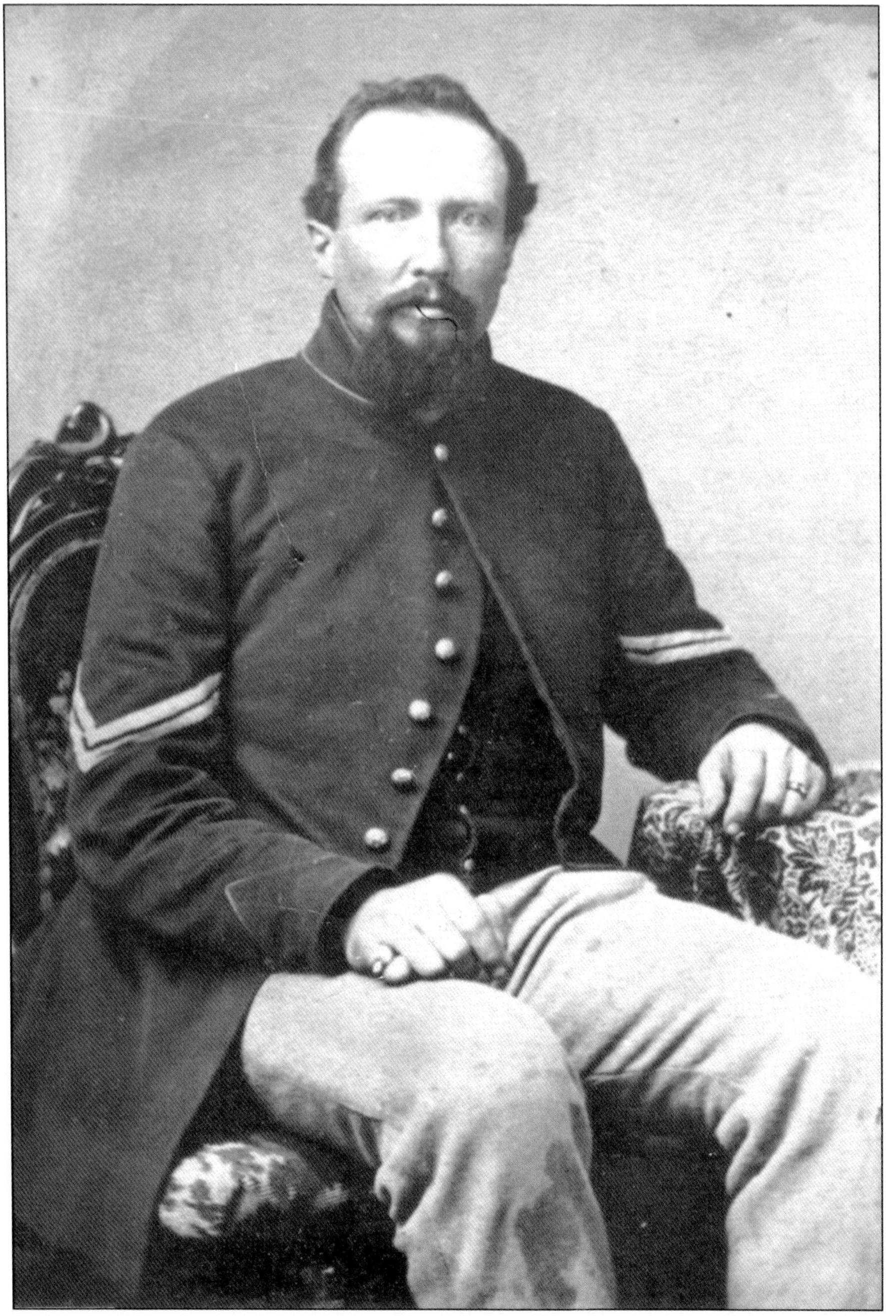

Sgt. James Thackery Ramer (1840–1892) was called into military service on August 14, 1862. Along with 96 other men, he reported for duty at Fort Snelling, where he was sworn into Company B of the 7th Regiment, Minnesota Volunteers. Furloughed to help with the harvest, Ramer was ordered back to Fort Snelling and sent to Fort Ridgely at the Lower Sioux Agency to quell the Sioux uprising that had started on August 18, 1862. After the army had put down the uprising and hanged 38 Sioux warriors, Ramer, along with the 7th Regiment, was ordered south to participate in the remainder of the war along the Mississippi River. Ramer was mustered out on August 16, 1865, and returned to Winona. (Kunz.)

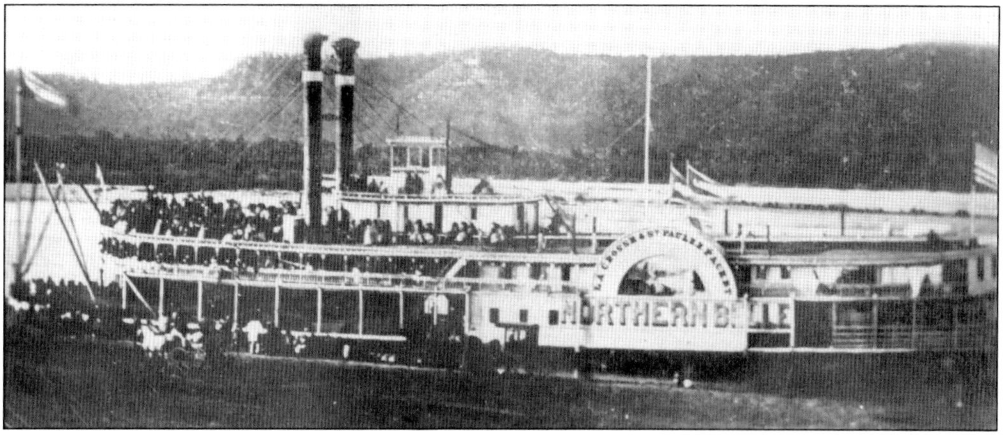

The *Northern Belle* of the La Crosse & St. Paul Packet Line carried the troops of Company K from Fort Snelling to the war, passing Winona on June 22, 1861.

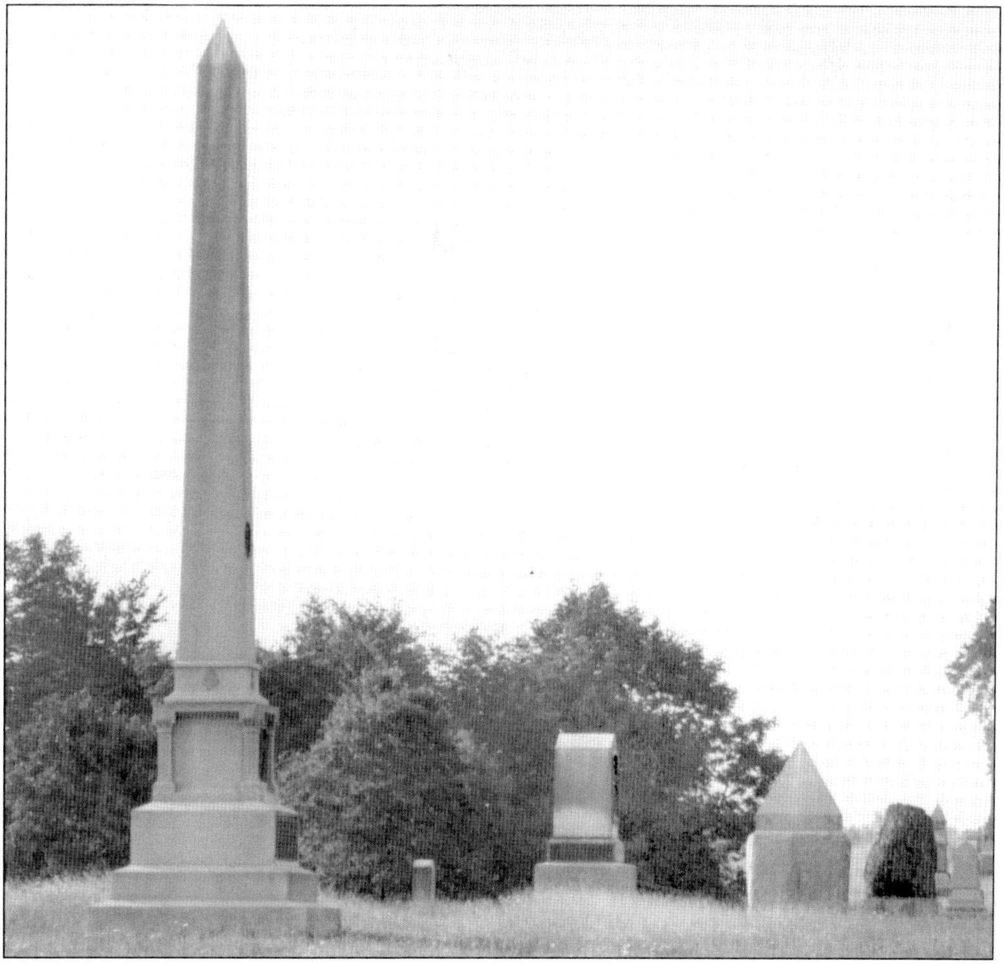

This monument at Gettysburg, Pennsylvania, is dedicated to the 1st Regiment of the Minnesota Volunteers for their role in repelling Pickett's Charge on July 3, 1863, during the Battle of Gettysburg. It was erected by the state of Minnesota in 1893.

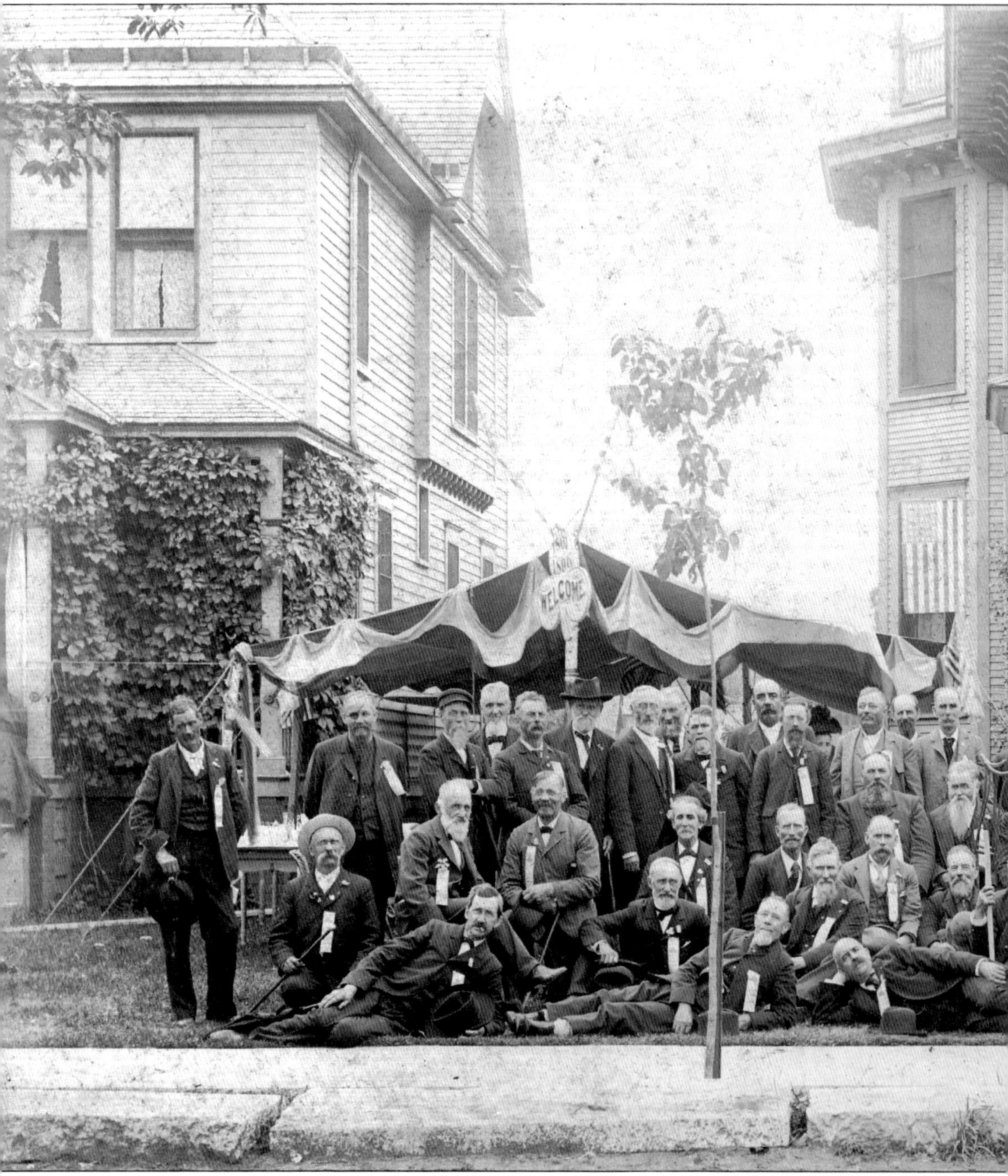

The 29th annual reunion of the 1st Minnesota Regiment was held in Winona on Wednesday, June 3, 1896, at Alonzo Holland's house at 411 West Sanborn Street and Leverett C. Johnson's house at 407 West Sanborn Street. It was Holland's house that was decorated for the occasion. The veterans had met in Winona five years earlier. There were 61 veterans in attendance at the reunion, and of those, only six were living in Winona County. These six included Paul Nelson and Hezekiah Bruce, both living in Ridgeway and part of Company F. Charles W. Merritt was living in Homer and was also from Company F. The remaining three veterans, Matthew Marvin, Alonzo

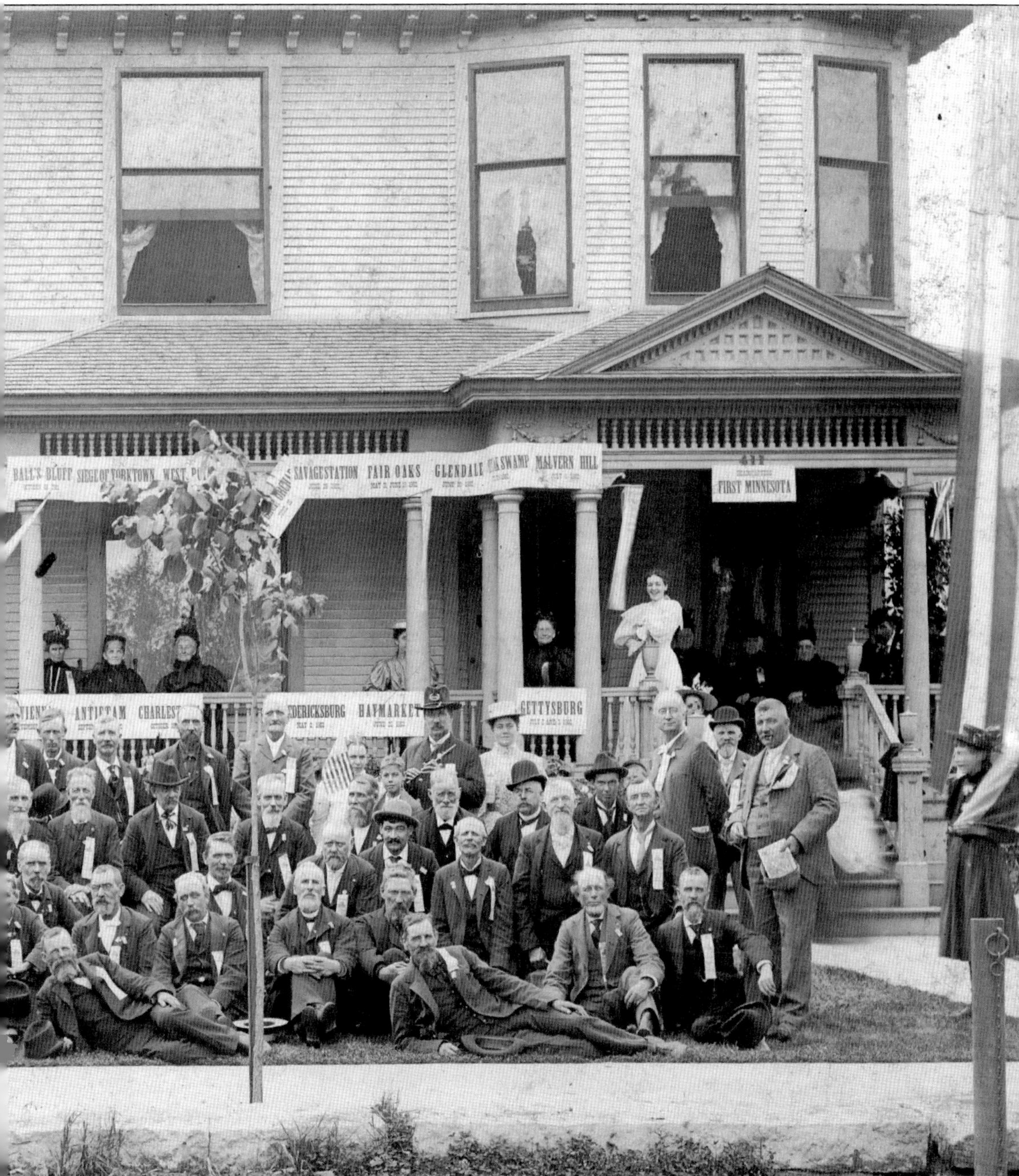

Holland, and John Einfeldt, lived in Winona and were members of Company K. Other members of Company K in attendance were Mark J. Kennedy of Kimball, Samuel S. Tenney of Wabasha, John J. Manning of Redfield, and Charles Ely of DeSmet, South Dakota. The veterans had arrived in Winona the previous evening on board the steamer *Henrietta*. There was a crowd to greet them when the booming of a cannon announced their arrival. As the veterans traveled to Winona, they could vividly recall when the *Northern Belle* and the *War Eagle* conveyed the regiment, 1,000 strong, to the warfront. Of those, only 262 went entirely through the war and returned.

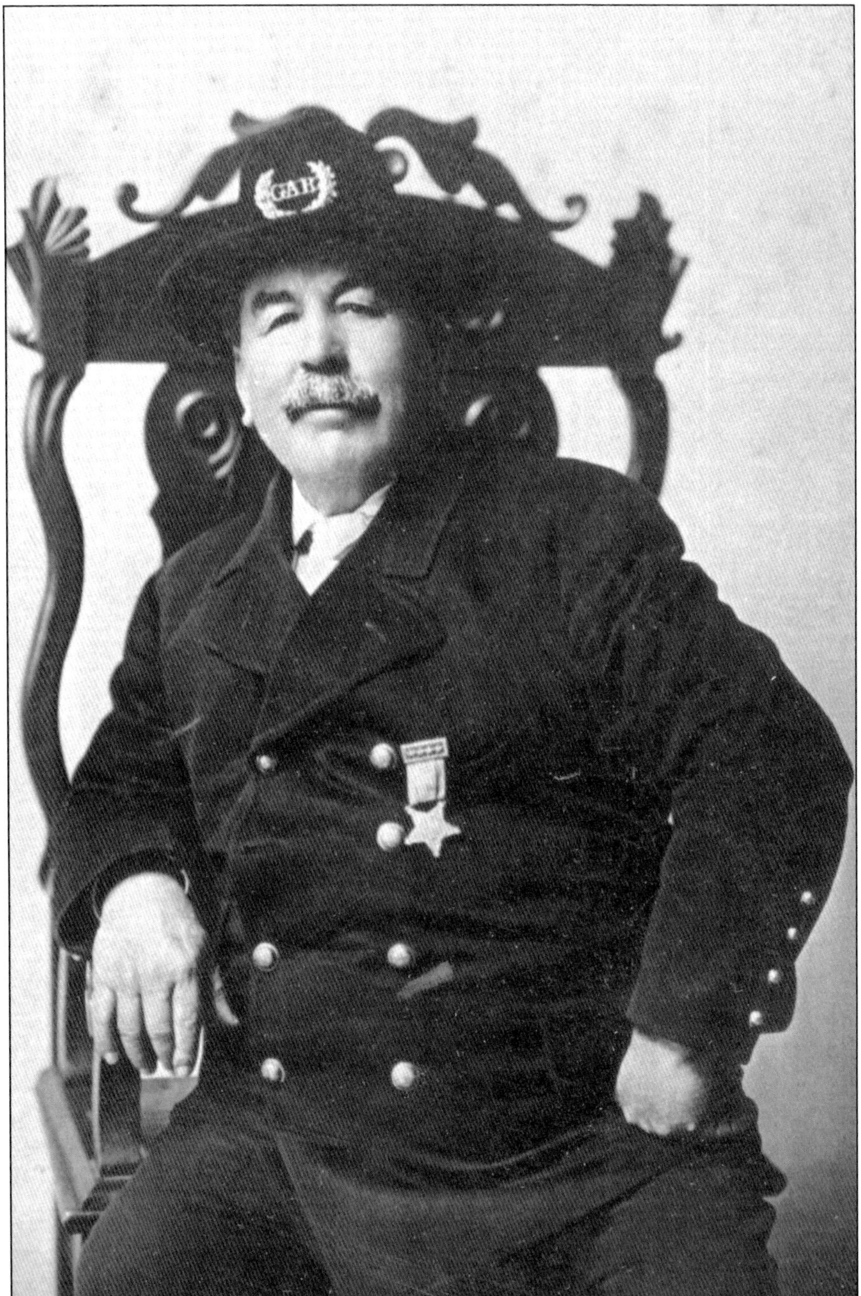

Samuel R. Van Sant (1844–1936) enlisted in the Union army as a teenager in September 1861. He fought with Company A of the 9th Illinois Cavalry for three years against the South along the Mississippi River and was mustered out in September 1864. After the war, he returned to Rock Island, Illinois, to work on the riverboats. He invented a special type of steamboat that was designed to move huge log rafts on the Mississippi River. He moved his business to Winona in 1883, and 10 years later, was elected to the Minnesota legislature and served two terms, the second as speaker of the house. He served as Minnesota governor from 1901 to 1905 and as the national commander of the Grand Army of the Republic from 1909 to 1910.

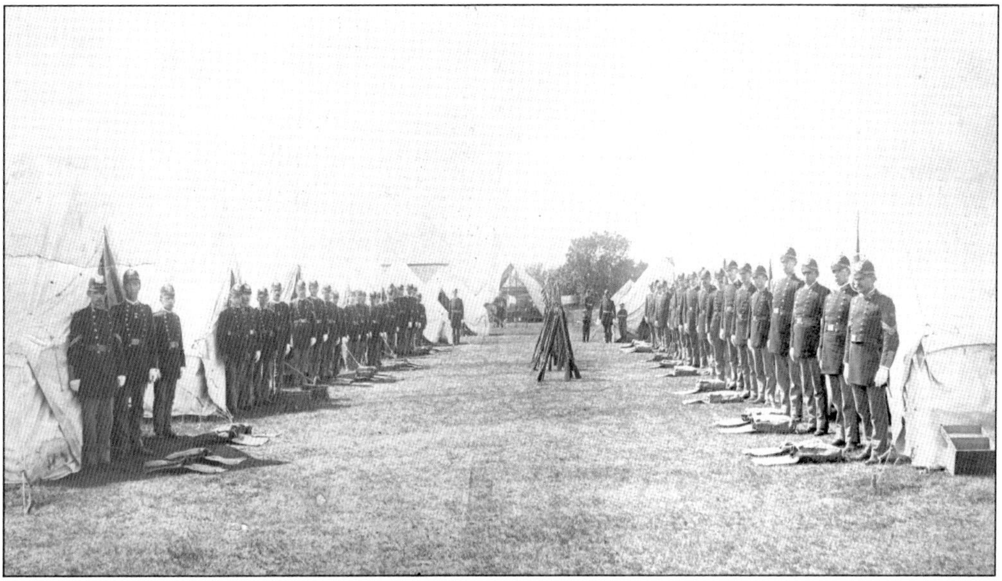

Company C of the Winona National Guard is pictured at an encampment at Camp McGill near Mankato, Minnesota, during the week of July 4, 1887. Camp McGill was located along the Minnesota River about one mile from Mankato. The troops pictured here are in their dress uniforms and prepared for a parade.

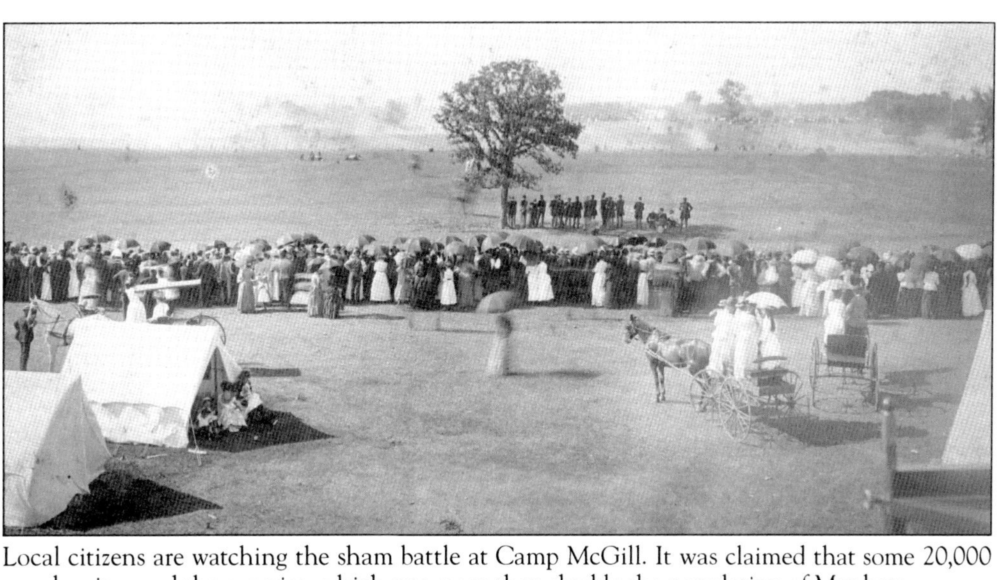

Local citizens are watching the sham battle at Camp McGill. It was claimed that some 20,000 people witnessed the exercise, which was more than double the population of Mankato.

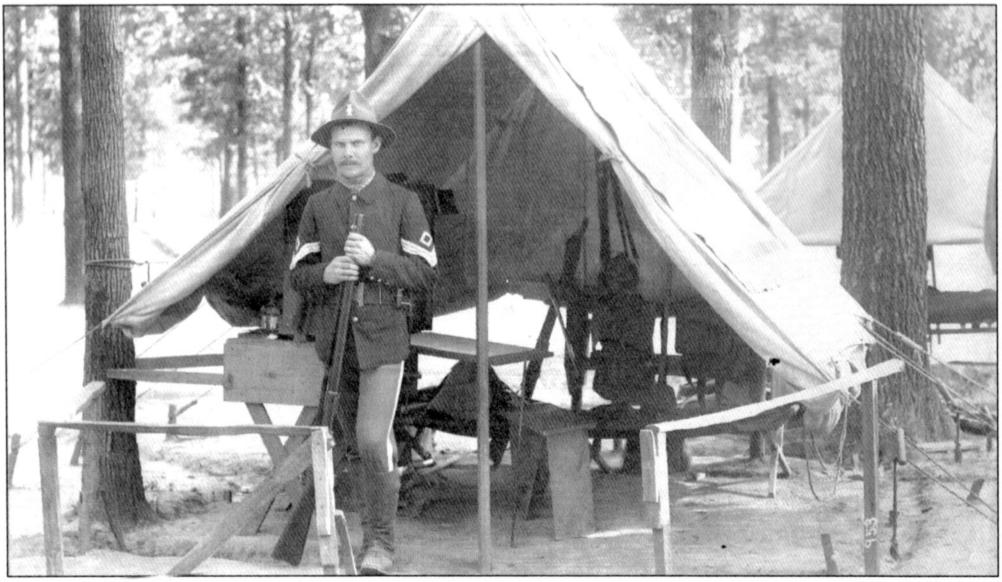

First Sgt. Charles A. Sinclair, "The Terrible Swede," of Company K of the 14th Minnesota Volunteer Infantry was stationed at Camp George N. Thomas in Chickamauga-Chattanooga National Military Park near Chattanooga, Tennessee. When the war with Spain in Cuba ended on August 12, 1898, Company K was ordered to return to St. Paul, Minnesota, arriving on September 23, 1898. (Holbrook.)

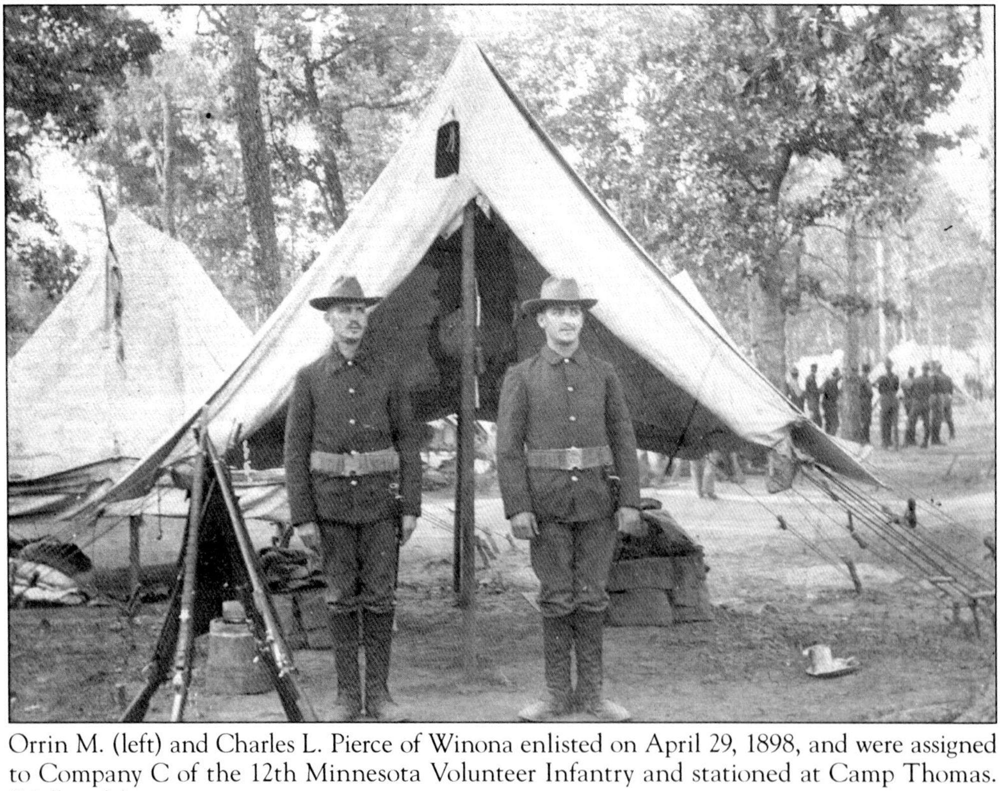

Orrin M. (left) and Charles L. Pierce of Winona enlisted on April 29, 1898, and were assigned to Company C of the 12th Minnesota Volunteer Infantry and stationed at Camp Thomas. (Holbrook.)

Leon J. Wetzel (1891–1917) was sailing on the USS *Jacob Jones* when a German submarine, while on escort duty in the Atlantic Ocean, torpedoed it. The ship was struck midship, rupturing the fuel tanks and splitting it in half. About 50 seamen were killed immediately, and another 15 were trapped when the ship sank. A few days after the sinking, Leon Wetzel was reported missing and presumed lost at sea. The *Jacob Jones* was the first American ship lost due to enemy action in World War I, and Wetzel was the first serviceman from Winona County killed in action in the war.

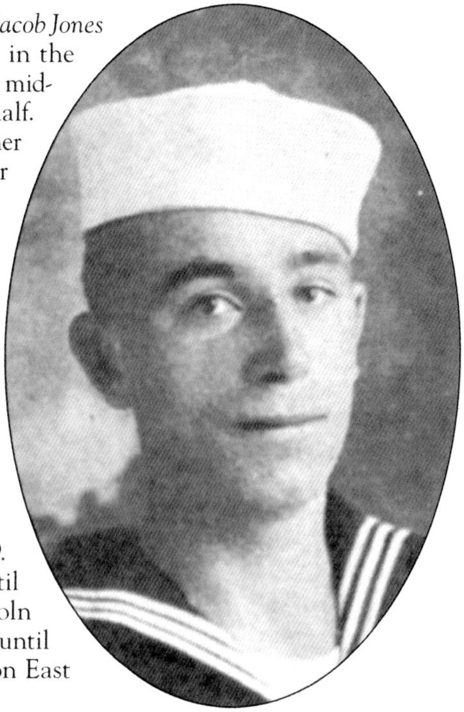

The Leon J. Wetzel Post of the American Legion in Winona, Minnesota, was given its charter in July 1919. The post's meetings were held at various locations until 1944, when the group purchased the former Lincoln Hotel building. The post remained at this location until November 2008, when it moved to its new hall on East Sarnia Street.

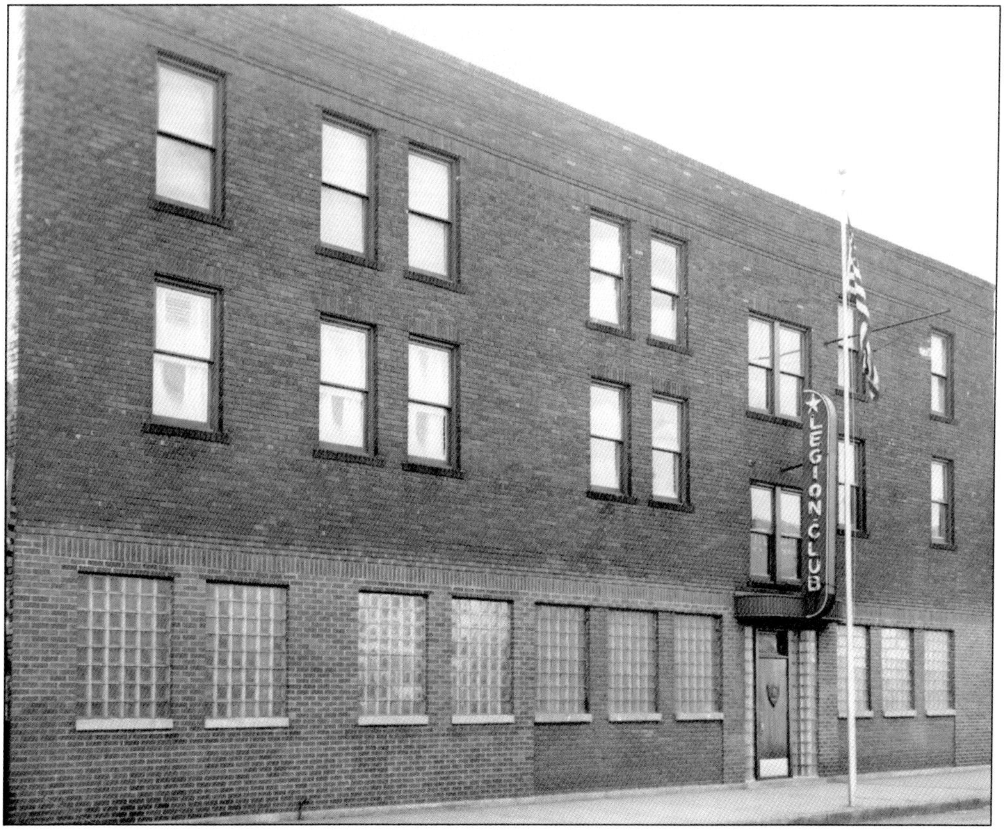

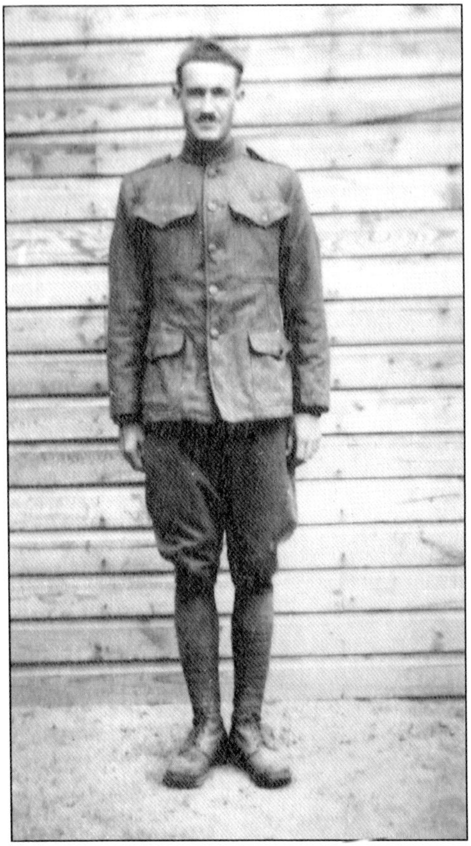

Cpl. Claude R. Graham (1893–1977) enlisted in the army on July 24, 1918. After basic training at Camp Wadsworth near Spartanburg, South Carolina, he was assigned to Company E of the 3rd Pioneer Infantry and sent to France on September 5, 1918. Corporal Graham saw action in the Meuse and Argonne offensives. Following the Armistice, the 3rd Pioneer Infantry was assigned to Camp Guthrie at the French port city of Saint Nazaire. There, the soldiers were assigned to occupation duty in Germany. The 3rd Pioneer Infantry was sent to the United States in July 1919 on the transport *Mexican*, arriving in New York on July 21, 1919. Corporal Graham was discharged on July 30, 1919. (Graham.)

A destroyed Boche (German) stronghold in France is shown in this photograph. (Graham.)

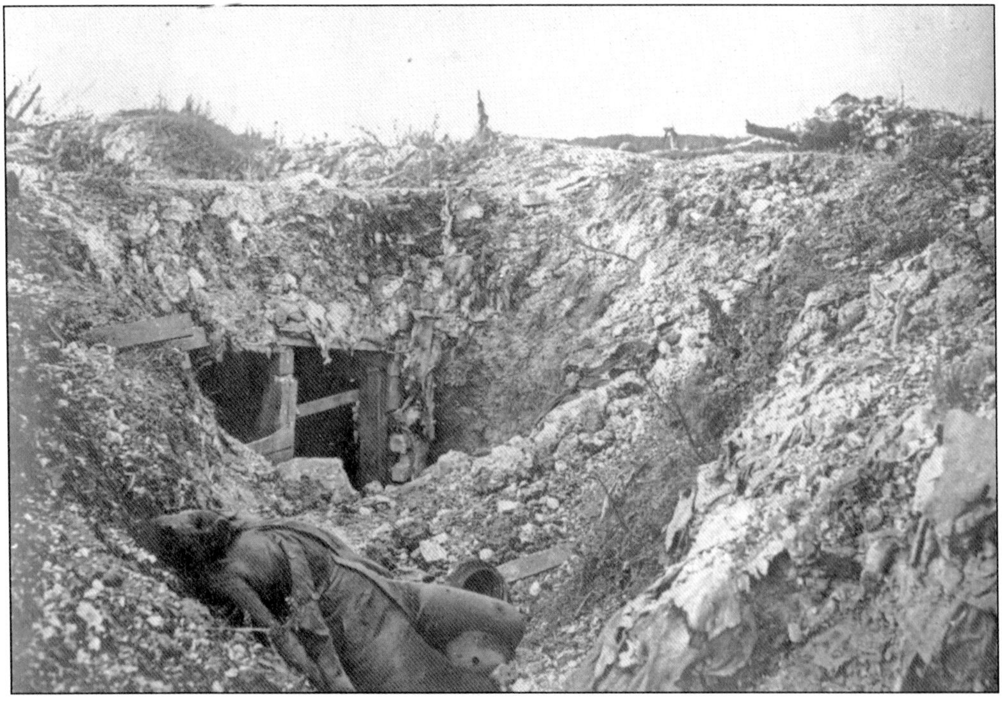

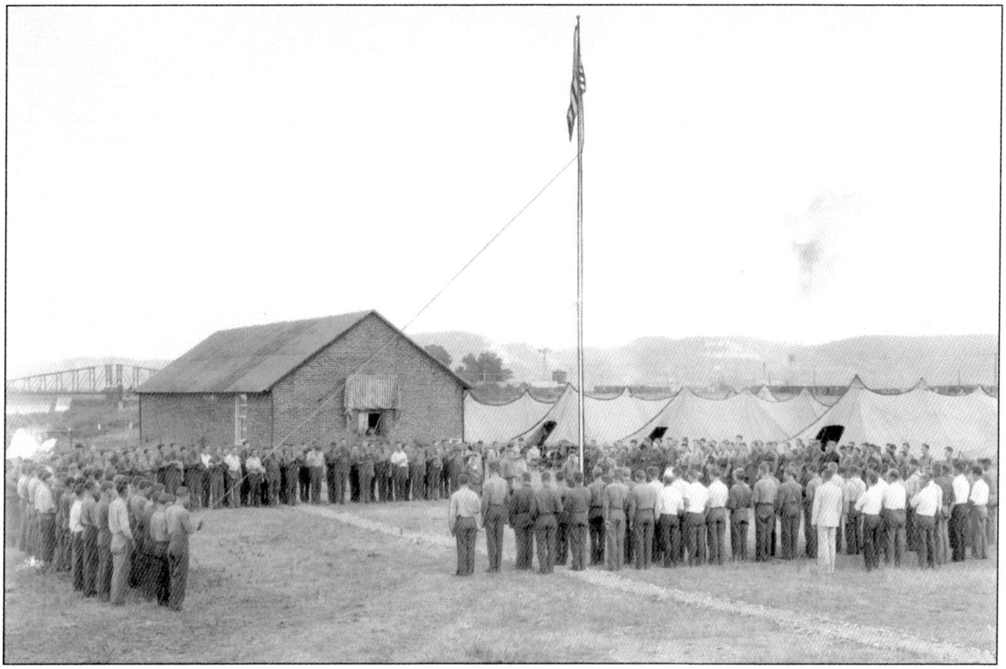

This July 1933 photograph was taken at the Winona Civilian Conservation Corps (CCC) Camp Floyd B. Olson, located along Louisa Street at the far end of East Sanborn Street. The photograph shows the men, not in uniform, standing in formation during the flag raising. Later, permanent buildings were constructed, and the brick building was probably used as the headquarters. Seen in the background is the Burlington Railroad Swing Bridge.

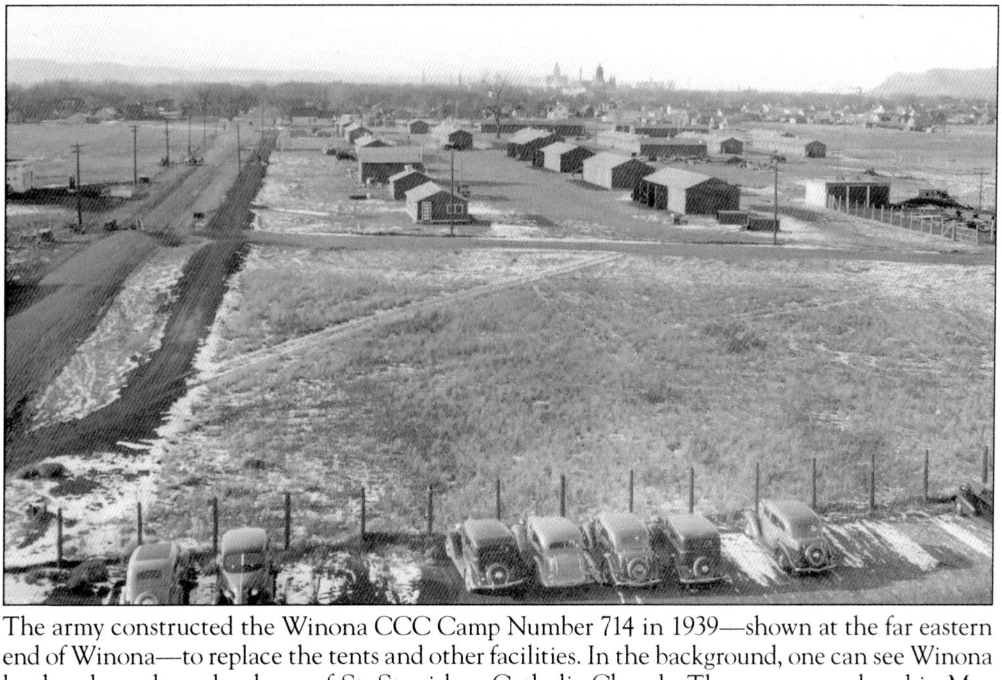

The army constructed the Winona CCC Camp Number 714 in 1939—shown at the far eastern end of Winona—to replace the tents and other facilities. In the background, one can see Winona landmarks such as the dome of St. Stanislaus Catholic Church. The camp was closed in May 1942 and the buildings were dismantled.

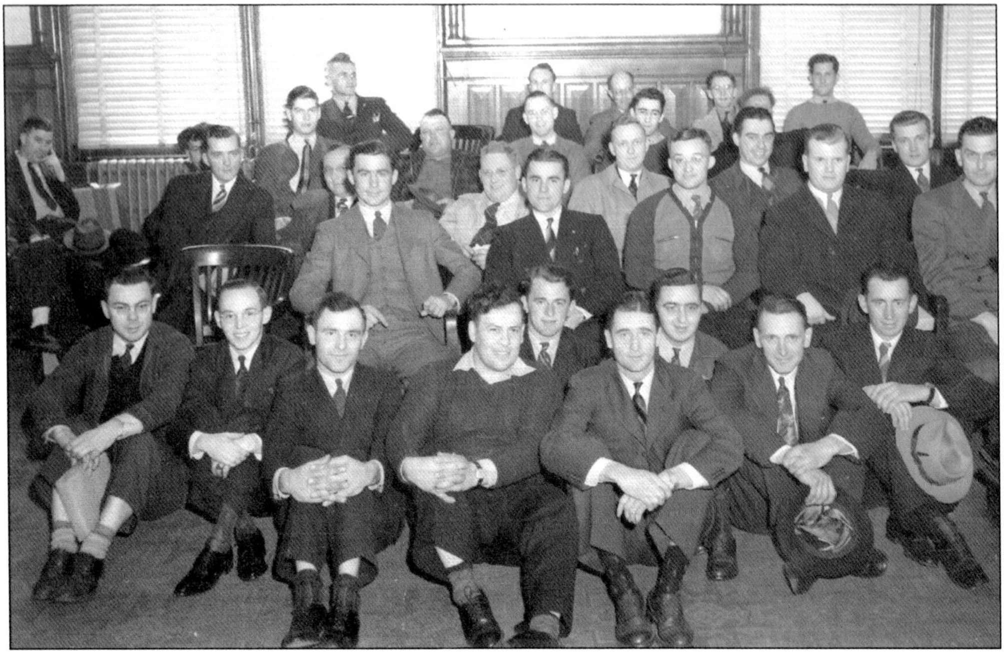

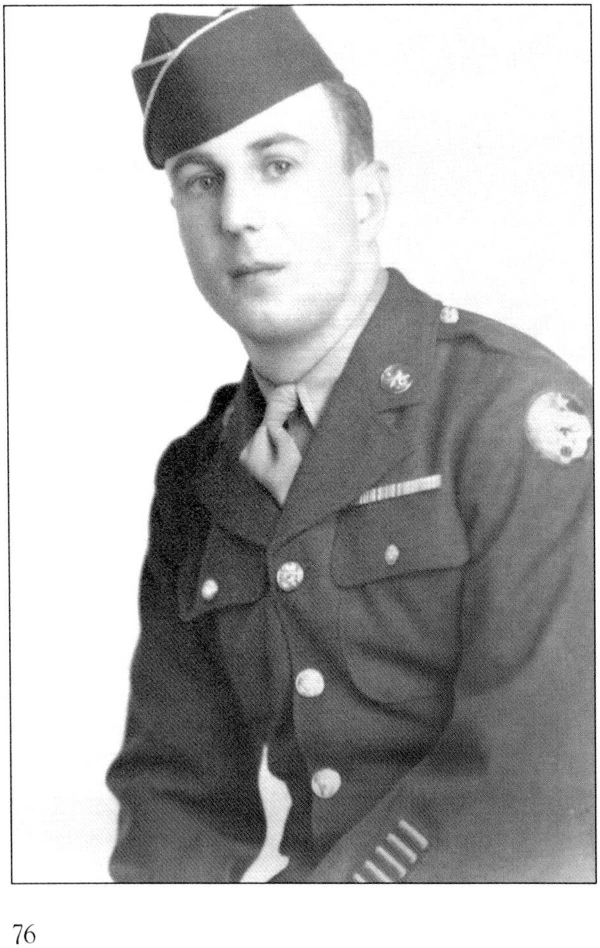

Paul P. Drwall (back row, second from left, in front of window) was one of 176 draftees leaving for Fort Snelling on April 10, 1942. The men, pictured in the courtroom of the Federal Building and post office, were sent off on buses with speeches and the municipal band playing lively military music.

Pfc. Paul P. Drwall (1918–1974) had volunteered for the draft and entered the army on April 9, 1942. Following induction at Fort Snelling, Paul was sent to Camp Roberts, which is nine miles north of Paso Robles, California, where he was assigned to the 79th Infantry Training Battalion. Following training, Drwall was sent to Alaska and assigned to the Signal Corps. Following 30 months in Alaska, Drwall was reassigned. He was discharged from the army on November 1, 1945, at Topeka, Kansas.

While he was stationed in Alaska, Private Drwall lived and worked in an earth-covered hut like the one he is standing in front of in this photograph. (Legion.)

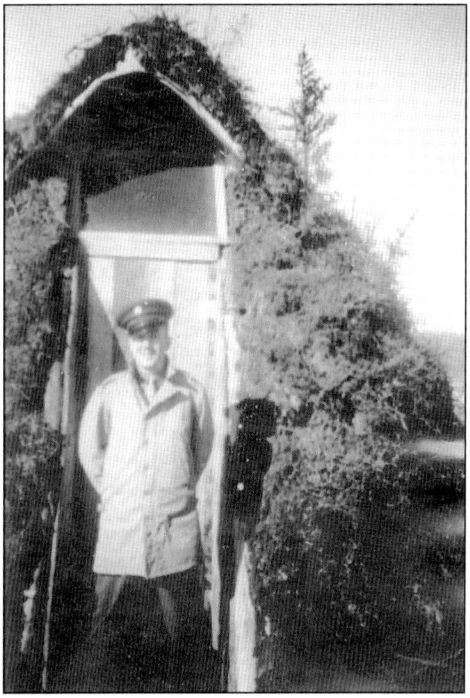

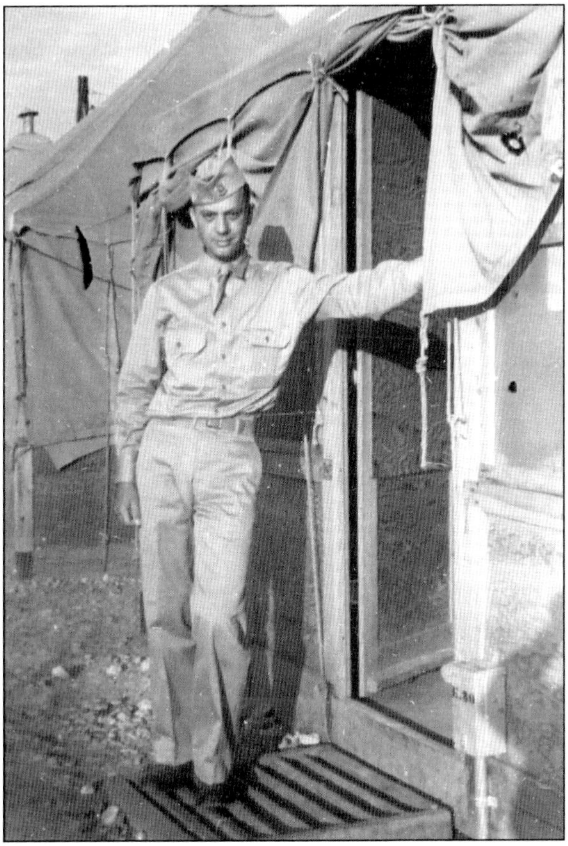

Paul Libera (1917–1999), a St. Mary's College graduate, was drafted in March 1942 and stationed at Camp Barkeley, Texas. Following his training, Corporal Libera was transferred to England and then to France, where he remained for the duration of the war. Following his return to Winona, Libera enlisted in Winona's Army Reserve Company. (Legion.)

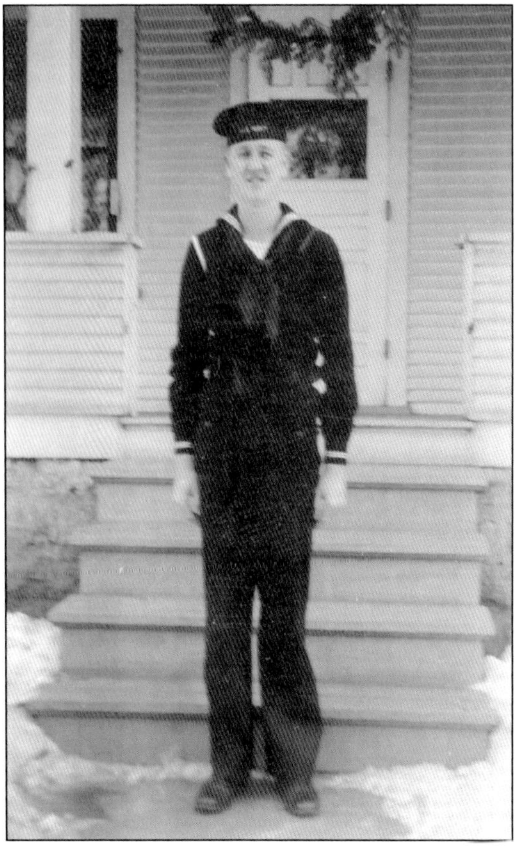

Eugene "Gene" Pelowski was the golf pro at Westfield Golf Club when he enlisted in the navy in 1942. After his basic training in San Diego, he was assigned to the Quartermaster Corps and received further training in Ohio. He served on light navy cruisers as a storekeeper. Pelowski had mostly been assigned to warships in the Atlantic theater of the war. After around 40 months of service, Pelowski returned to Winona and his position as Westfield Golf Club's pro. (Legion.)

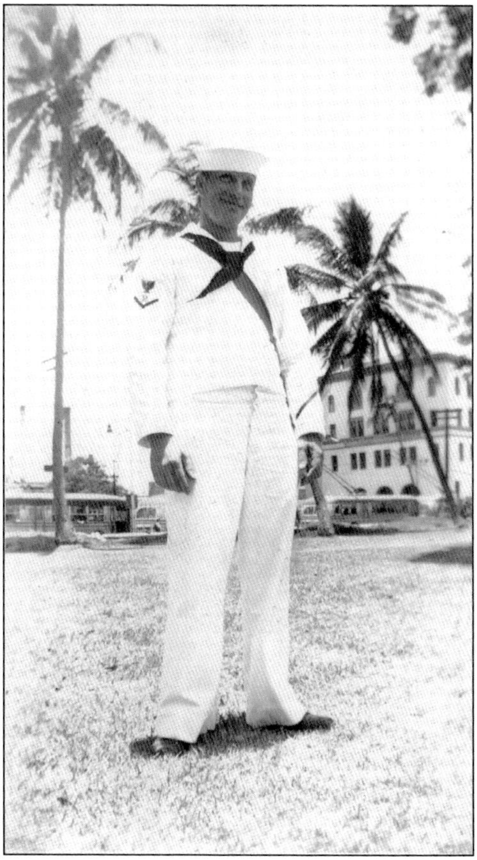

Edward E. Czaplewski (1905–1944), a father of five, enlisted in the navy in January 1942. After his basic training at the Great Lakes Training Station, he was assigned to a duty station at Pearl Harbor, Hawaii. Later, while serving in San Francisco, Edward died on April 1, 1944, in a rail yard under apparently unusual circumstances. Edward's remains were returned to Winona for burial in St. Mary's Cemetery on April 11, 1944. In December 1946, Edward's widow, Margaret, received the medals due her husband. (Legion.)

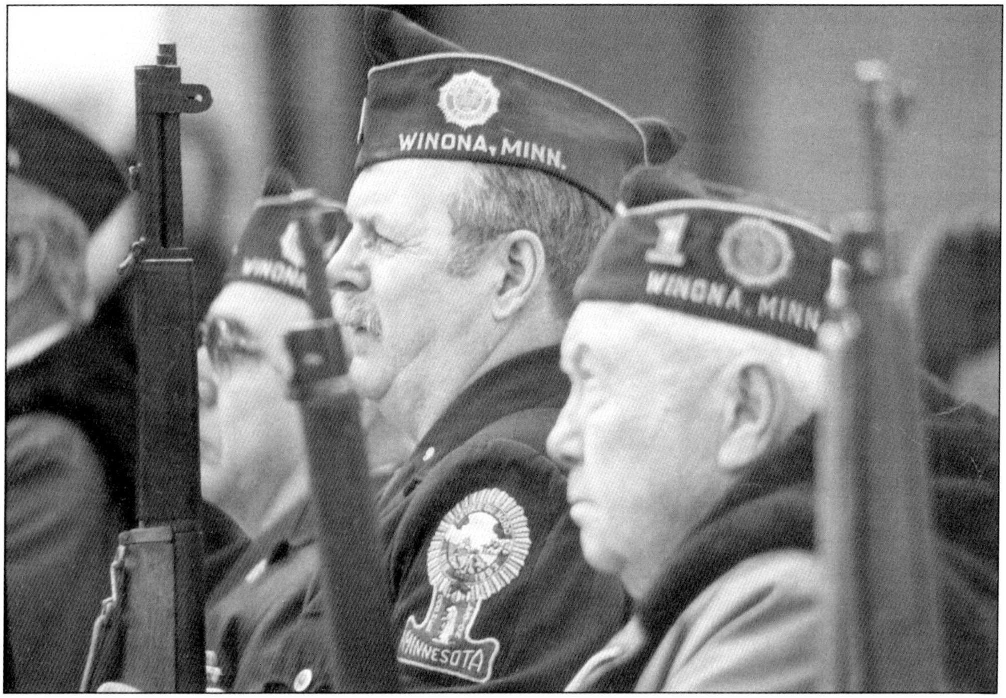

The Winona American Legion firing squad is standing at attention during taps at Veterans Day services at Plaza Square on Friday, November 11, 1983. From left to right are Clarence W. Schneider, World War II; Stuart V. Clemence, Korea; and Eugene W. Schueler, World War II.

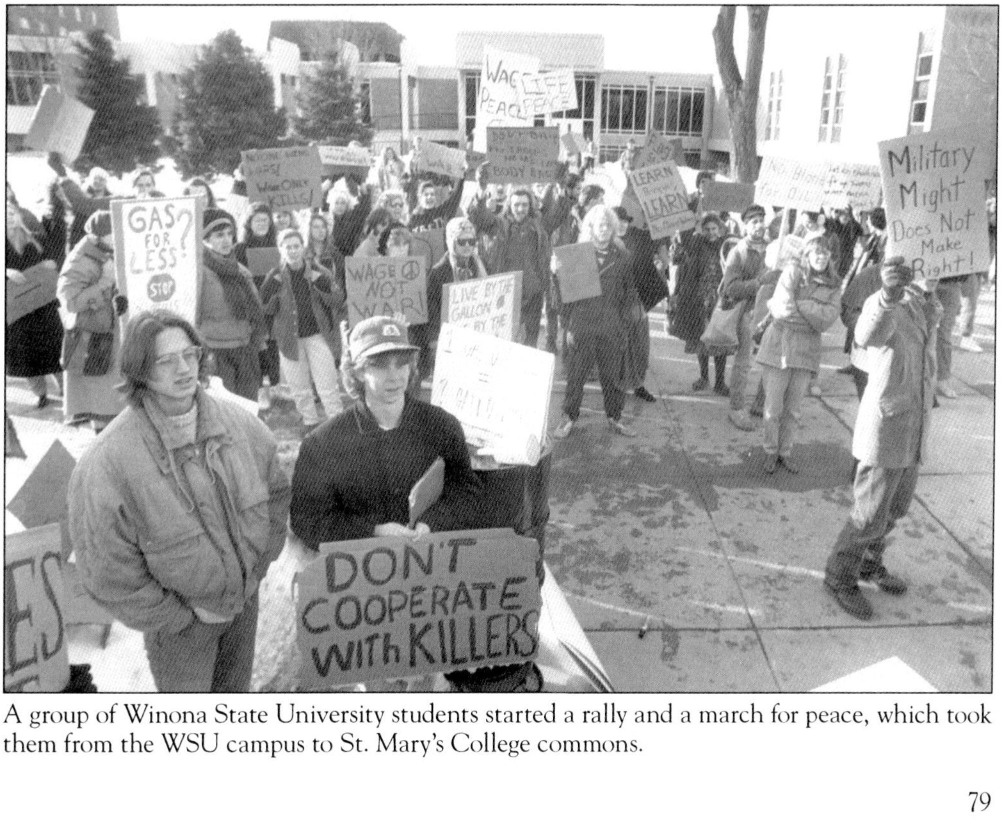

A group of Winona State University students started a rally and a march for peace, which took them from the WSU campus to St. Mary's College commons.

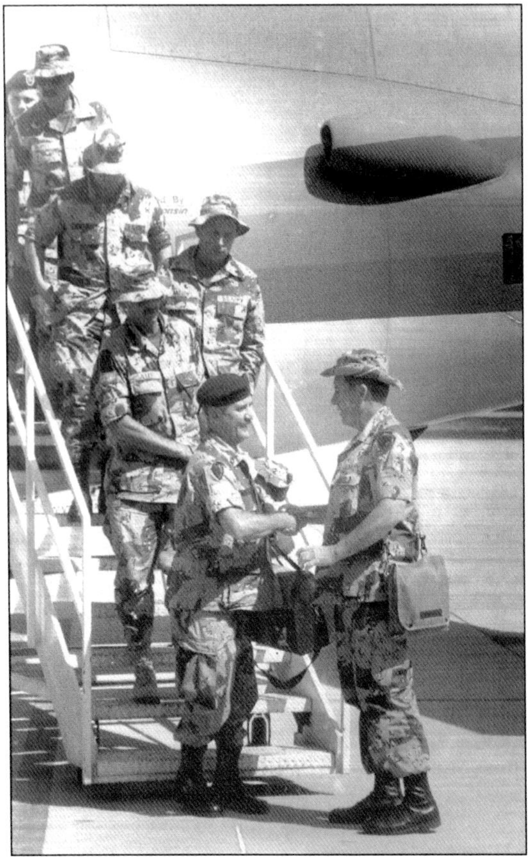

Reserves from the 407th Civil Affairs Detachment are returning to the La Crosse Airport from Operation Desert Storm on Saturday, April 20, 1991.

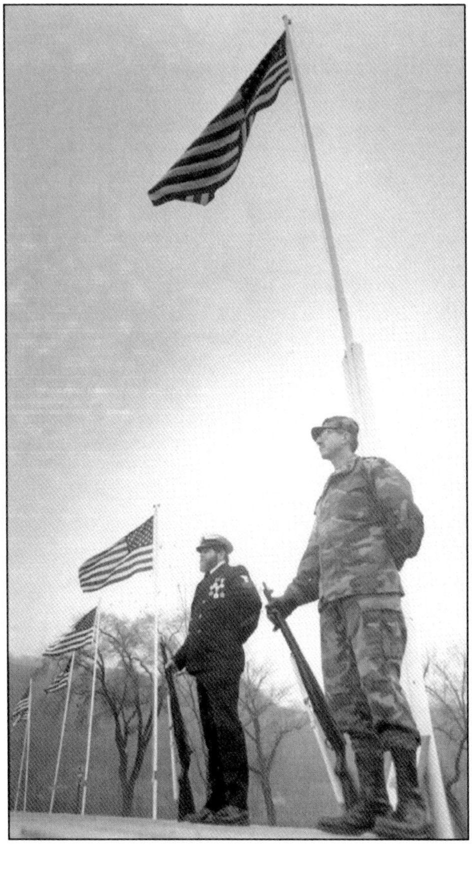

Jerry Obleglo (right) and Daniel Foster are two veterans standing at attention during the Veteran's Day Vigil at Lake Park.

Seven

Health and Sickness, Hospitals and Cemeteries

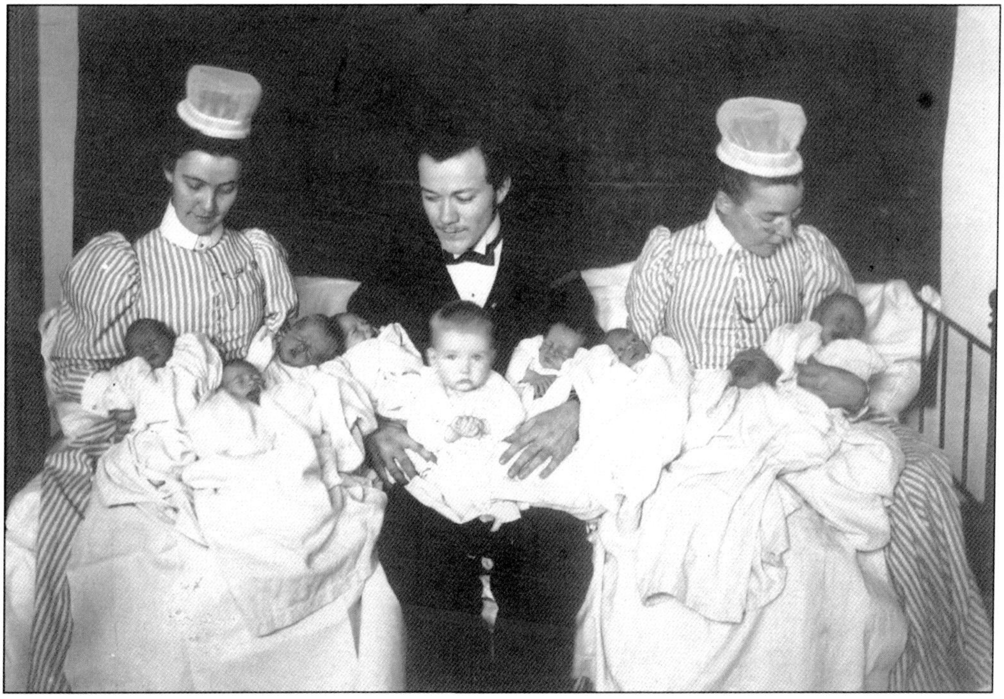

Dr. William F.C. Heise is pictured around 1900 with two nurses and nine babies at the Winona General Hospital. Doctor Heise started his practice in Winona in 1898 and performed the first operation at the hospital.

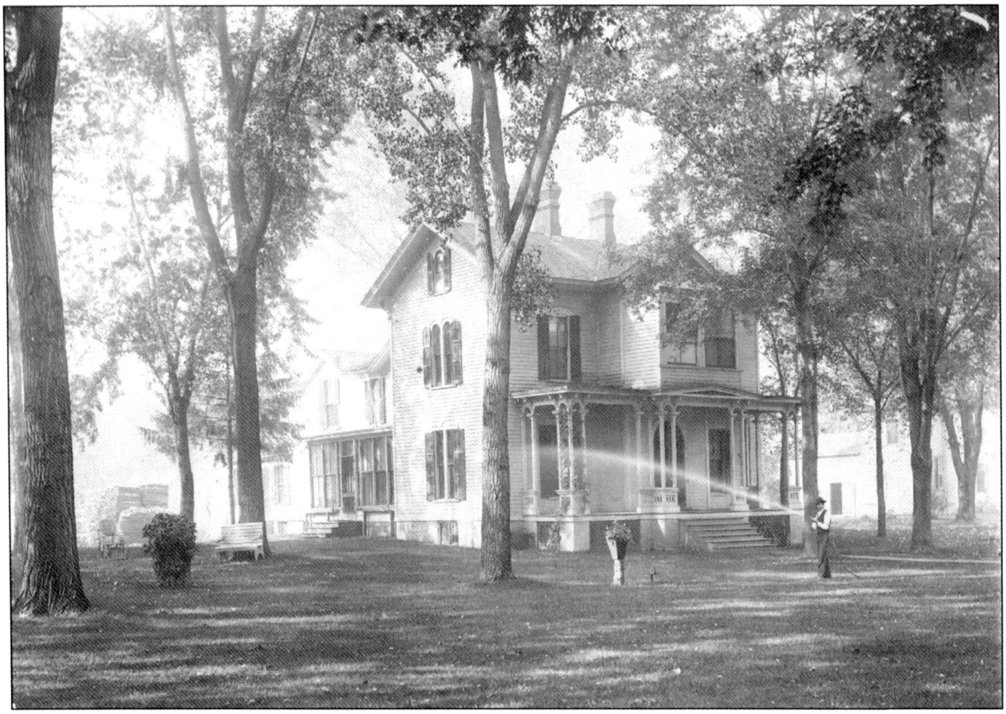

The Benton H. Langley home at 261 West Sanborn Street became Winona's second hospital in May 1895. It was closed in the spring of 1899 and became a dormitory for the normal school. It was remodeled in 1902 to become the east lodge of Morey Hall, a dormitory for ladies, until 1911, when it was sold to Jacob Stirneman. (Ruggles.)

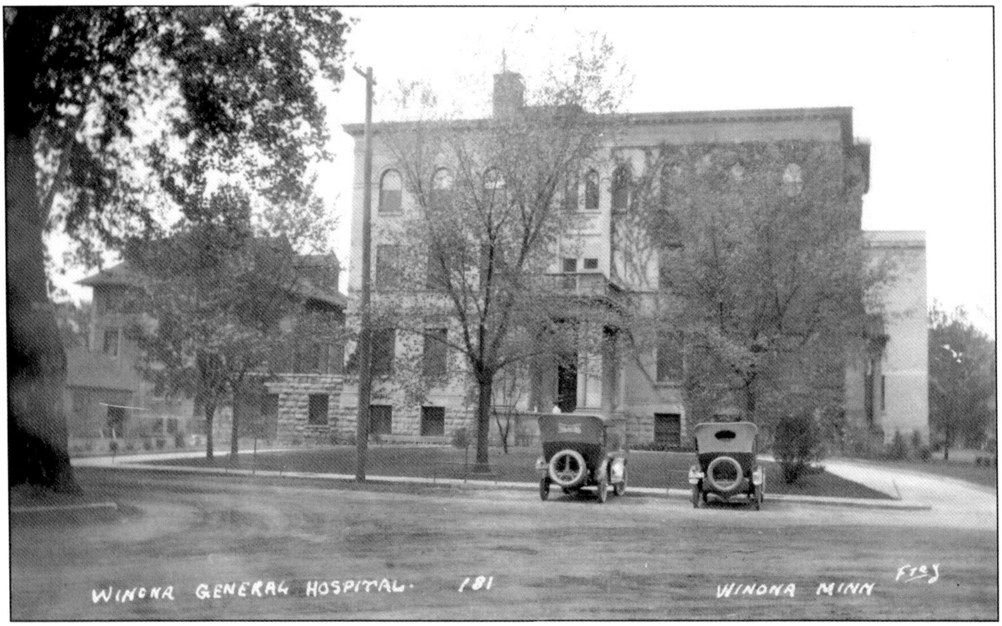

The Winona General Hospital (right) and nurses' home (left) are seen at the southwest corner of West Wabasha and Ewing Streets. The hospital was built in 1899, and the nurses' home was built in 1910. The buildings were razed in 1964 to make way for an apartment complex.

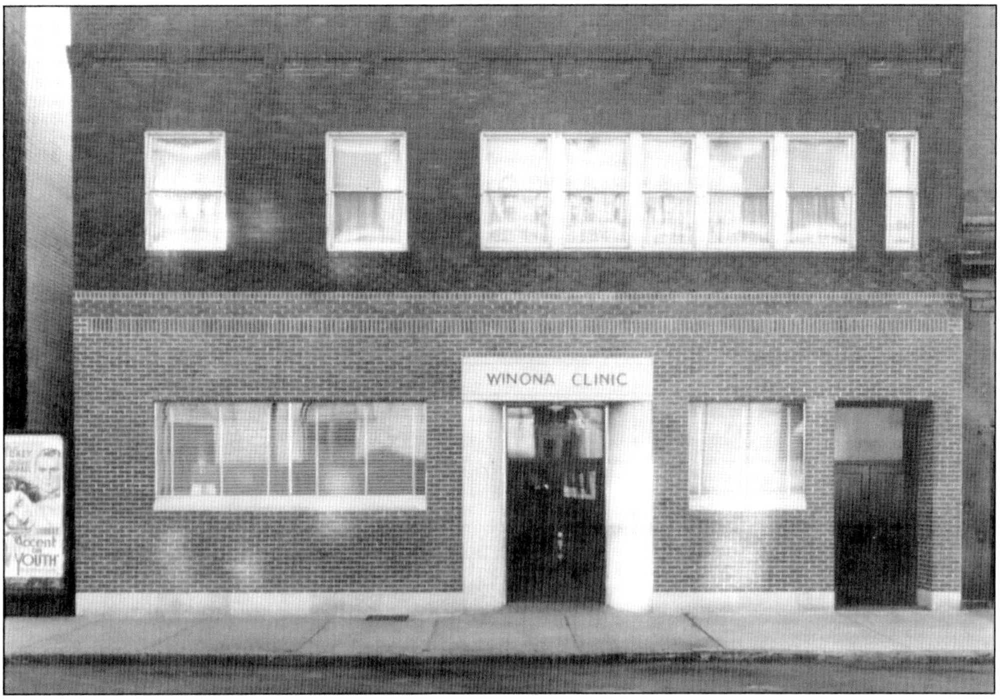

The Winona Clinic, located in the Kissling Building at 172 Main Street, opened on August 29, 1921. Dr. Edmund M. McLaughlin, Dr. Bertolet P. Rosenberry, and Dr. Walter W. Nauth founded the clinic in 1920. It was moved to its Sarnia Street location in October 1963. The building was converted into the Professional Building and destroyed by fire in February 1974.

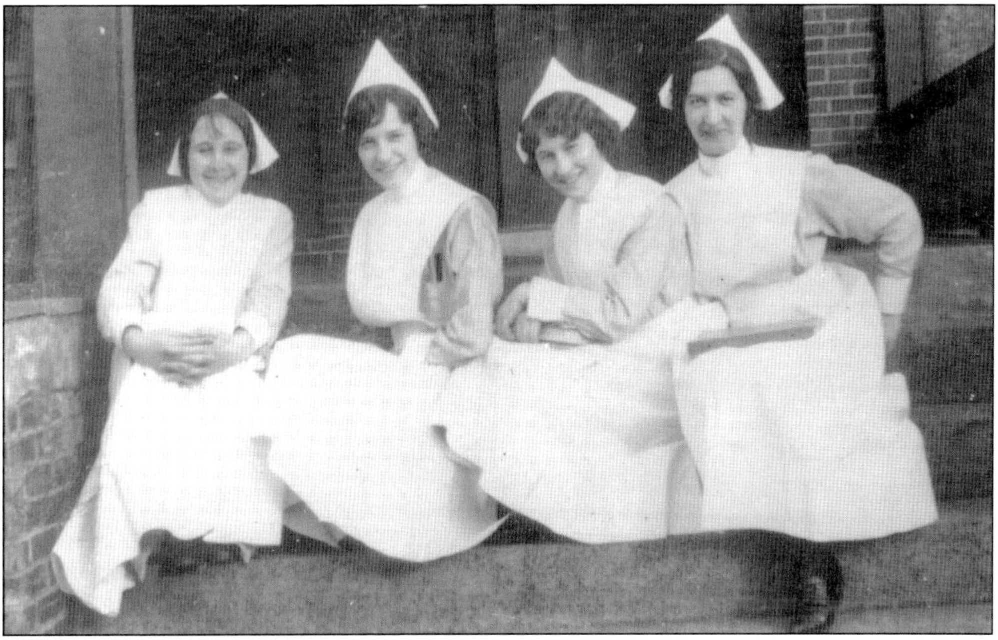

Four of the six student nurses from the class of 1926 are pictured sitting on the steps at the nurses' home. From left to right are Susannah McMartin, Clara Sobotta, Stella Slaby, and Mary (Prondzinski) Robb. (Sobotta.)

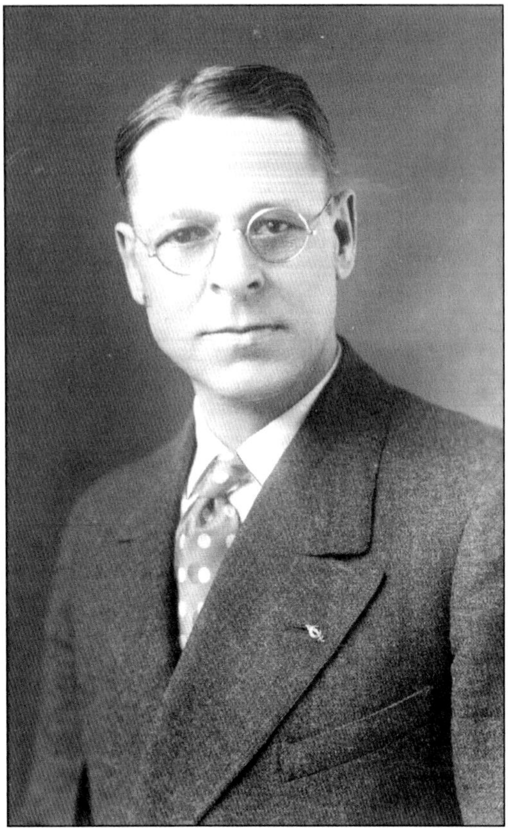

Dr. Walter W. Nauth (1885–1950) started his surgery practice in Winona in 1917 and was a founding member of the Winona Clinic. Following World War I, Doctor Nauth, along with Doctor Rosenberry, operated the Winona unit of the US Public Health Service to provide treatment to former servicemen at the Winona General Hospital, which was under contract to provide these services. Due to ill health, Doctor Nauth retired from his practice in 1940.

Dr. "Honey" Nauth and a nurse can be seen in the operating room of the Winona General Hospital in 1926. (Sobotta.)

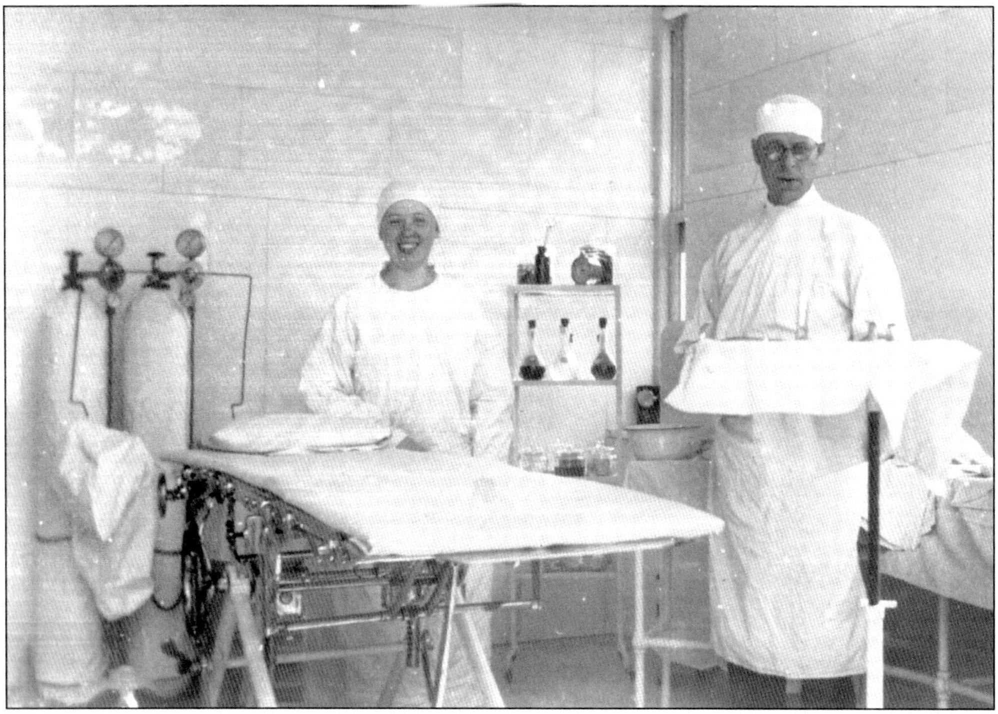

Hazel M. (Feller) Talsma (1907–1971) graduated from Winona General Hospital's class of 1929 and continued working at the hospital until she married Fred Talsma and moved to Racine, Wisconsin. Hazel was an active member of the nursing staff until her marriage in 1931. (Sobotta.)

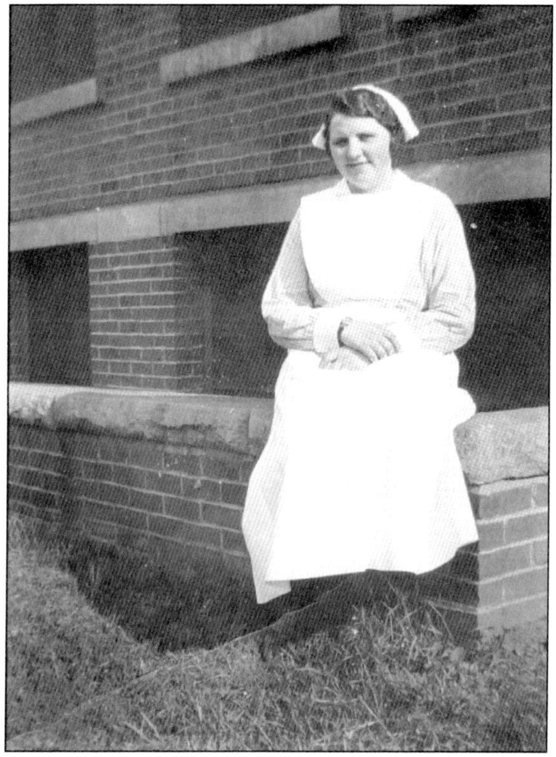

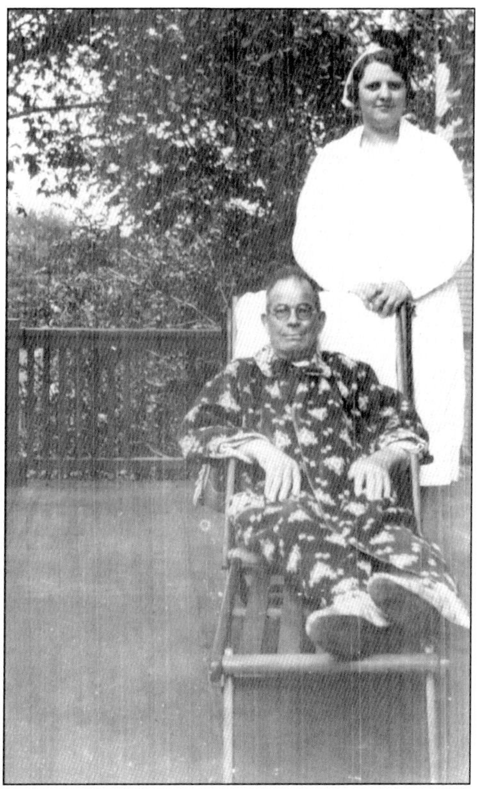

In April 1930, an ill John Latsch is resting under the attentive eyes of his nurse, Hazel Feller, on a lounge chair on the deck of the Winona General Hospital's roof. (Sobotta.)

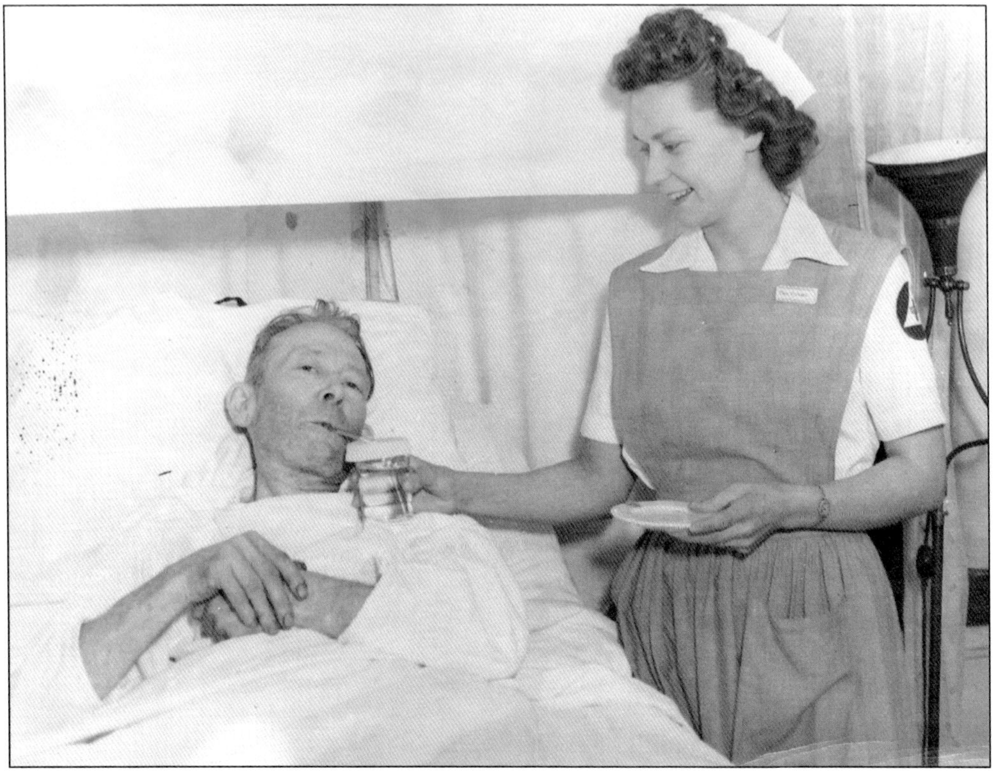

A Red Cross volunteer nurse's aide is helping a thirsty patient with a drink of water. These volunteers filled in during World War II to allow nurses to serve in the military. (Hardtke.)

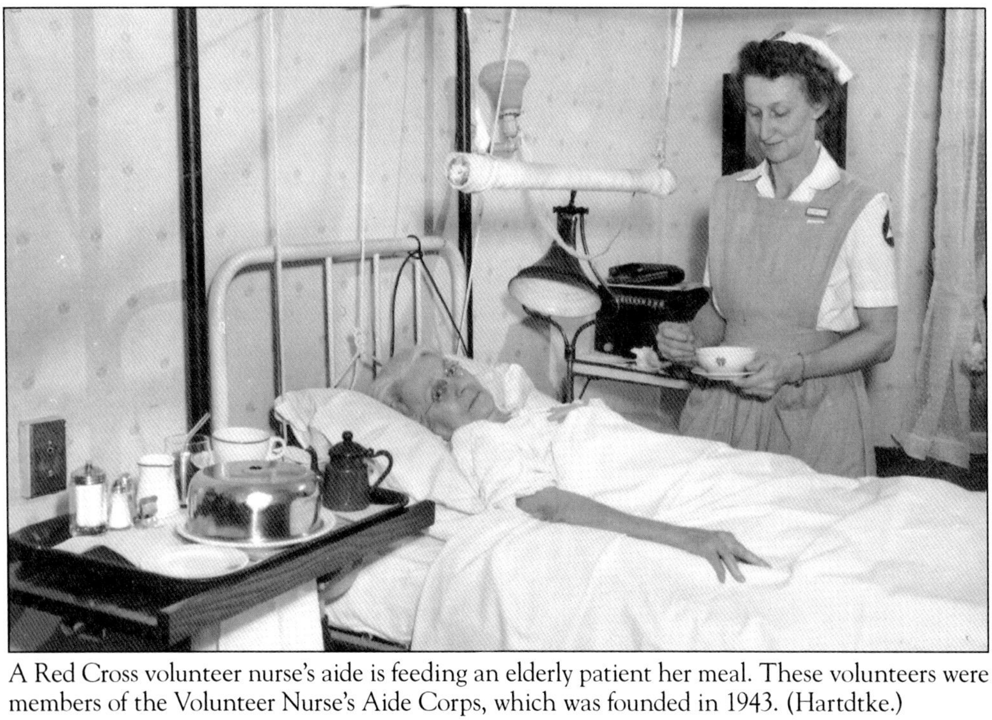

A Red Cross volunteer nurse's aide is feeding an elderly patient her meal. These volunteers were members of the Volunteer Nurse's Aide Corps, which was founded in 1943. (Hartdtke.)

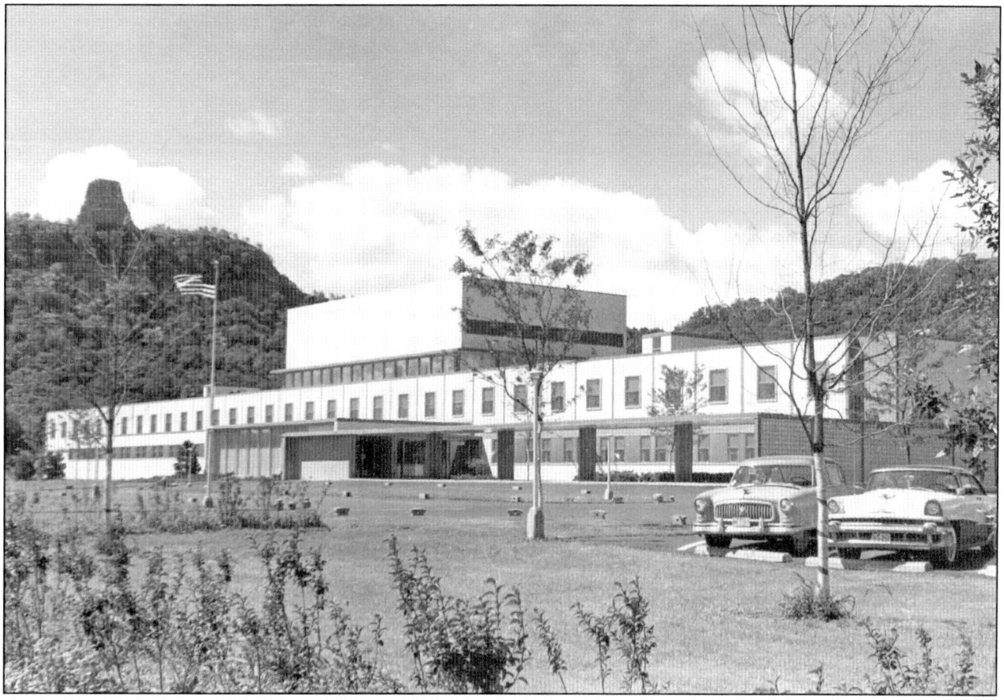

Community Memorial Hospital, located along Mankato Avenue at the east end of Lake Winona, opened to the public on Saturday, August 11, 1962. When it was built, the hospital was equipped with 120 beds and had a staff of 265, which included 39 physicians and 134 nursing personnel.

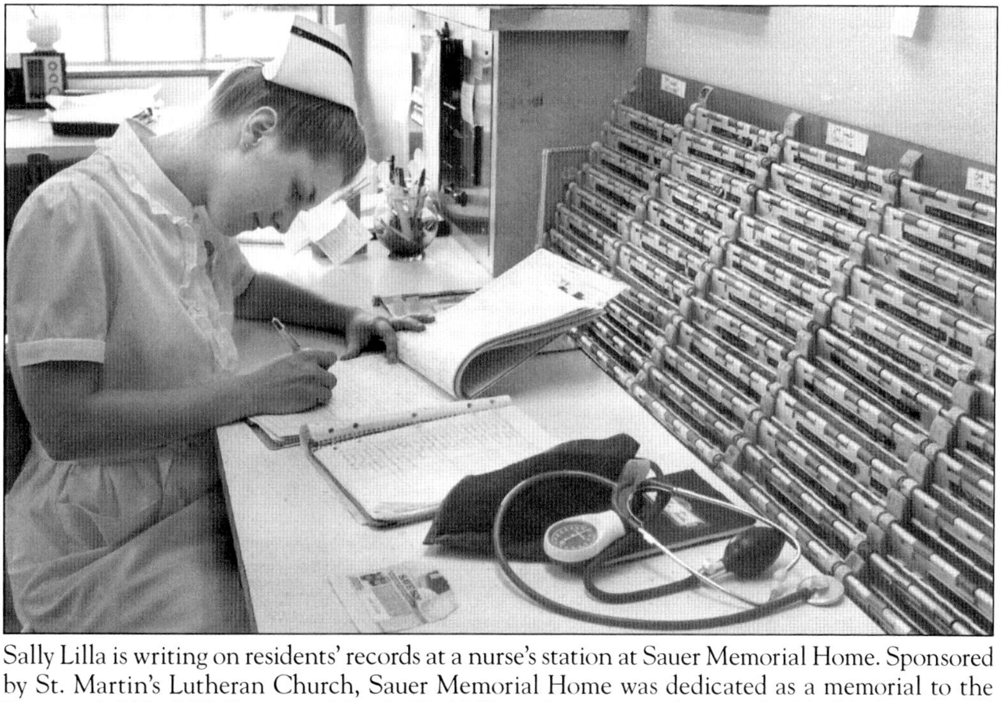

Sally Lilla is writing on residents' records at a nurse's station at Sauer Memorial Home. Sponsored by St. Martin's Lutheran Church, Sauer Memorial Home was dedicated as a memorial to the Reverend Alfred W. Sauer on March 27, 1966, with accommodations for 80 elderly men and women. It is located at 1635 Service Drive.

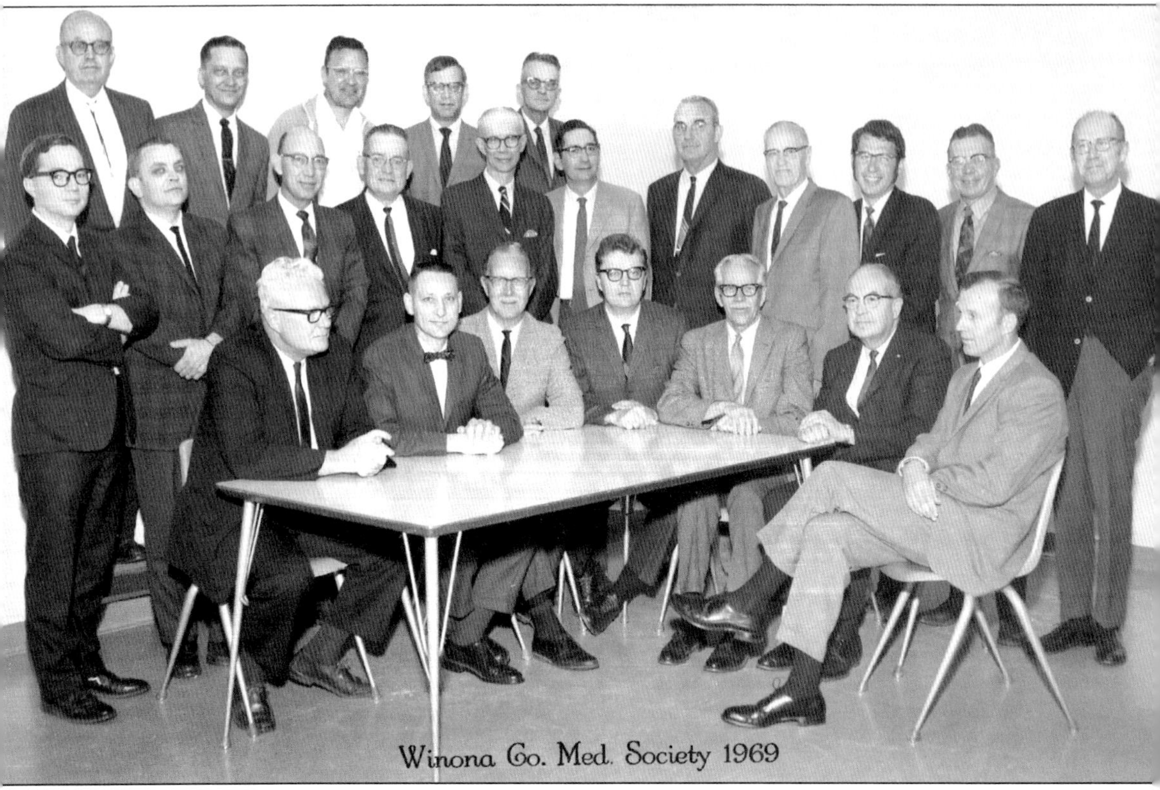

The Winona County Medical Society of 1969 was photographed in Community Memorial Hospital's third-floor auditorium on June 14, 1969. Pictured from left to right are (first row) Paul R. Heise, Arnold W. Fenske, Philip vR. Heise (vice president), Curtis M. Johnson (president), Herbert vR. Heise (secretary-treasurer), Leonard F. Johnston, and James V. Testor; (second row) Horace J. Andersen, George L. Garber, William O. Finkelnburg, Lewis I. Younger, William vR. Heise, Roger F. Hartwich, John A. Tweedy, Howard W. Satterlee, Charles F. Schafer, Frederick J. Vollmer, and George L. Loomis; (third row) Dalmon V. Boardman, Warren W. Haesley, Dale J. Hawk, Sidney O. Hughes, and Henry J. Roemer. Not pictured are Thomas L. Brannick, Daniel Degallier, Andrew E. Edin, Carl vR. Heise, John F. Hick, Charles W. Rogers, Robert B. Tweedy, and Louis J. Wilson.

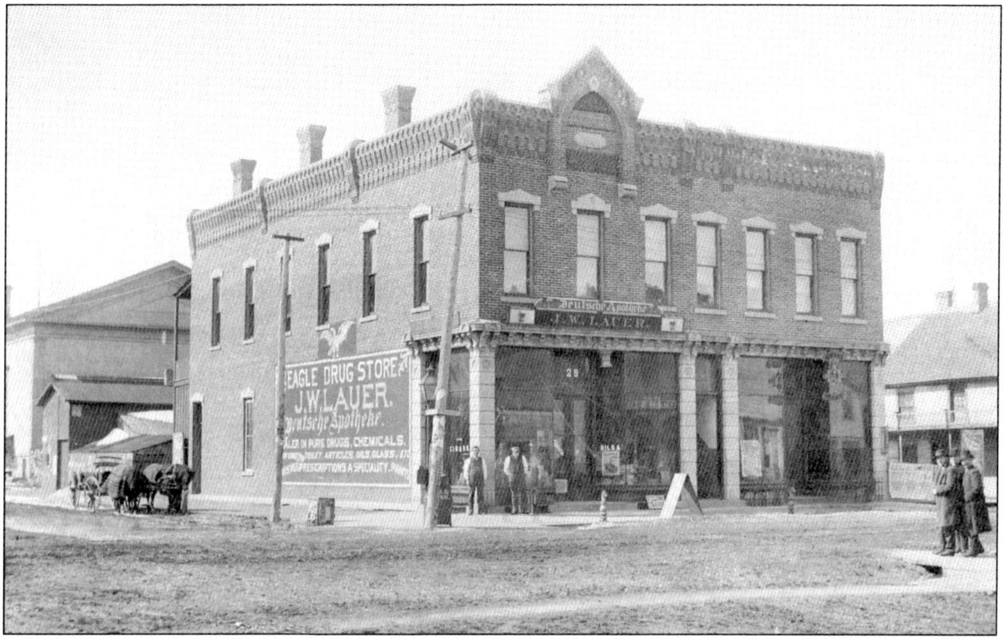

Joseph W. Lauer's Eagle Drugstore, founded in 1881, was located at the southwest corner of Franklin and East Third Streets. Of the two men pictured standing in front of the store, Lauer is the man to the left.

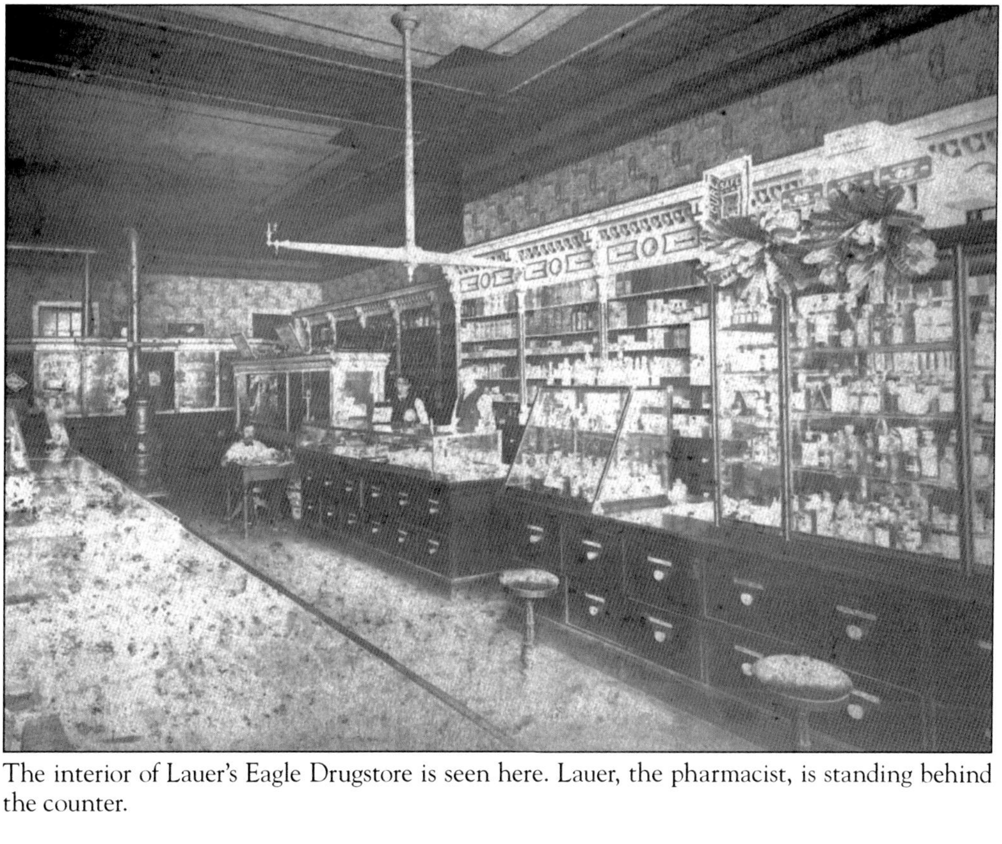

The interior of Lauer's Eagle Drugstore is seen here. Lauer, the pharmacist, is standing behind the counter.

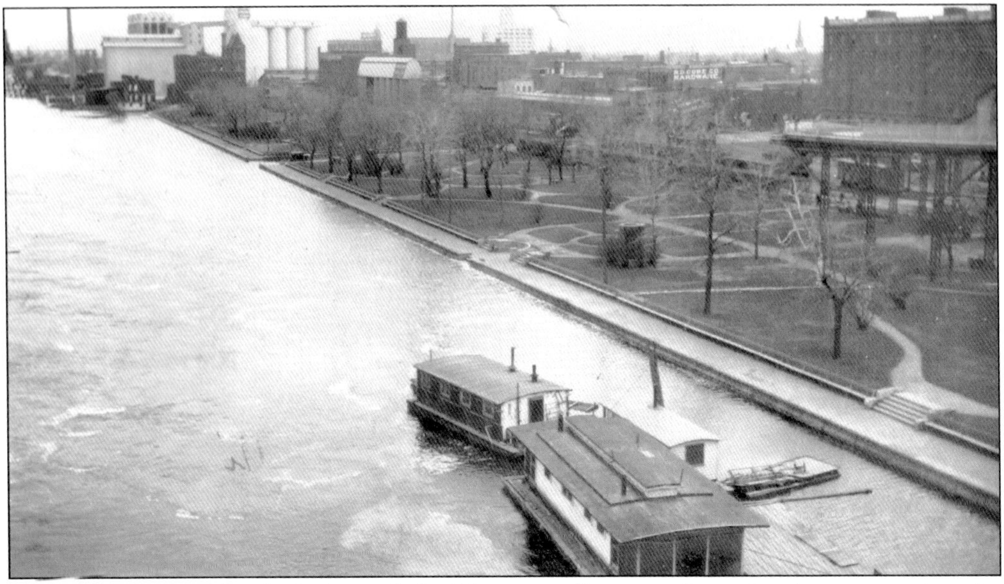

Spring flooding in April 1916 raised the Mississippi River to above flood stage, causing the floodwater to cover the "Death Road," and crossing the Wisconsin bottoms to the old ferry bridge and the High Wagon Bridge to cover Winona with up to 10 inches of water.

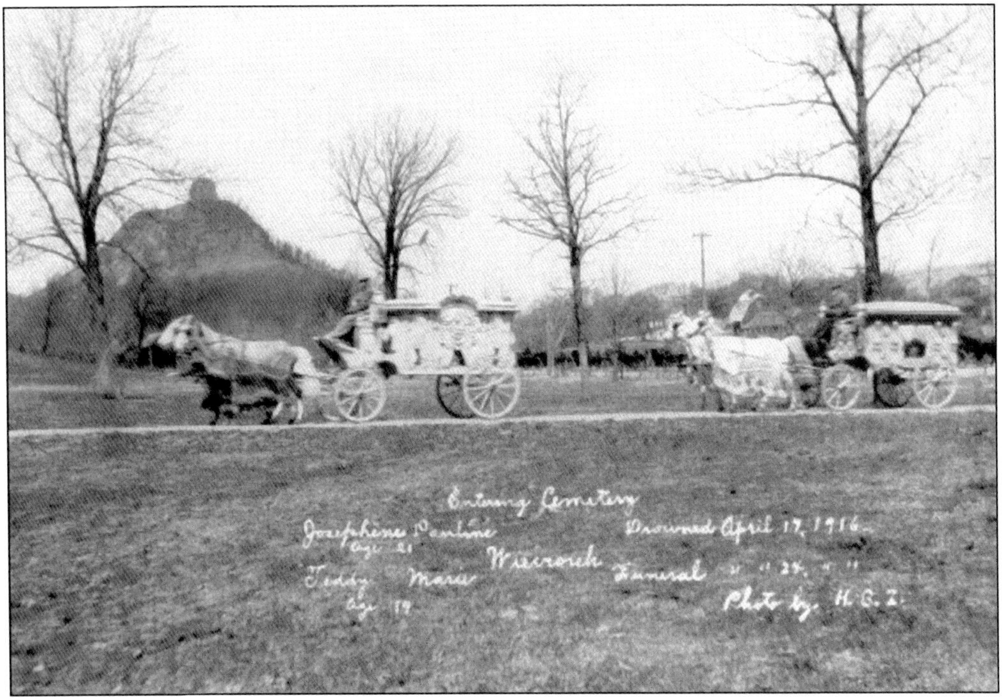

Stopped by high water while attempting to cross the Wisconsin Bottoms Causeway, an automobile carrying the Ben Crogan family of four and a buggy carrying Josephine (21 years old) and Theodosia (19 years old) Wieczorek plunged into the high water as they tried to turn around. The Wieczorek sisters' funeral service was held on April 24, 1916, at St. Stanislaus Catholic Church and was followed by this procession, which carried their remains to St. Mary's Catholic Cemetery for internment in Section G, Lot 2.

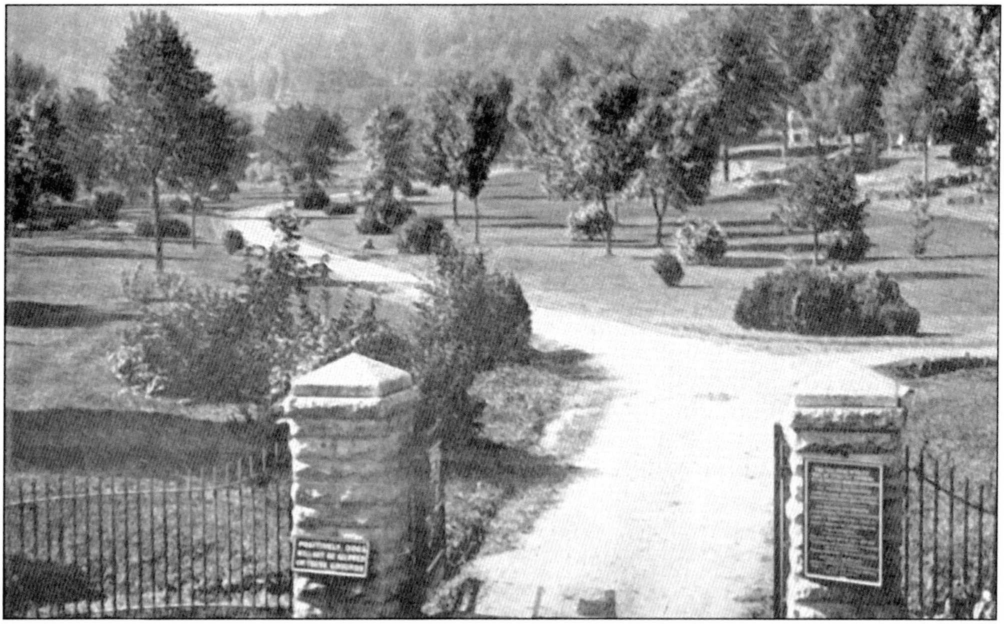

Woodlawn Cemetery was founded in June 1862 in a small, eroded valley in the north-facing bluffs on the south side of Lake Winona. It first consisted of 40 acres, but was soon increased to 200 acres, much of which cannot be used. The first official burial was of Benjamin Lowe, but J. Scott Clark had been buried in this valley some eight years earlier.

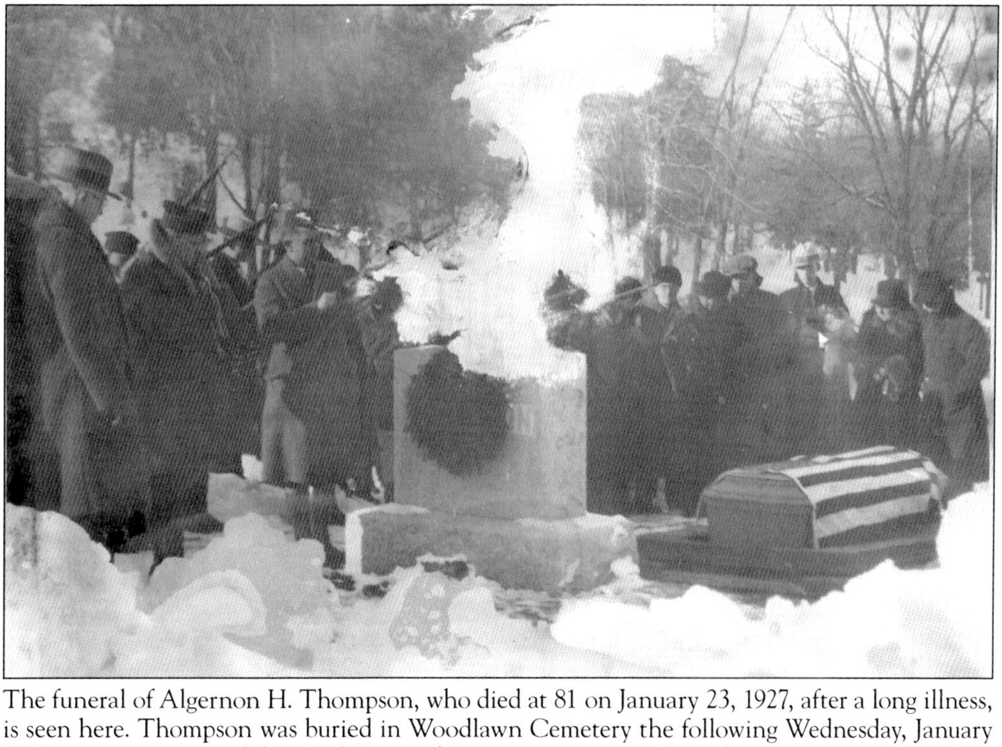

The funeral of Algernon H. Thompson, who died at 81 on January 23, 1927, after a long illness, is seen here. Thompson was buried in Woodlawn Cemetery the following Wednesday, January 26. He was a veteran of the Civil War and was at Appomattox Courthouse when Robert E. Lee surrendered his troops. He lived his entire adult life in Winona County.

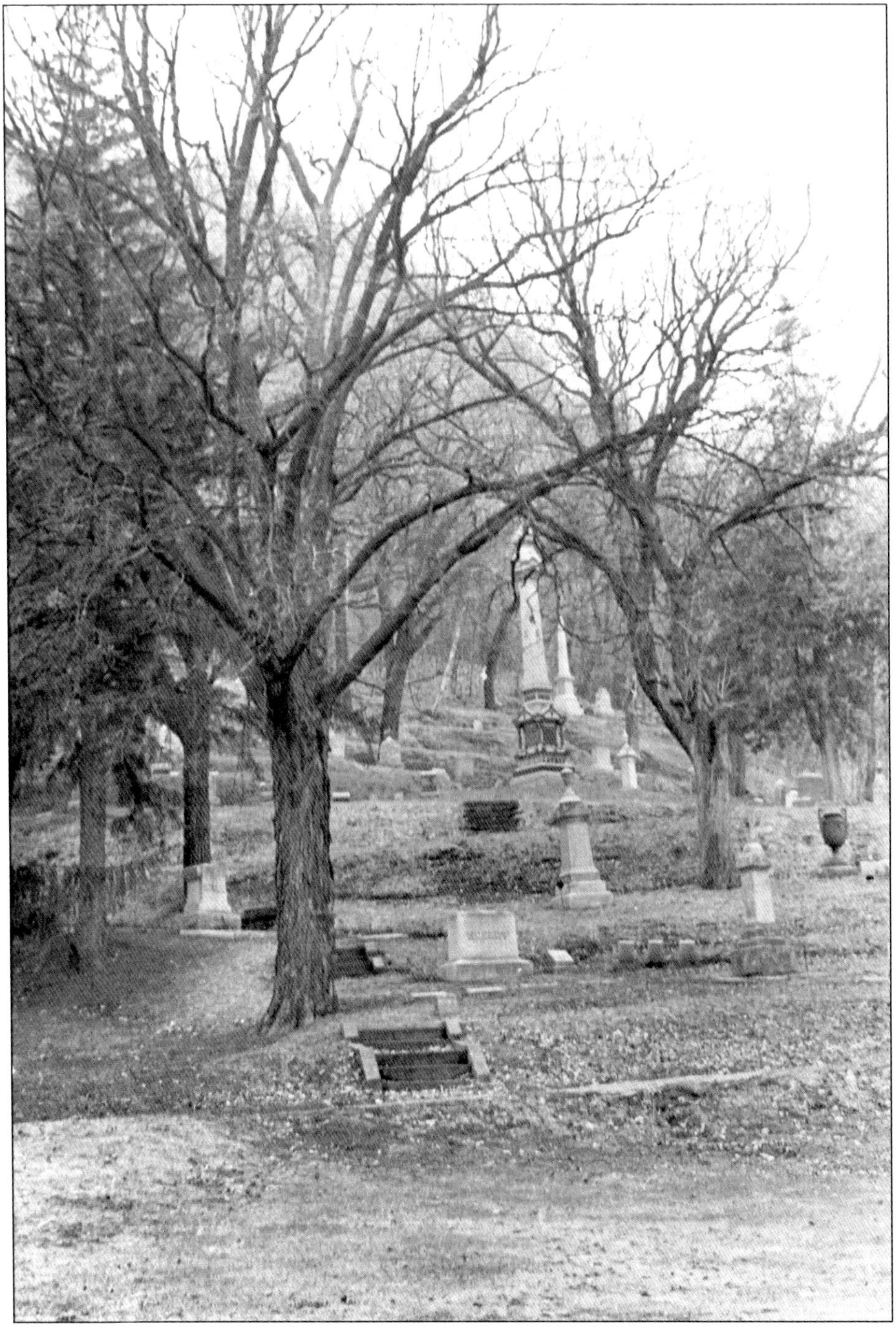

These tombstones in Woodlawn Cemetery mark the final resting place of many of Winona's citizens. Woodlawn Cemetery was designed as an arboretum and contains a multitude of different types of trees. Much of the cemetery is on the side of the bluff and has been terraced to accommodate the gravesites. St. Mary's Cemetery, the other cemetery in Winona, is located at the southeastern edge of the city. It was originally deeded to the Bishop of St. Paul in 1864. The deed was then passed into the hands of the Bishop of Winona, and in 1911, it was deeded to the Diocese of Winona.

Eight

Educational and Religious Leadership

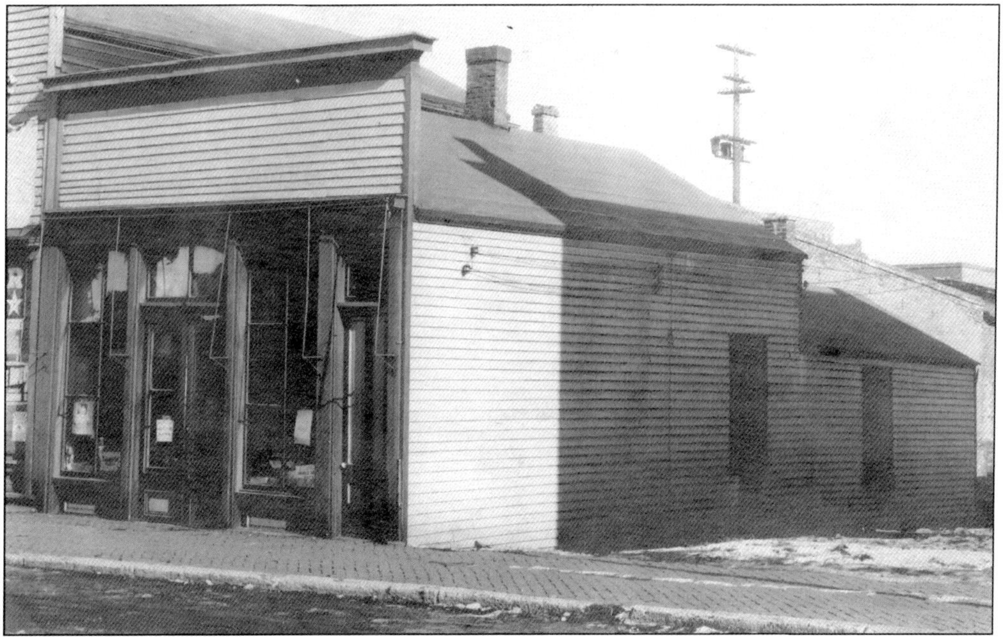

Winona's first school building was located at 118 Johnson Street. It was built by Henry T. Wickersham, an early Winona hardware merchant, in 1856. The building was used as a school for two years, 1857 and 1858, with Mary E. Ford as the teacher in 1857. The building had a variety of purposes after being a school, including a tailor shop owned by John H. Hughes and a confectionery run by his daughter, Fannie Hughes. Before it was razed in 1925, its final use was as a livery stable.

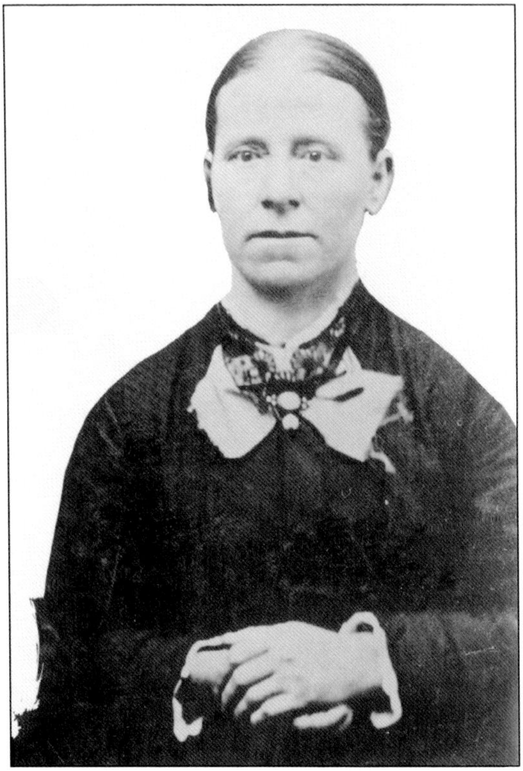

Mary Willis (1836–1885), considered Winona's first regular schoolteacher, began her teaching career in 1853 in Winona. She had arrived in Winona with her parents earlier that year, but settled in Chatfield, Minnesota, the following year, where her father was the clerk of court. Willis taught school in Chatfield until she married Josephus Gillett in 1858.

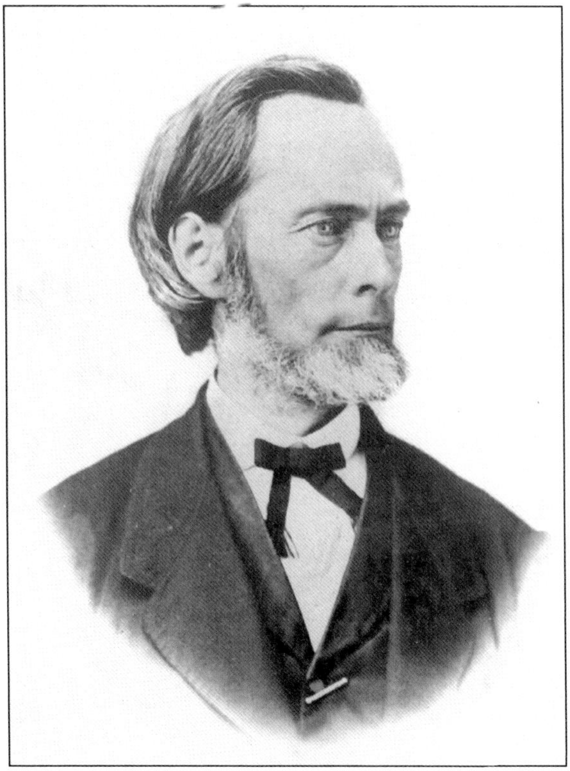

Rev. David Burt (1822–1881) was educated at Oberlin College, Ohio, and at the Andover Theological Seminary. In 1858, he became the third pastor of the First Congregational Church in Winona. Because of his educational experiences, Reverend Burt was appointed to be the first superintendent of the Winona Public Schools in 1862, a post he held until 1864, when he resigned. Reverend Burt was later appointed as the state superintendent of public instruction in 1875, and he died in Northfield, Minnesota, in 1881.

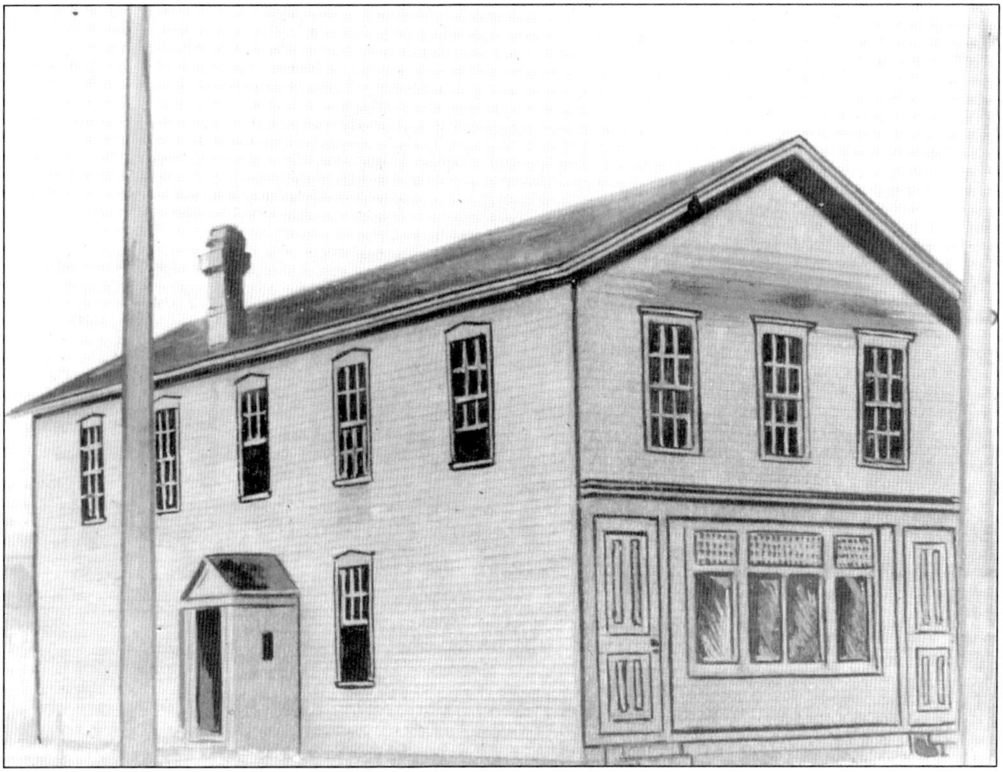

Pictured is a drawing of the first normal school for teacher training, which was established in Winona in 1859 and opened in September 1860. The legislation that established this school required that a subscription of $7,000 be provided by the community. The city also donated this public building, located at the northeast corner of Lafayette and Fourth Streets, to be used by the school at no charge. The school opened with John Ogden as its principal and William Stearns as the tutor.

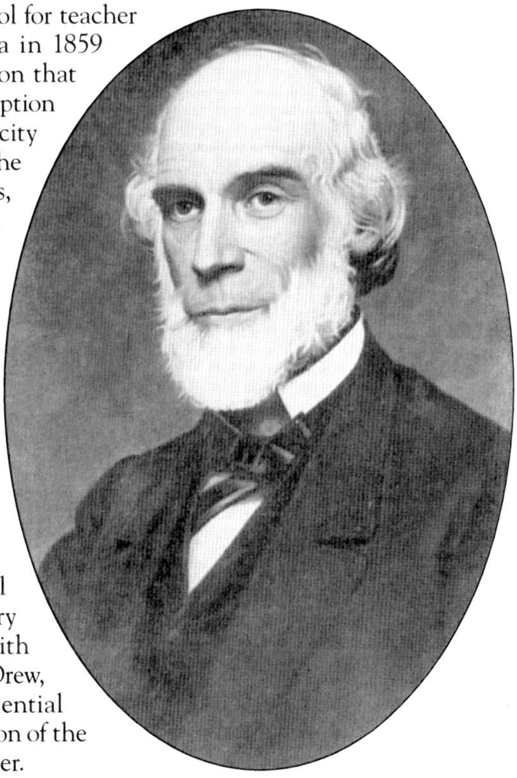

Dr. John D. Ford (1813–1867) is considered the "Father of Minnesota's Normal School System." He had secured the legislation necessary to establish the school in Winona. Along with David Burt, Sylvester J. Smith, and William S. Drew, Doctor Ford was appointed to the first prudential committee established to direct the organization of the first normal school west of the Mississippi River.

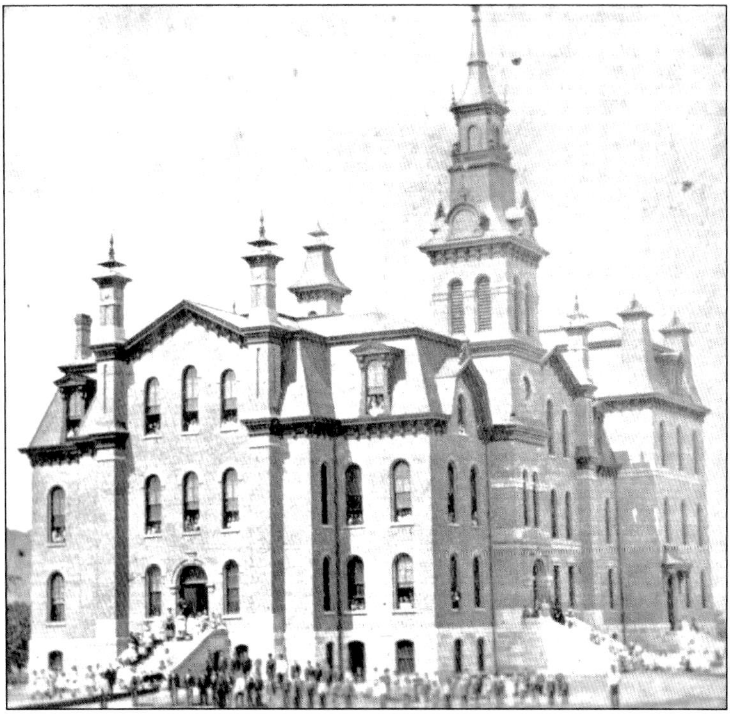

The first permanent normal school building in Winona was built at a cost of about $50,000, with half of the funds coming from the citizens of Winona. The building was occupied in September 1869 and completed in December.

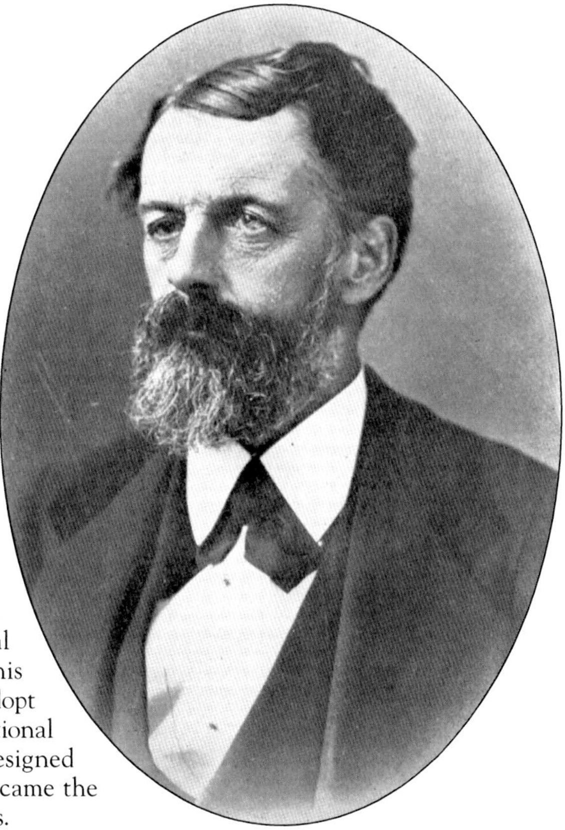

William F. Phelps (1822–1907), the second principal of the normal school, was appointed to the position in 1864. Phelps, an organizer and disciplinarian, was the man who could carry the normal school onto a permanent basis. Due to his educational background, he was able to adopt changes necessary to improve the educational experience of the students. After he resigned his position at the normal school, he became the superintendent of Winona Public Schools.

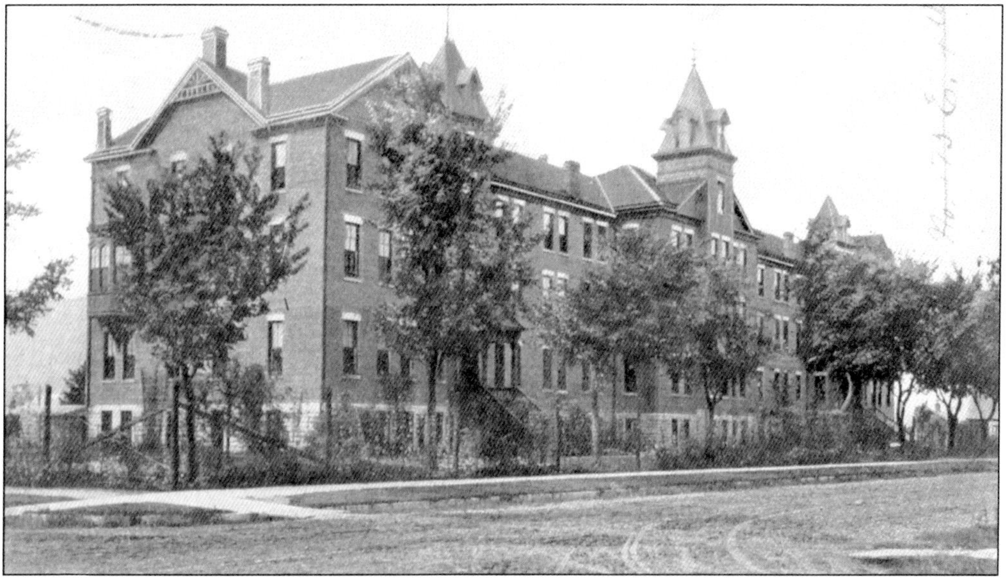

Pictured is a postcard showing the Ladies Seminary, which was located on property that had been purchased from Mary Curtis by the Milwaukee School Sisters of Saint Francis. Originally built in 1885 as a boarding school for girls, St. Mary's Academy was closed after two years. A portion of it was briefly reopened as a short-lived hospital operated by the Sisters of Saint Joseph of Carondelet. After the hospital closed, Bishop Joseph B. Cotter transferred the title of the building to the Academy of Our Lady of Lourdes in Rochester. The Ladies Seminary was opened as a school for young women in September 1894 with 59 students enrolled. After the College of Saint Teresa was established, the building was renamed Saint Mary's Hall. (Quinn.)

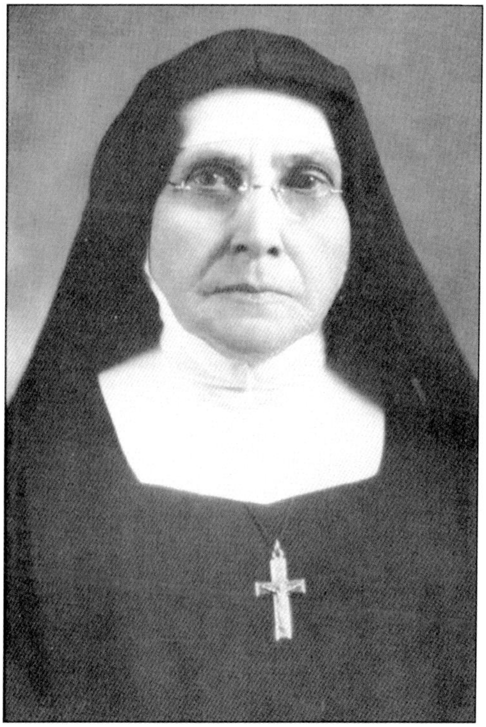

Sister Mary Leo (1860–1951) was born Emma Tracy and admitted as a postulant to the sisters of the Third Order of Saint Francis of the Congregation of Our Lady of Lourdes in Rochester, Minnesota. Sister Leo was the first superior of the Winona Seminary, which she organized in 1894. Under her leadership, the seminary grew into the College of Saint Teresa. Sister Leo was the college's first president, a post she first held until 1928 and then again from 1933 to 1939. She was given the title of "Mother" around 1916. (Quinn.)

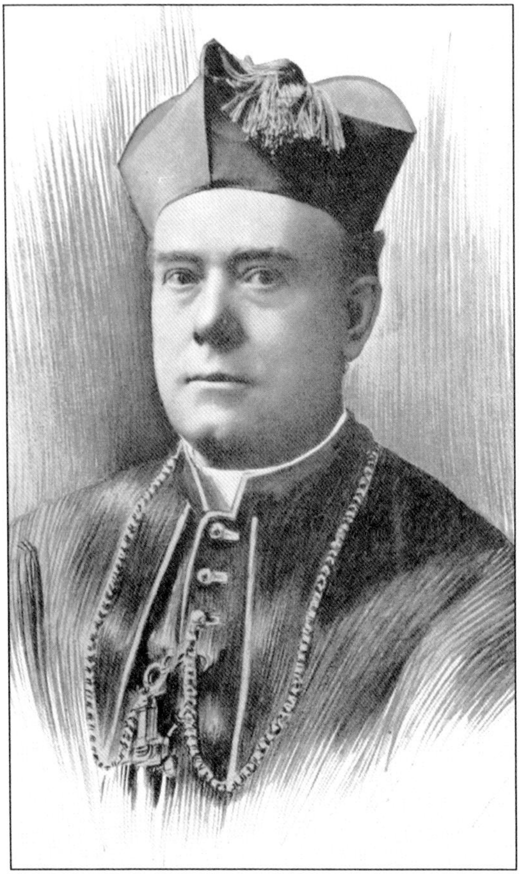

Rt. Rev. Joseph B. Cotter (1844–1909) was the first Catholic bishop of Winona. Reverend Cotter was ordained in 1871, shortly before coming to Winona, and was consecrated as bishop in 1889 when the Diocese of Winona was formed. During his ministry he was a liberal churchman, but he was also an advocate of the temperance movement. Bishop Cotter had an interest in education and helped the organization of the Ladies Seminary in Winona.

After being under construction for a year, this house, built by Bishop Cotter across the street from the Ladies Seminary, was completed in July 1894. The house, located on the northwest corner of Wabash and Cummings Streets, was designed and erected by Charles G. Maybury at a cost of approximately $16,000, all paid for by assessments of the Catholic parishes of the diocese. The house was made of red brick, and its interior was finished in solid oak. After Bishop Cotter's death, the house was purchased by the seminary as a residence for women and renamed Assisi Hall in honor of the birthplace of Saint Francis.

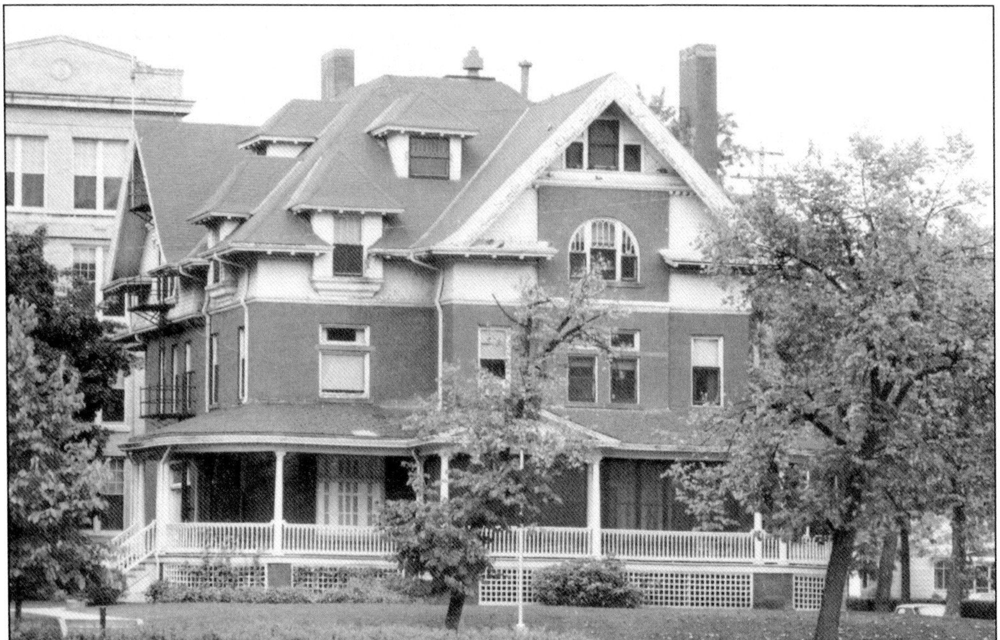

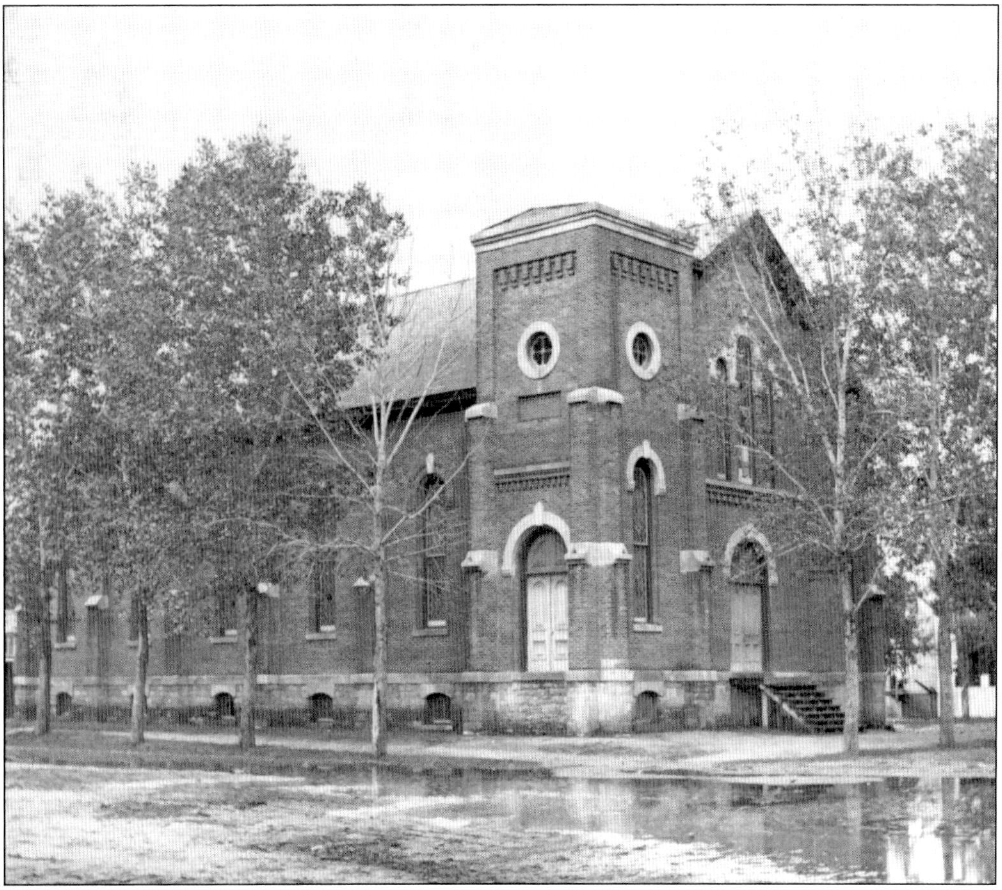

Bishop Cotter's church, the Pro-Cathedral of Saint Thomas, was located on the southwest corner of Wabasha and Center Streets. The church was dedicated in August 1872 and replaced a small wooden building that had been constructed in 1857.

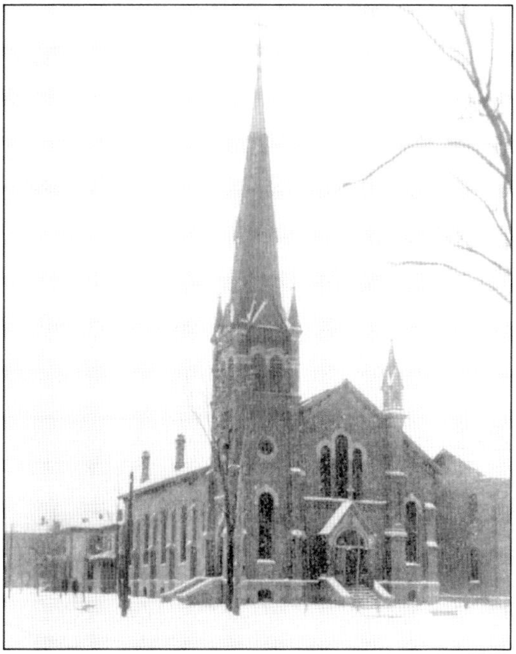

The steeple, spires, and stone stairways were added to the Saint Thomas Pro-Cathedral during the fall and early winter of 1888. A bell, donated by the late John Courtney, was installed in the steeple and rang for the first time on Christmas 1888. John Courtney, a parishioner of Saint Thomas, died in March 1888 at the age of 70.

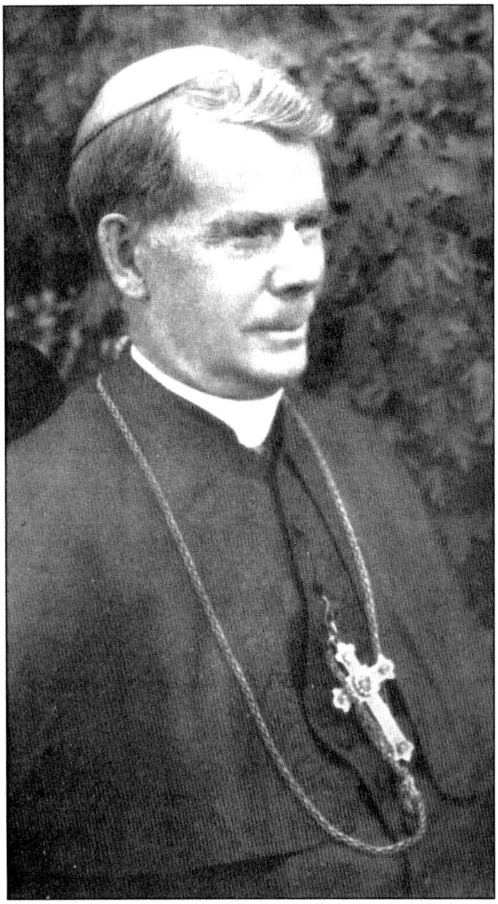

Rt. Rev. Patrick R. Heffron (1860–1927) was ordained into the priesthood in 1884 and was installed as the second bishop of the Diocese of Winona in 1910. Soon after he was installed as bishop, he began a program of expanding Catholic educational opportunities in the diocese. In 1911, he founded the Cotter School for Boys and had a building constructed to house the school in 1911. This was followed by the opening of St. Mary's College on Terrace Heights in 1913. In 1915, Bishop Heffron survived an assassination attempt by Fr. Louis Lesches, a deranged priest. During his tenure, Heffron established nearly 40 Catholic schools in the diocese.

Pictured is St. Mary's Hall, the original St. Mary's College building authorized for construction by Bishop Heffron and dedicated on September 17, 1913. Bishop Heffron had purchased the Christian C. Beck mansion and 160 acres of property on Terrace Heights from Margarethe Beck for $28,000. Bishop Heffron used the Beck mansion for the college, and after St. Mary's Hall was completed, he made it his home. The small structure on the left of the building is a passageway to a dormitory and gymnasium building, which was opened in 1922. (Wright.)

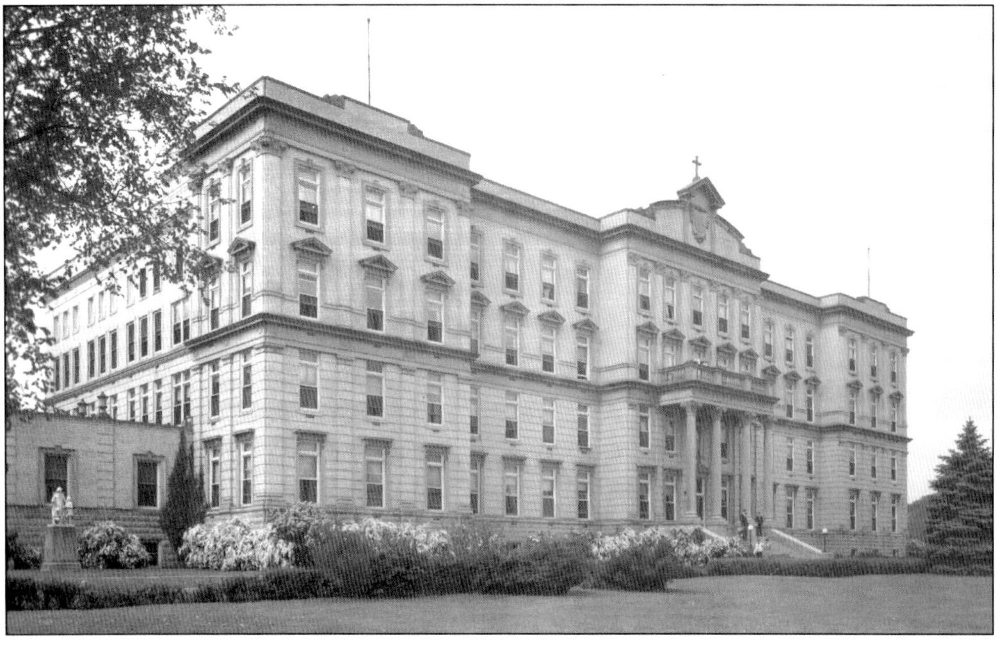

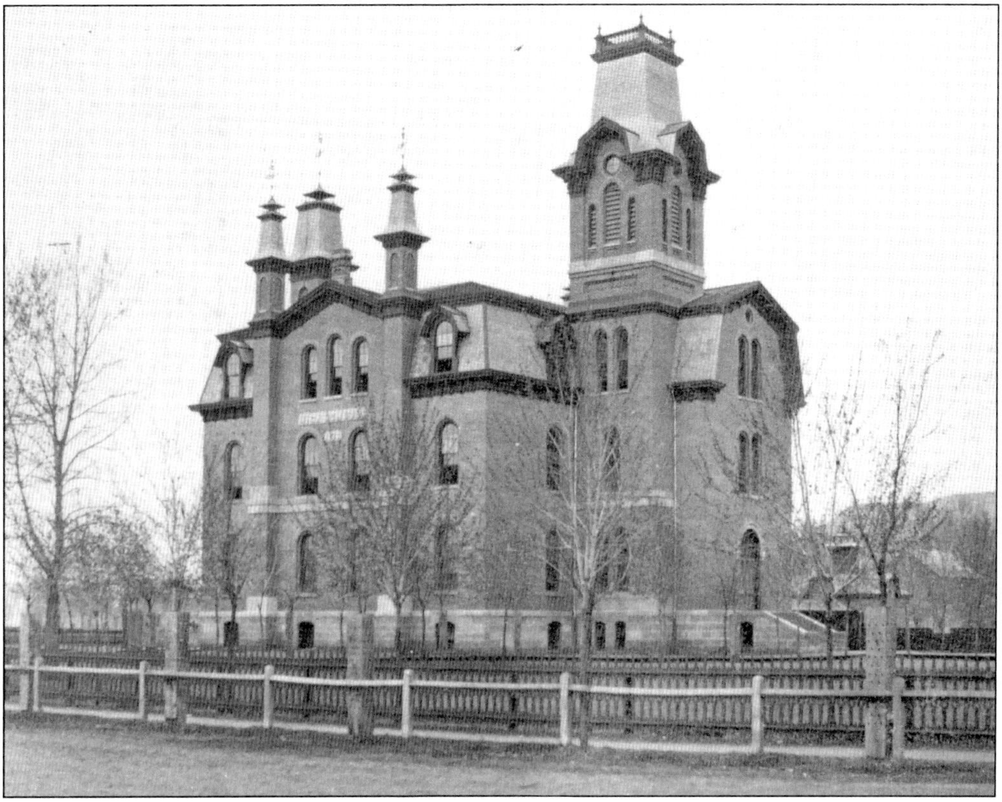

Early schools in Winona relied on rental buildings as a place for students to be taught. Central High School, located at the southeast corner of Broadway and Walnut Streets, was the third building to be designed as a school. The building, designed by Gurdon P. Randall, was built by Conrad Bohn at a cost of $36,700. The school opened for classes in September 1867 and could accommodate up to 600 pupils. (Tenney.)

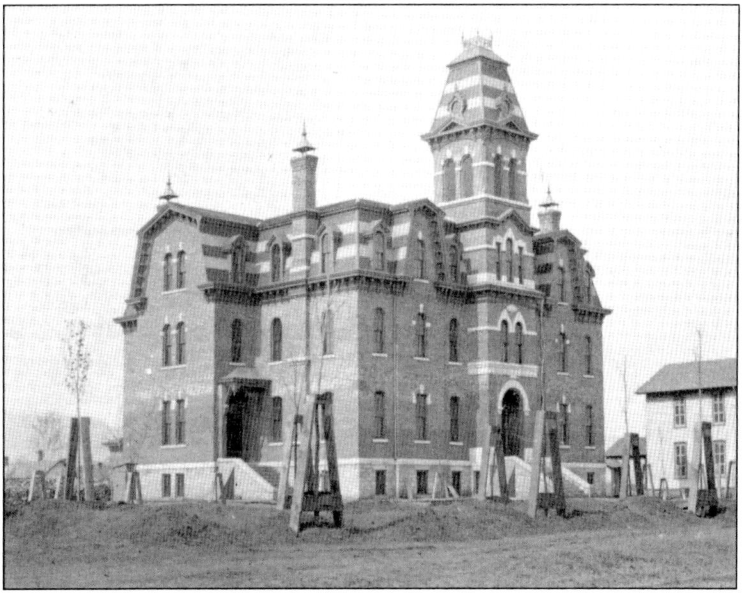

Madison Elementary School, designed by Charles G. Maybury and opened in August 1875, was located at the southeast corner of Wabasha and Dakota Streets. (Tenney.)

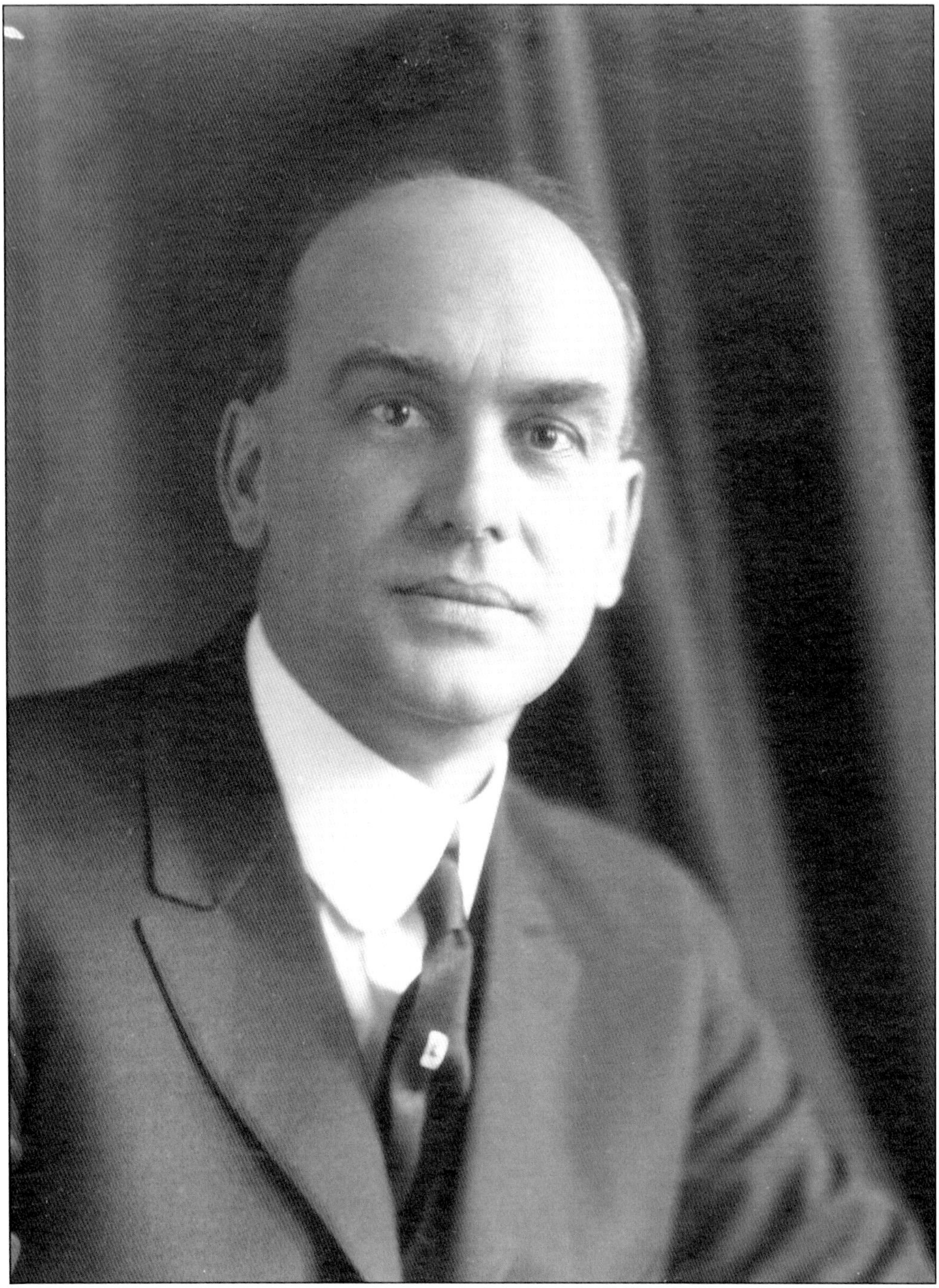

Rev. Alfred W. Sauer (1881–1955) served the congregation of St. Martin's Lutheran Church for almost 50 years. Under Reverend Sauer's leadership, St. Martin's Church began English service in 1910, and in 1930, a new parish school—first started by Rev. Philip Von Rohr—was erected at a cost of $75,000. In 1951, Reverend Sauer directed some major renovation to the church. Sauer, who was ordained in 1905, came to St. Martin's Church shortly thereafter. He was also involved in the founding of St. Matthew's Lutheran Church in Winona.

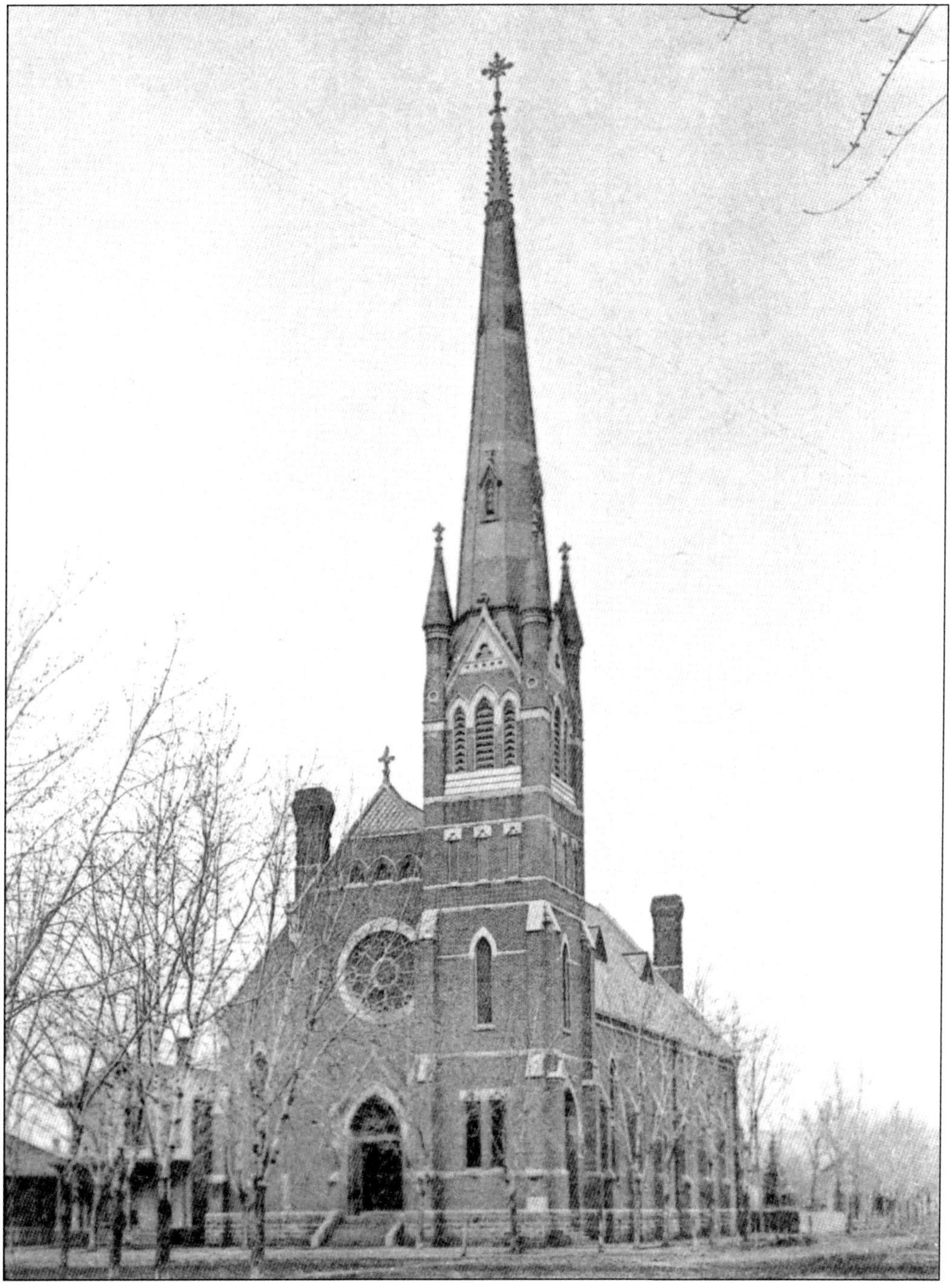

St. Martin's Evangelical German Lutheran Church was established in 1856 by Rev. L.F.E. Krause and had seven members. In 1866, Reverend Sauer's father-in-law, the Reverend Philip Von Rohr, became pastor of the church and remained at the helm for 43 years. The congregation grew, and in 1886, a new church was designed by Charles G. Maybury and built at a cost of $19,000 at the northwest corner of Broadway and Liberty Streets. Later renovations in 1956 took the roof of the steeple off and refaced the brick with stone.

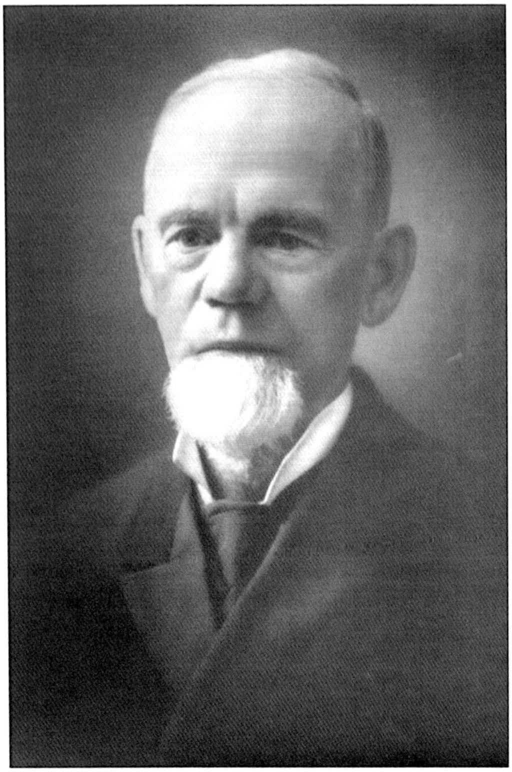

Rev. William McKinley (1834–1918) began his Methodist ministry in Winona in 1866. After three years, he was transferred to a church in St. Paul. After a hiatus of five years, Reverend McKinley returned to Winona's Central Methodist Church until 1880, when he left to service other churches. He returned to Winona again in 1899 as the pastor of the Olive Branch Methodist Church. During a good share of his life as a pastor, Doctor McKinley suffered from various illnesses and was often disabled. In his later life, he was known as the "Dean of Minnesota Methodism."

Dedicated in 1872, the new chapel of the Methodist Episcopal Church was located at the southwest corner of Lafayette and Fifth Streets. The church, designed by Charles G. Maybury, was constructed at a cost of nearly $16,000. The church was completely destroyed by fire on January 27, 1895. It was replaced by a large church on the northwest corner of Broadway and Main Streets a couple of years later.

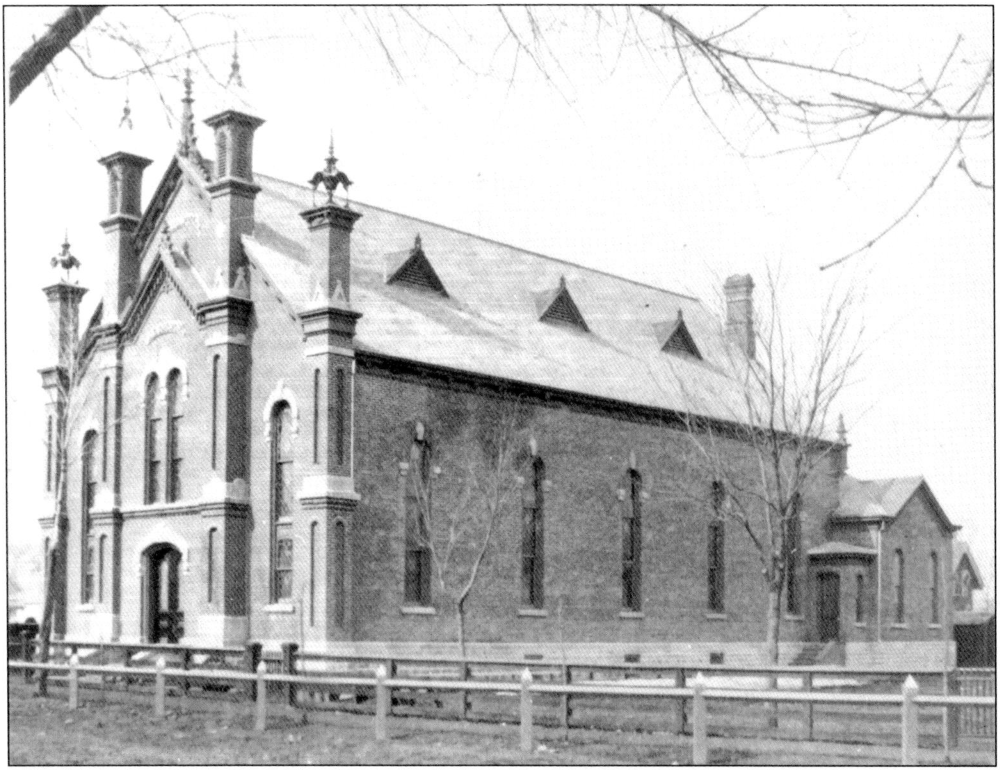

Nine

The Arts and Entertainment

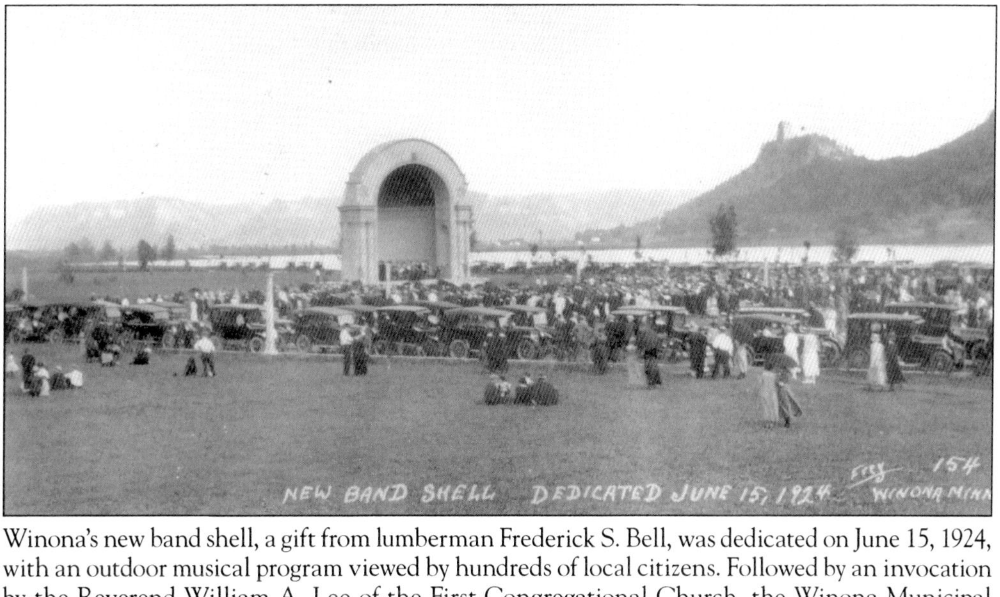

Winona's new band shell, a gift from lumberman Frederick S. Bell, was dedicated on June 15, 1924, with an outdoor musical program viewed by hundreds of local citizens. Followed by an invocation by the Reverend William A. Lee of the First Congregational Church, the Winona Municipal Band, under the direction of Orville W. Reese, opened with Sousa's spirited "US Field Artillery March." This was followed by a selection by the mixed chorus under the direction of Horace G. Seaton, and the stringed orchestra directed by Mildred Brown. The band shell was designed by Edwin H. Clark, a Chicago architect, and rested on a number of wooden pilings that were driven deep into the ground. The soil itself was set in place by earlier dredging operations.

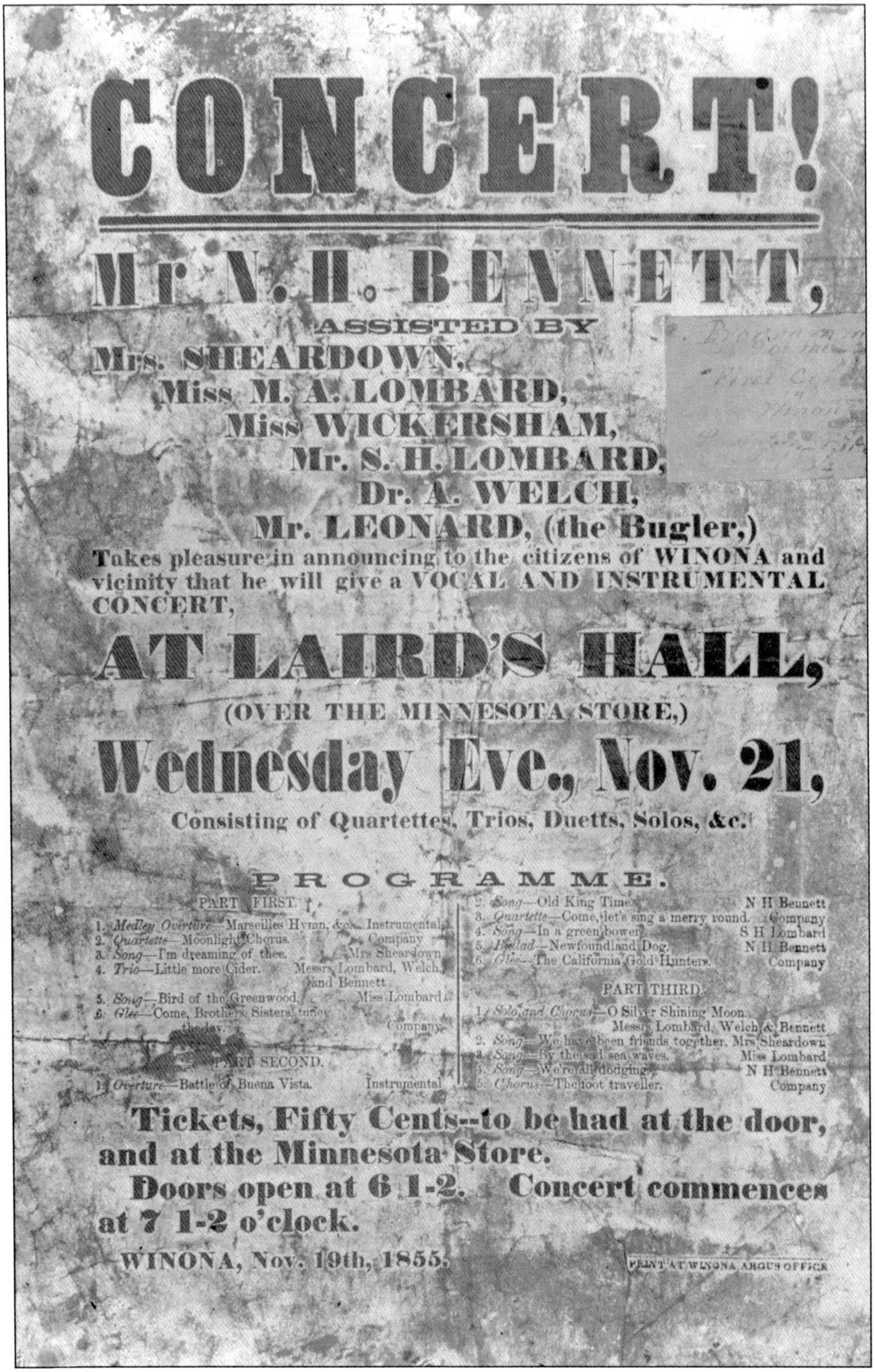

This poster announces the first musical concert that was held in Winona, on the evening of November 21, 1855, in Laird's Hall above James White's Minnesota Store near the levee along Front Street. Performing at the concert was N.H. Bennett assisted by Mary Sheardown, Maria Lombard, Martha A. Wickersham, Sanford H. Lombard (a merchant), Dr. Alfred Welch (a dentist), and Mr. Leonard on the bugle. It has not been reported how many attended this concert, but the population of Winona in 1855 was registered at 813 souls.

Pictured is a part of an 1865 Winona music group, the St. Cecilia Society. They included, from left to right, (first row) Maria Louise Worthington and Alice Langley; (second row) Mary Holcomb, Fred A. Clarke, and Philo G. Hubbell. (de Groot.)

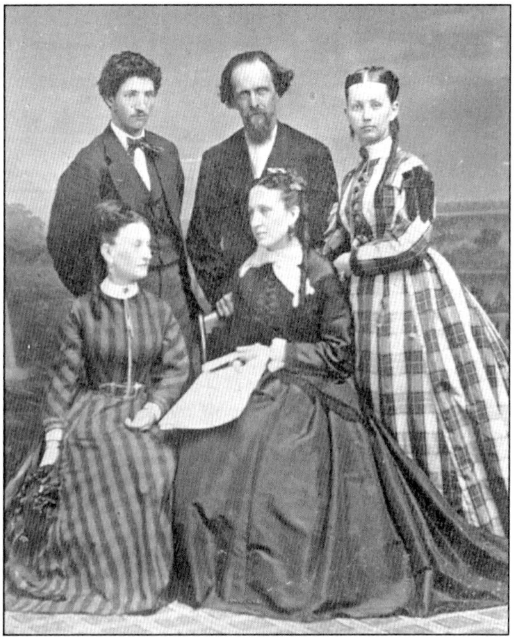

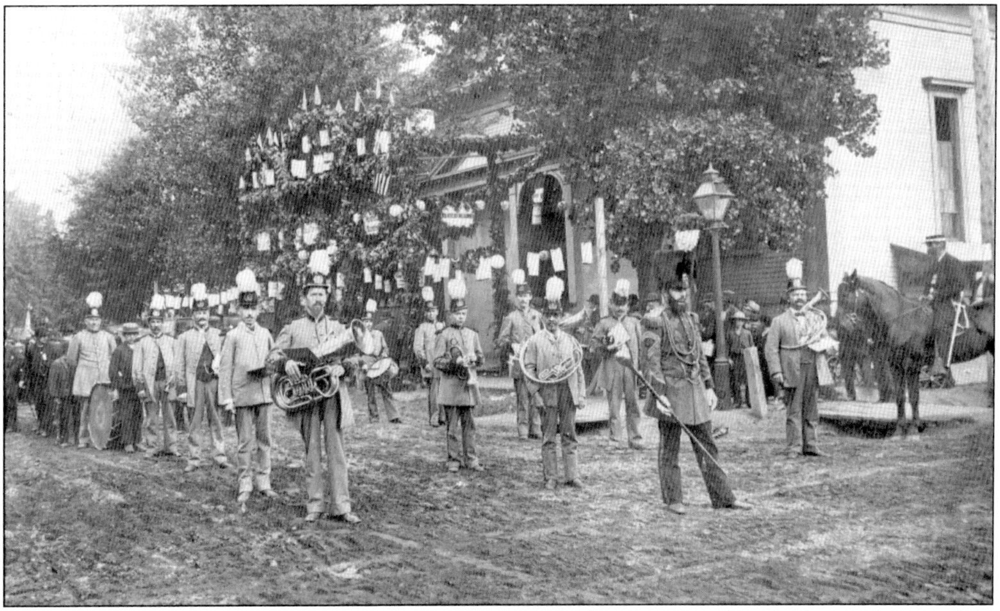

The Germania Band is lining up in front of the old Philharmonic Hall, which was destroyed by fire in June 1893. The building was located at the northeast corner of Franklin and Fourth Streets. The band lined up in preparation for the Turner Festival Parade in August 1870. The Turners were originally a German gymnastic society that became a social group. Shown in the photograph are Samuel Van Gorder on horseback and Frank Ctibor, the drum major. Listed from front to back are (left row) Conrad Wolpers, tuba; J. Henry Benz, second cornet; Christian Clausen, E-flat clarinet; Frank Voturba, B-flat clarinet; and Fred W. Becker, bass drum; (middle row) George F. Story, first tenor; and Fred Benz, second E-flat alto; (right row) Herman Rohweder, director and baritone; Henry Clausen, first alto; August Kircheck, first cornet; Henry Benz, E-flat clarinet; and William Becker, snare drum. (de Groot.)

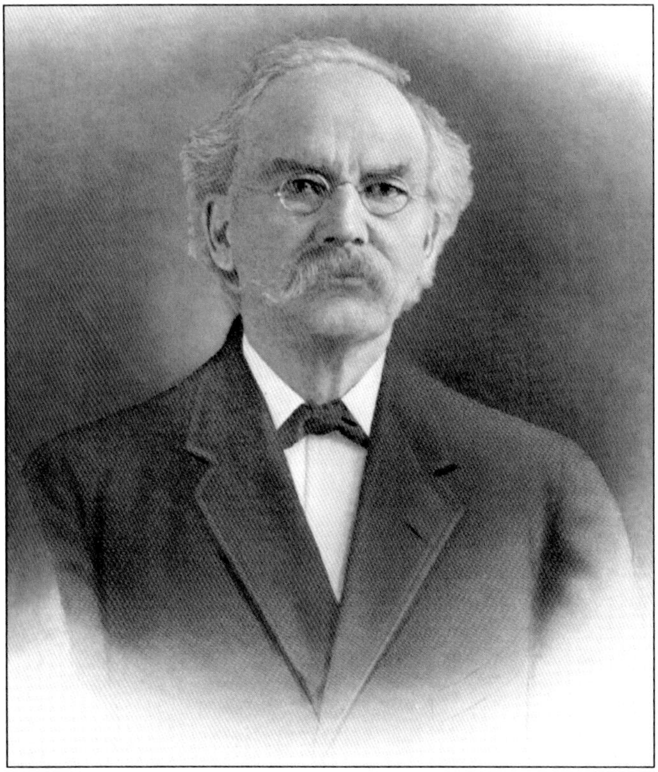

Herman Rohweder (1842–1921) immigrated to Winona in 1857; soon after arriving, he made an effort to organize a band with George W. Story. From these small beginnings, Professor Rohweder was able to organize the Germania Band, which was made up of 14 expert players. The Germania Band became a permanent institution in Winona and for many years gave weekly concerts in Central Park. (Curtis-Wedge.)

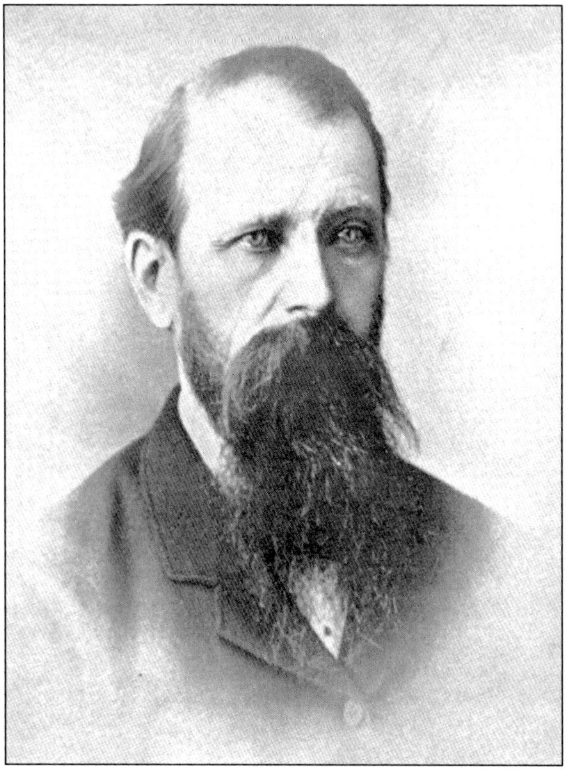

Gustave Anger (1826–1890) came to Winona in 1856 and opened a meat market in 1860. Having an interest in music, Gustave was a founding member of the Philharmonic Society, which was established in 1866. In addition, he was a member of the Maennerchor, or male singing society, of the Philharmonic Society and also served as its president for several years. In 1871, Anger built a new store for himself at 118 Walnut Street, which still exists today as a dental office. (Curtis-Wedge.)

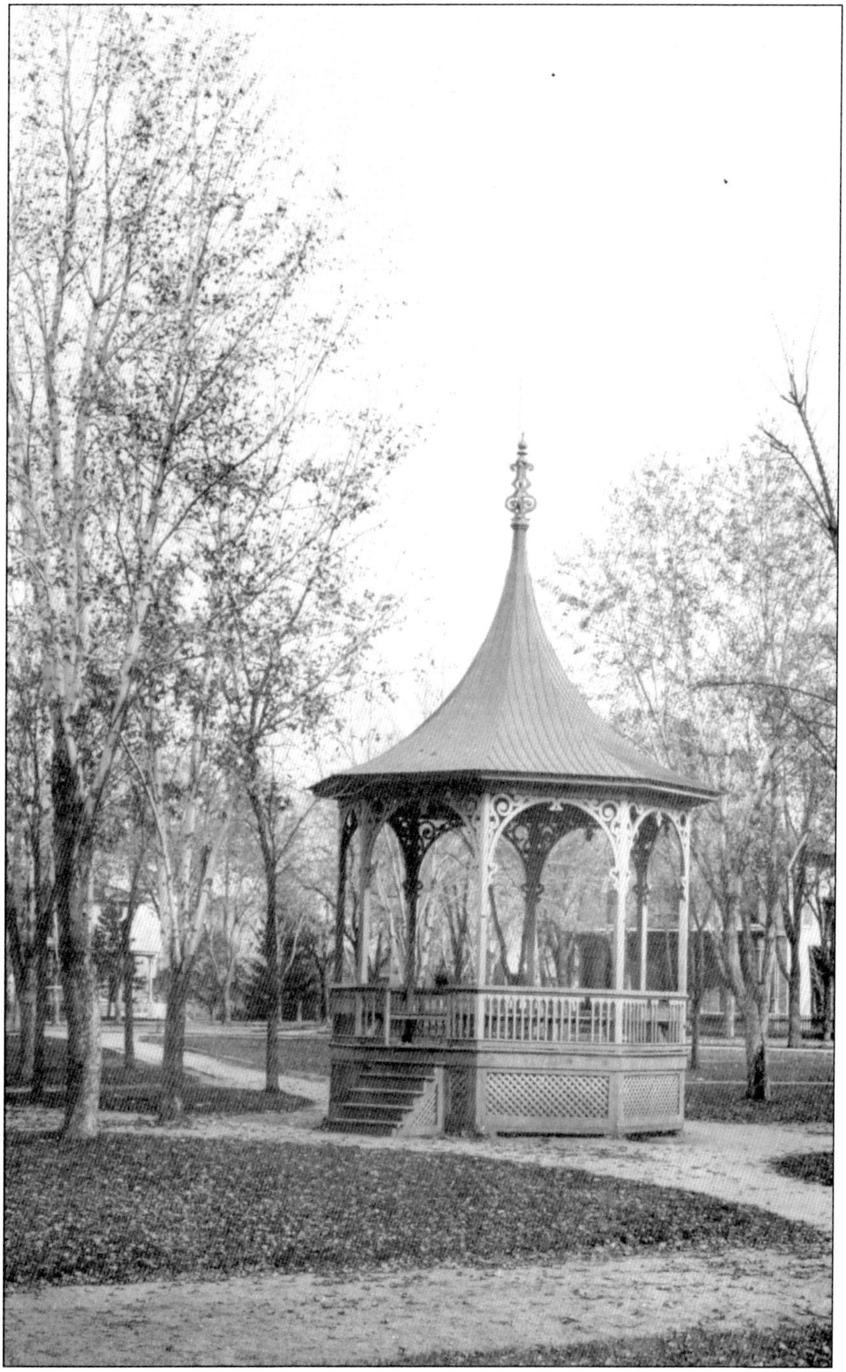

The Central Park Bandstand was one of four that had been built in the city parks over the years. This stand was the site of many summer band concerts that were put on by the Germania Band. This one, the earliest bandstand, was located in Central Park and built in the late 1870s, as the first of the park concerts occurred around 1877. Vandals destroyed this bandstand in September 1901, but it was not considered a loss, as it was to be removed and replaced by the Princess Wenonah Statue and Fountain. (Pratt & Owen.)

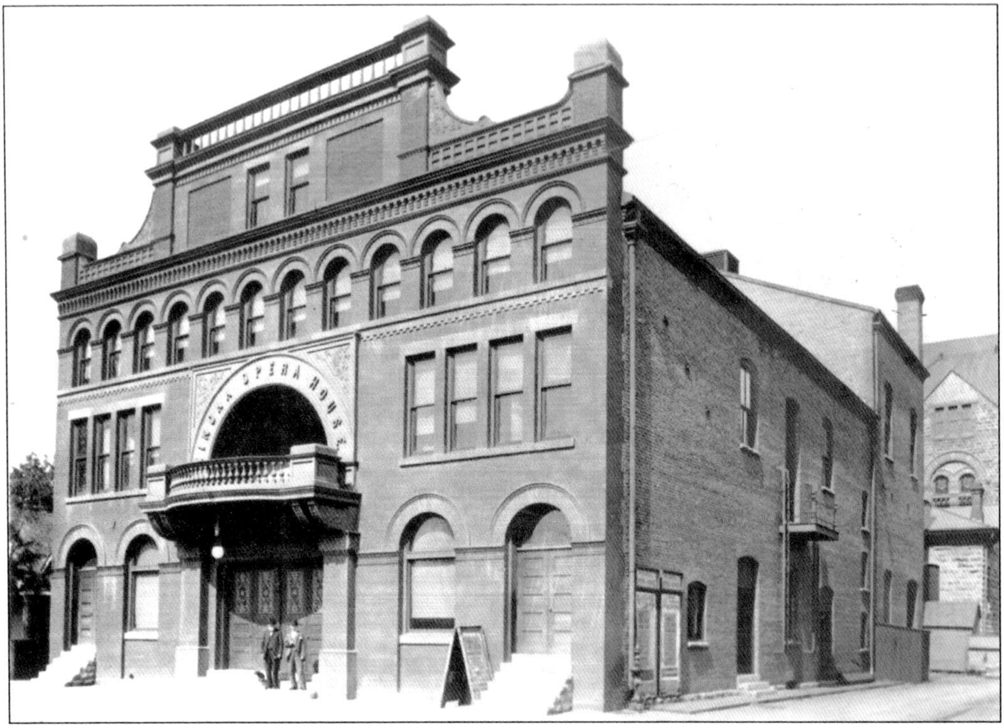

The Winona Opera House, located at 167 Johnson Street, opened in December 1892. The building was promoted and mostly paid for by Hannibal Choate, Addison B. Youmans, and Henry J. O'Neill and was to be used by the citizens of Winona for their entertainment.

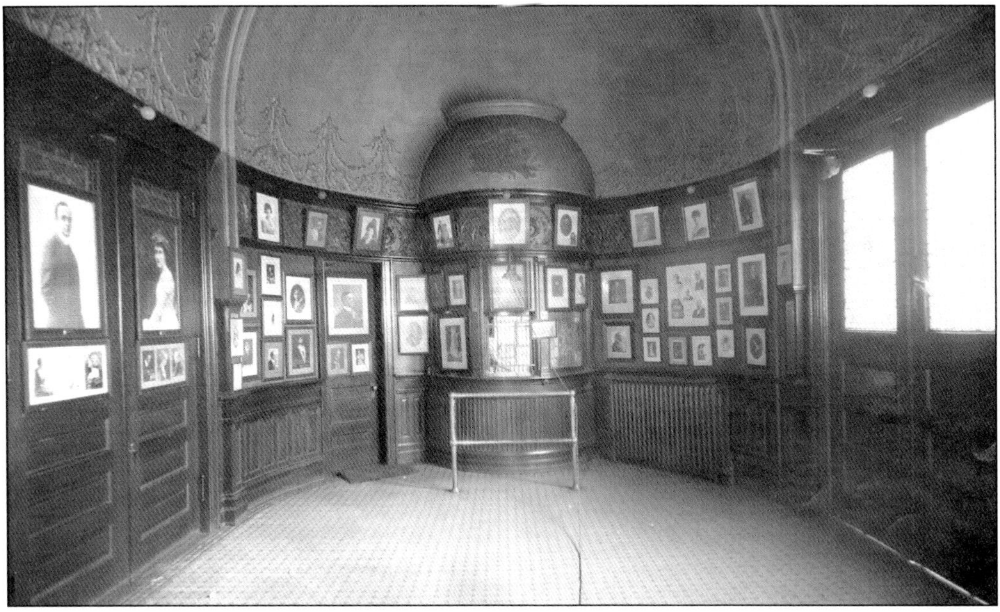

The Winona Opera House, in its day, was considered one of the finest theaters in the upper Midwest. The photographs seen here on the walls of the lobby and ticket booth were given to Orville E. Burlingame, the longtime manager, and are of some of the actors and actresses who played on the opera's stage.

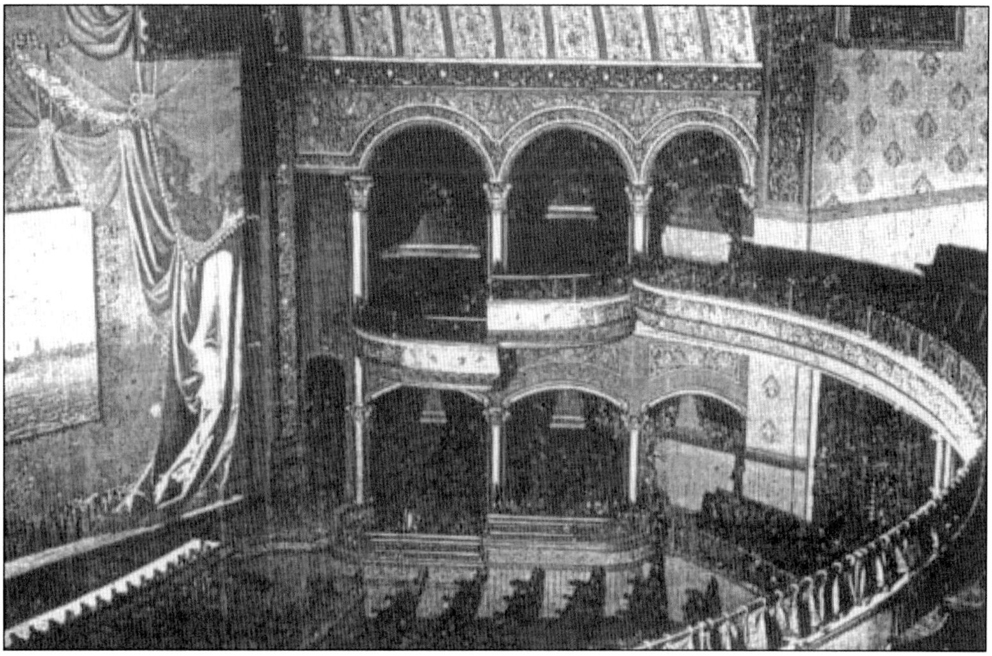

The Winona Opera House, built with a very elegant interior, box seats, and two large balconies, was able to accommodate 1,000 people. The seats were of crimson plush, the aisles were carpeted, and sculptured colonnades and abutments were everywhere. Fronting the audience was a giant, rippling damask curtain, thrusting its opaque protection before the square eye of the stage.

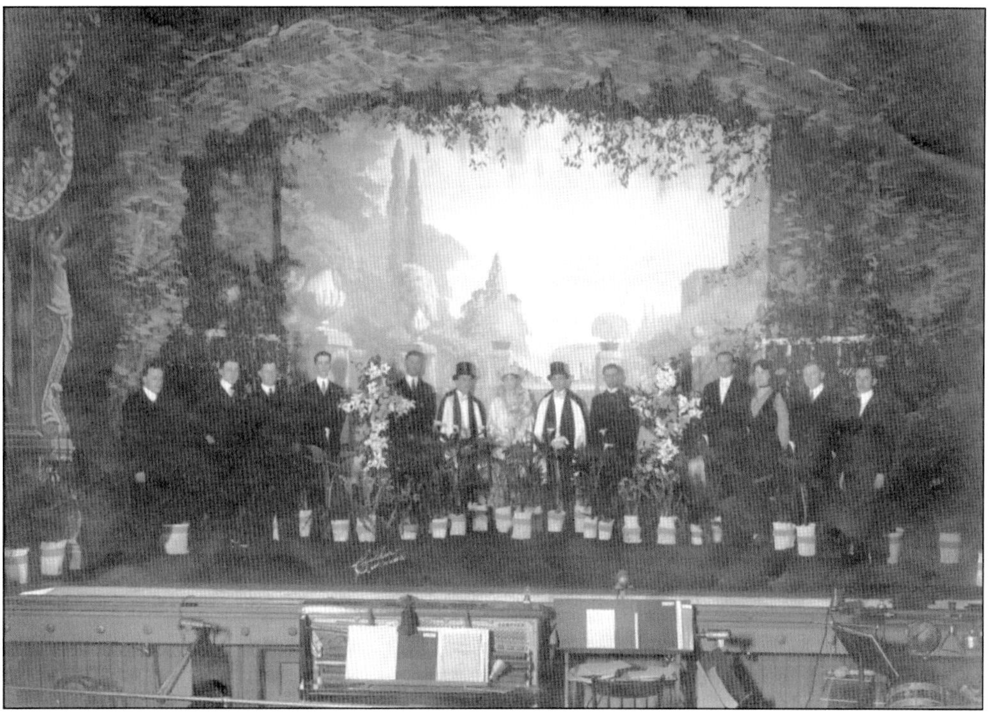

Pictured is the stage of the Winona Opera House at the end of an unknown production with the actors taking a bow. In front of the stage is the orchestra pit.

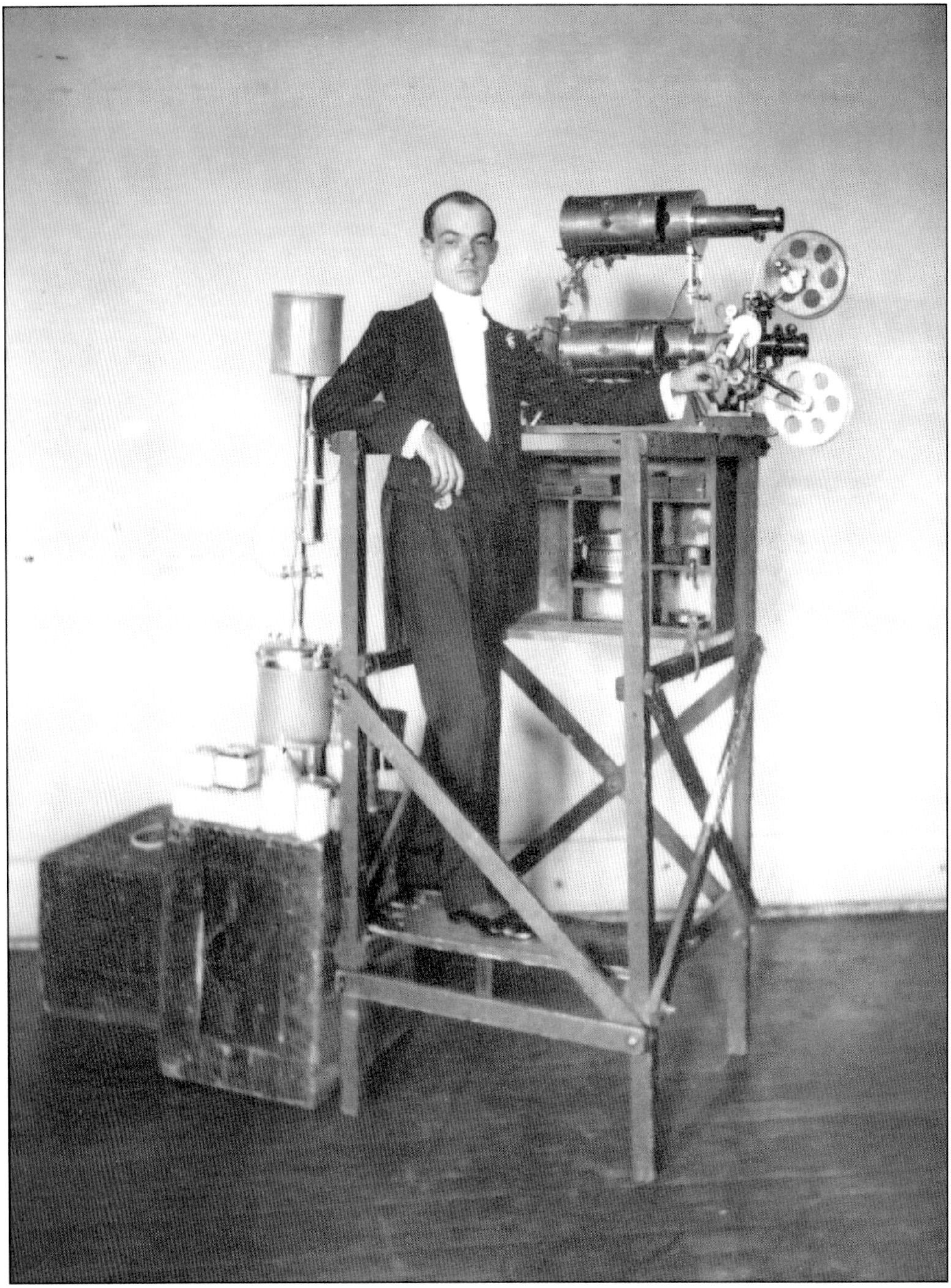

Ben A. Huntley (1876–1961) is pictured in formal evening wear, which he always wore while working, with his movie projector. Huntley was a vaudeville actor and an early veteran movie producer who worked out of Winona. He would photograph his wife, Myrtle E. (Barnes) Huntley, as she played various parts in his movies and in advertisements he photographed. Myrtle, a vaudeville star in her own right, traveled the circuit with her husband, her mother, and her stepfather. In addition to his movie production, Huntley also operated a business that equipped theaters to show movies.

Myrtle E. (Barnes) Huntley (1880–1974) is pictured in Robb's Grocery Store with Charles Arling in the movie production of *The Romance of a Traveling Man*, which was produced and filmed by her husband, Ben A. Huntley, in the spring of 1915. The movie was played by local talent and portrays a local girl who elopes with a traveling salesman as her father chases the couple to stop the wedding. (Huntley.)

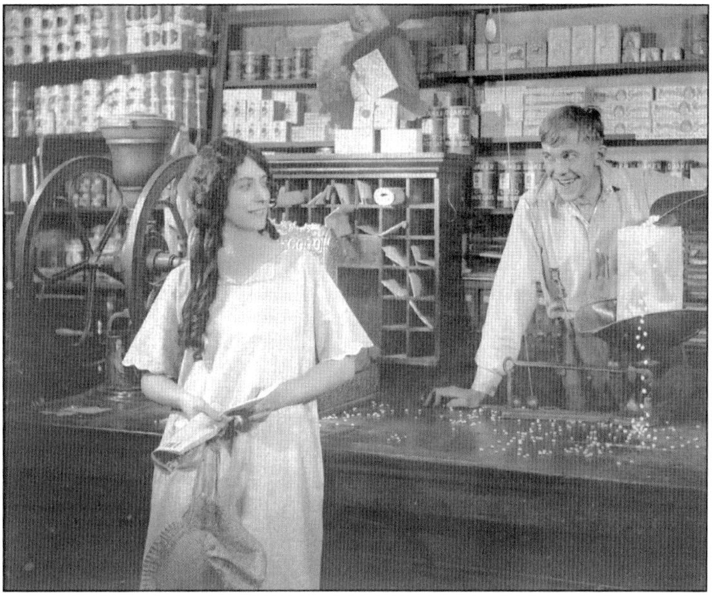

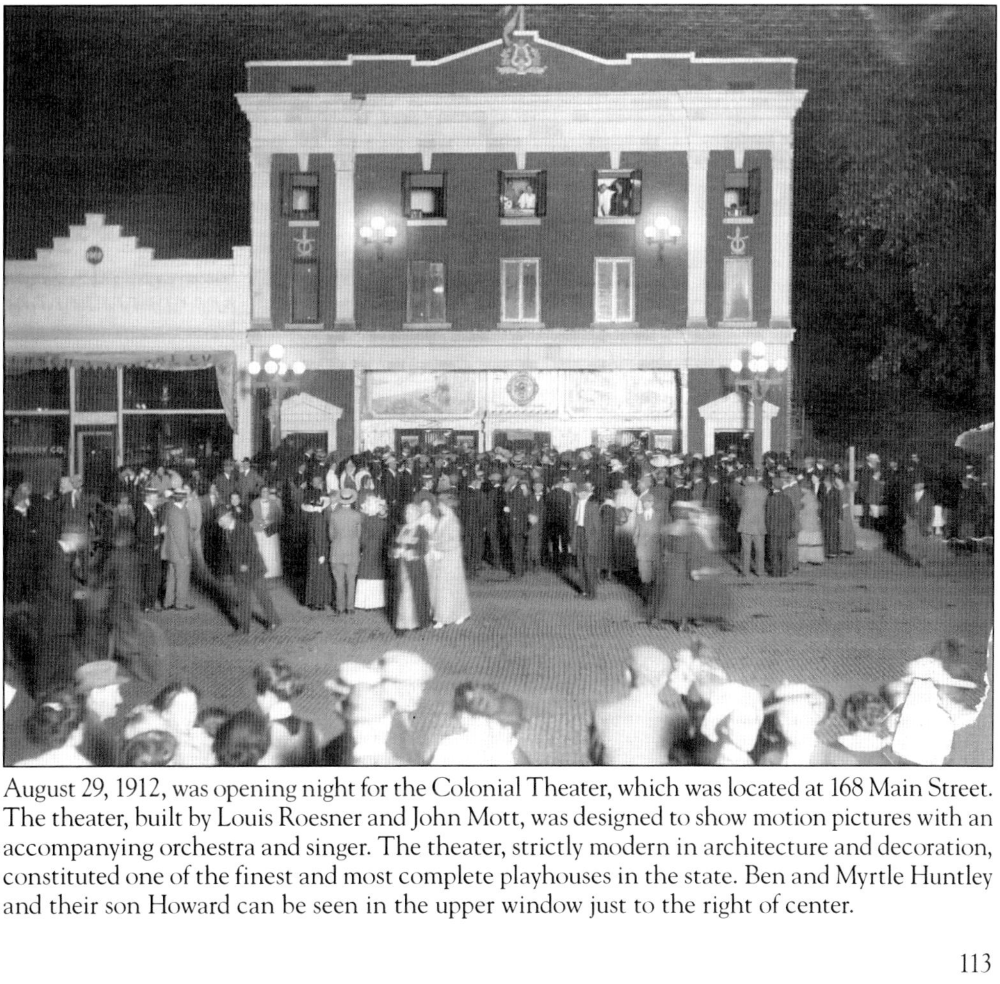

August 29, 1912, was opening night for the Colonial Theater, which was located at 168 Main Street. The theater, built by Louis Roesner and John Mott, was designed to show motion pictures with an accompanying orchestra and singer. The theater, strictly modern in architecture and decoration, constituted one of the finest and most complete playhouses in the state. Ben and Myrtle Huntley and their son Howard can be seen in the upper window just to the right of center.

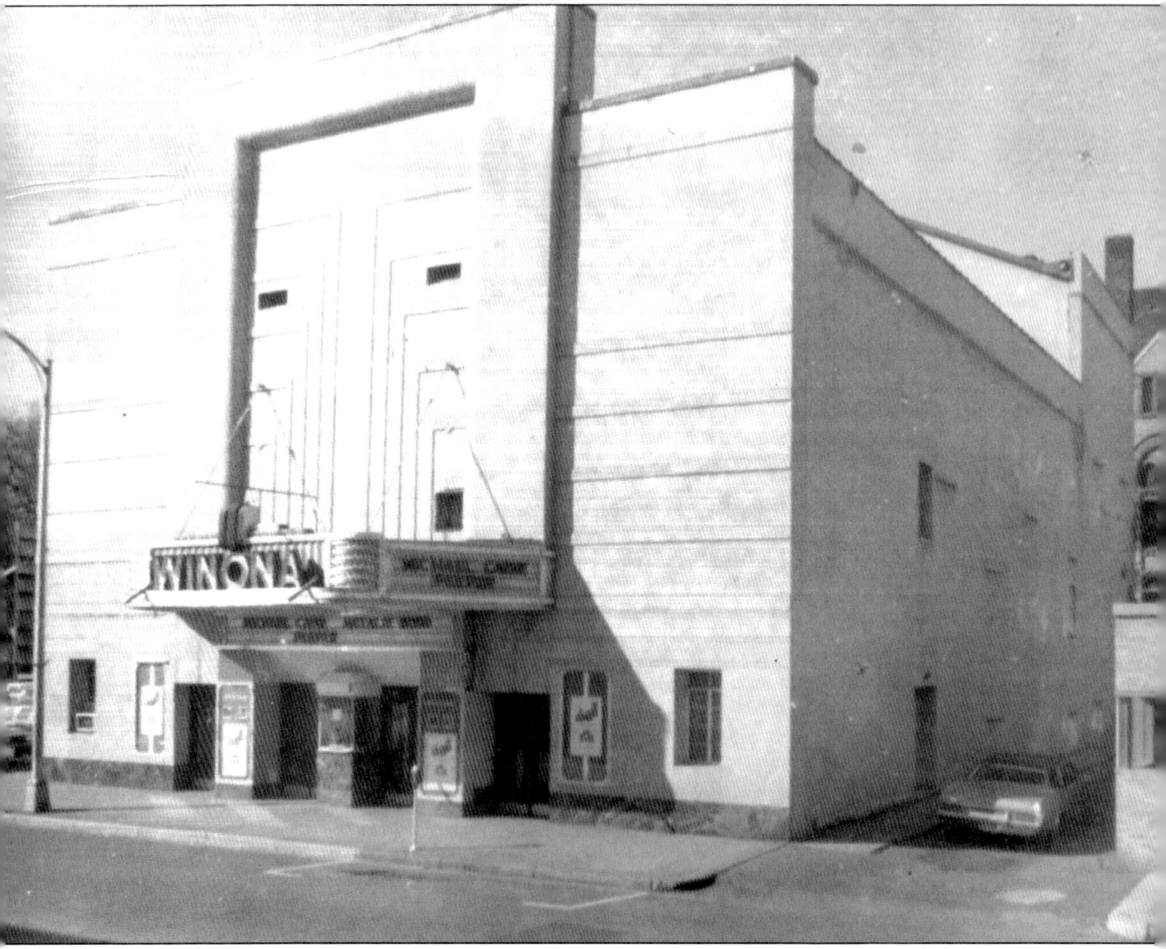

In 1926, the Winona Opera House was renamed the Winona Theater, and in 1936, the front of the building was "wrecked" when it was covered with black marble and a buff-covered stucco. In addition, the stage and balcony were removed as the interior was remodeled.

Ten

Lost Winona

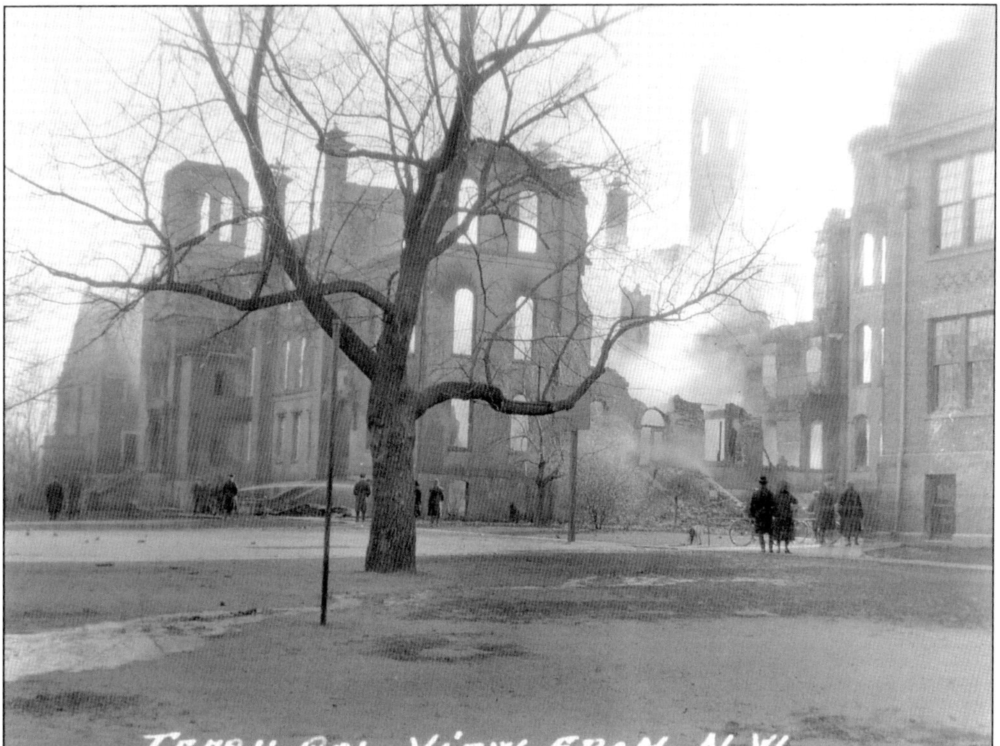

The Winona State Normal School was destroyed by fire early on Sunday morning, December 3, 1922. The building was built at a cost of $10,000 in 1866 with wings added in 1895. A major loss resulting from the fire was the college museum, which held the Woodman Collection of marine, mineral, and fossil specimens that a group of city businessmen had purchased from the Mississippi Valley Scientific Association in 1876. After the rubble was cleared, a new building was constructed and then dedicated on October 17, 1924.

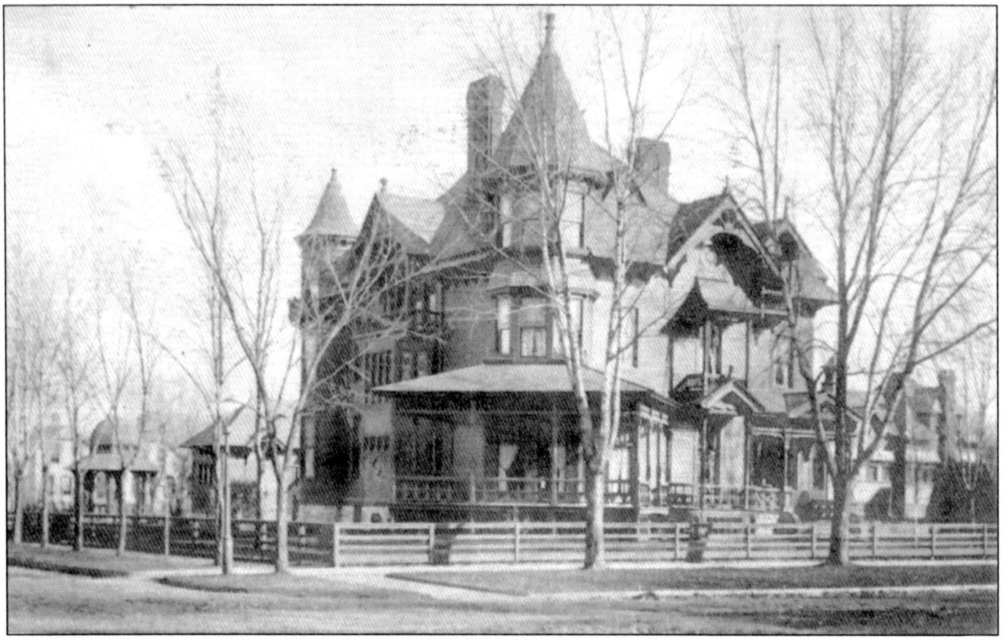

Charles Horton (1836–1913), one of the founders of the lumber milling industry in Winona, had this house built in 1883 at the northeast corner of Franklin and Broadway Streets. Designed in the Queen Anne style by William H. Wilcox of Chicago, it was valued at $10,000. The house was not occupied very much after Horton died and was razed in 1928 after the death of his wife.

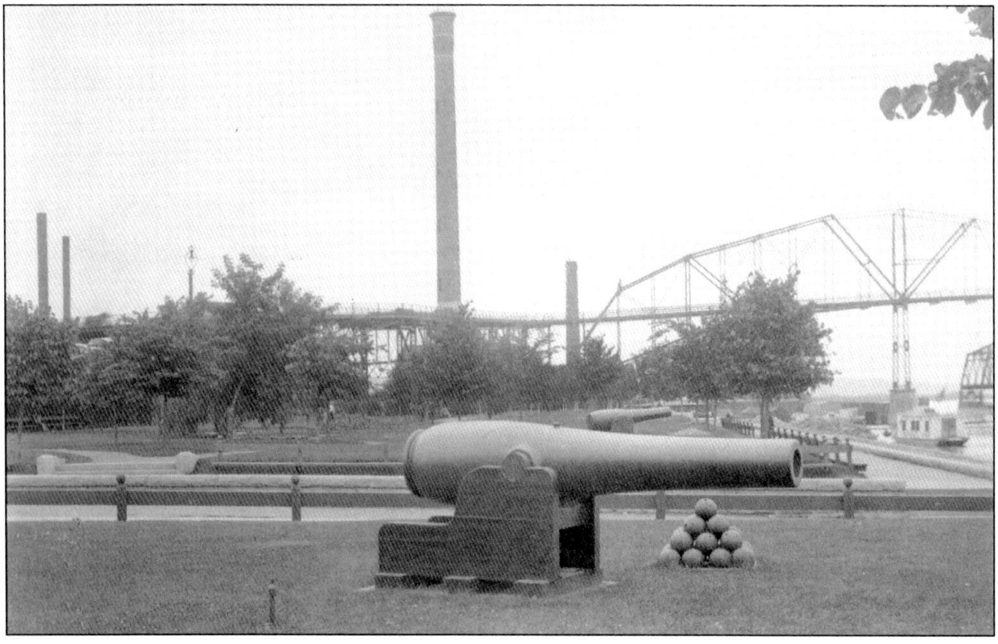

The Civil War cannons, standpipe, and high bridge, all located in or near Riverside Park, can no longer be seen. The cannons, captured by the First Minnesota Battery, had been in the possession of John Nicklin for many years. They were donated by the John Ball Post and placed in the park in 1899. The cannons were given as scrap for the war effort in 1942. The old standpipe, which was built in 1882 and used to regulate the city's water pressure, was dismantled in 1962.

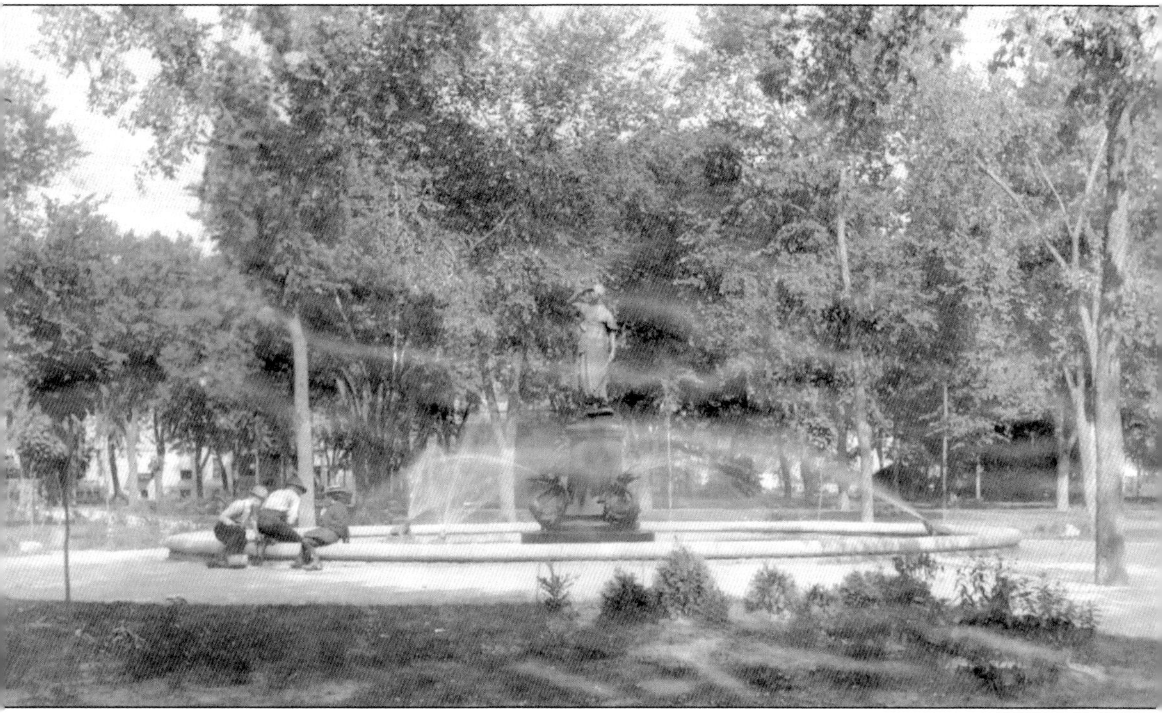

William J. Landon commissioned the Landon Fountain in 1901 as a memorial to his wife, Ida Cone Landon. Isabel Moore Kimball sculpted the statue of Princess Wenonah, along with three turtles and three pelicans, in New York City. After the fountain was constructed in the summer of 1902, the statues and granite pedestal were put in place on August 26, 1902. The fountain was removed from the park in May 1962 to make way for a new post office. Princess Wenonah was separated from her turtles and pelicans and soon found herself in Lake Park at the head of Main Street.

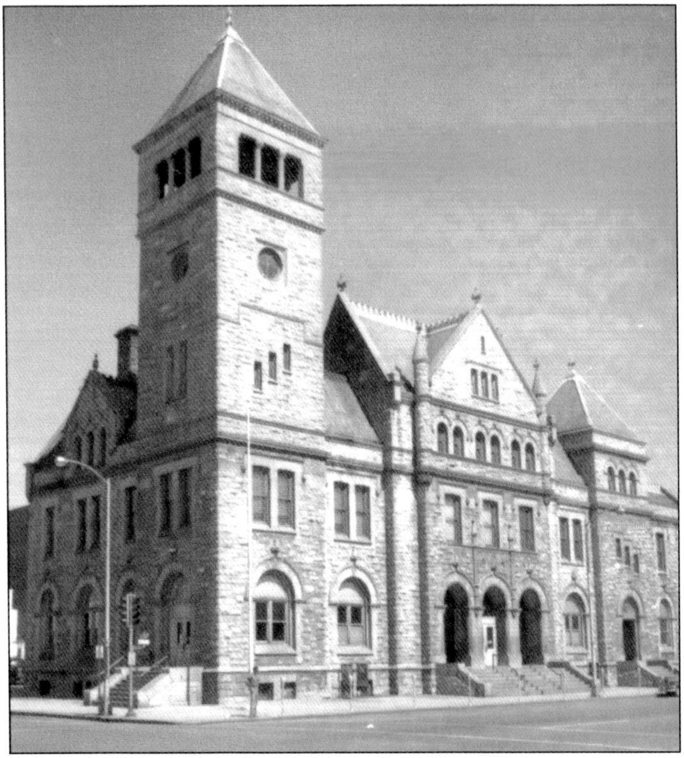

The Winona Post Office and Federal Court Building, located on the northwest corner of Fourth and Main Streets, was constructed of stone in a French Gothic design and opened on October 22, 1891. In the late 1950s, the business community petitioned for a new post office building in Central Park. The First National Bank purchased the old post office for $151,000 and razed the building in August 1963. The new bank building opened on the site in June 1965.

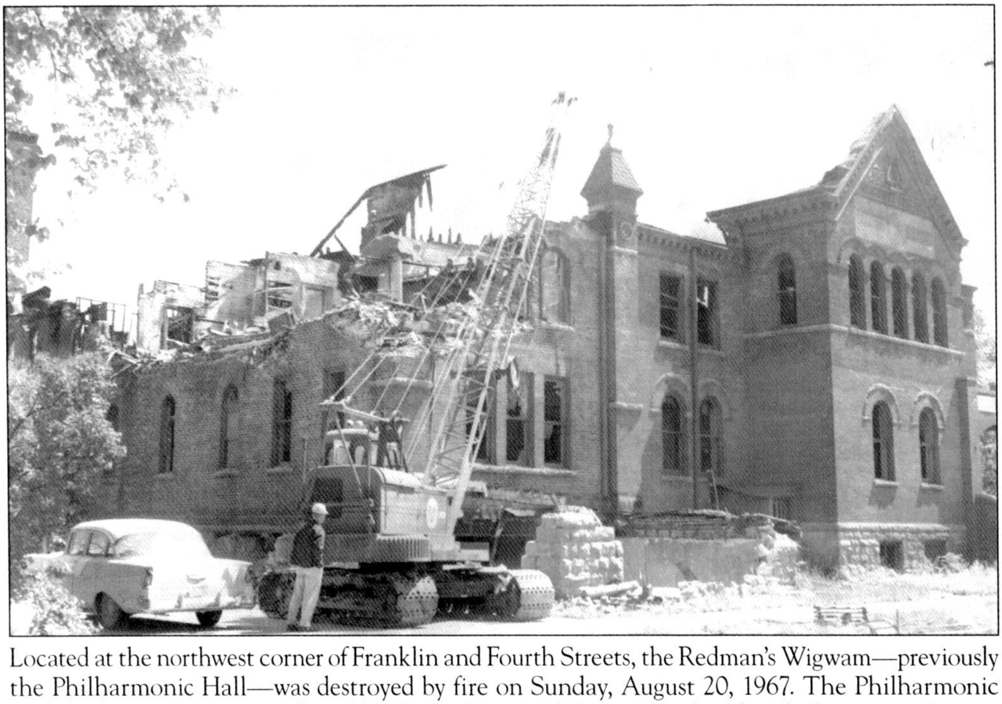

Located at the northwest corner of Franklin and Fourth Streets, the Redman's Wigwam—previously the Philharmonic Hall—was destroyed by fire on Sunday, August 20, 1967. The Philharmonic Hall, built in 1894, was purchased by the Redman's Club in 1918 after the Philharmonic Society was disbanded. After the fire was extinguished, the building was razed and the property used as a parking lot.

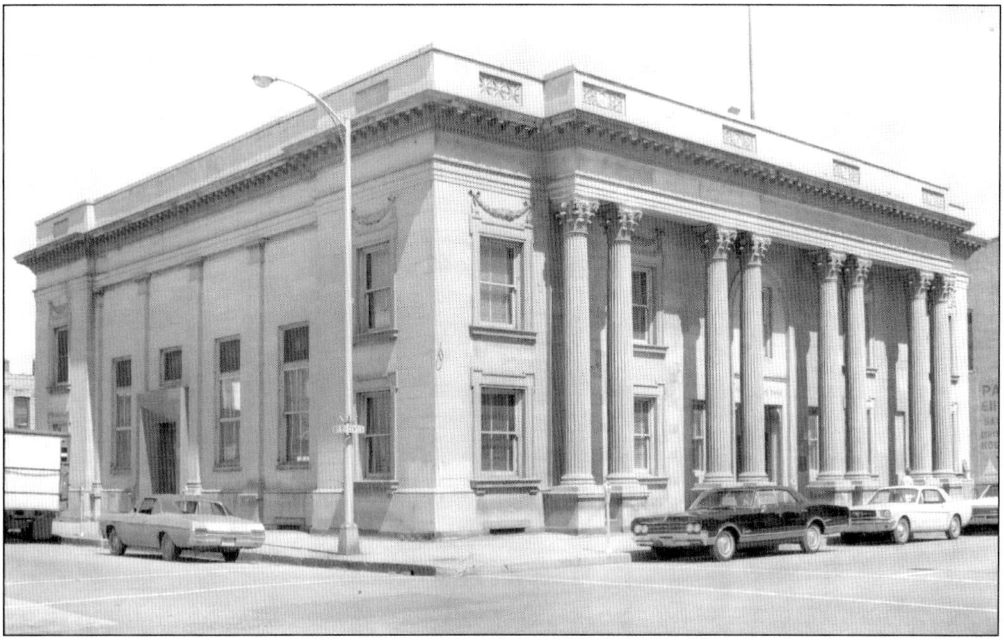

The First National Bank building, located on the northwest corner of Center and Fourth Streets, opened for business on December 21, 1908. Abandoned in June 1965 when the bank moved into new quarters at the site of the old post office, this stately structure was razed in July 1968 to make way for a parking lot for the Levee Plaza project.

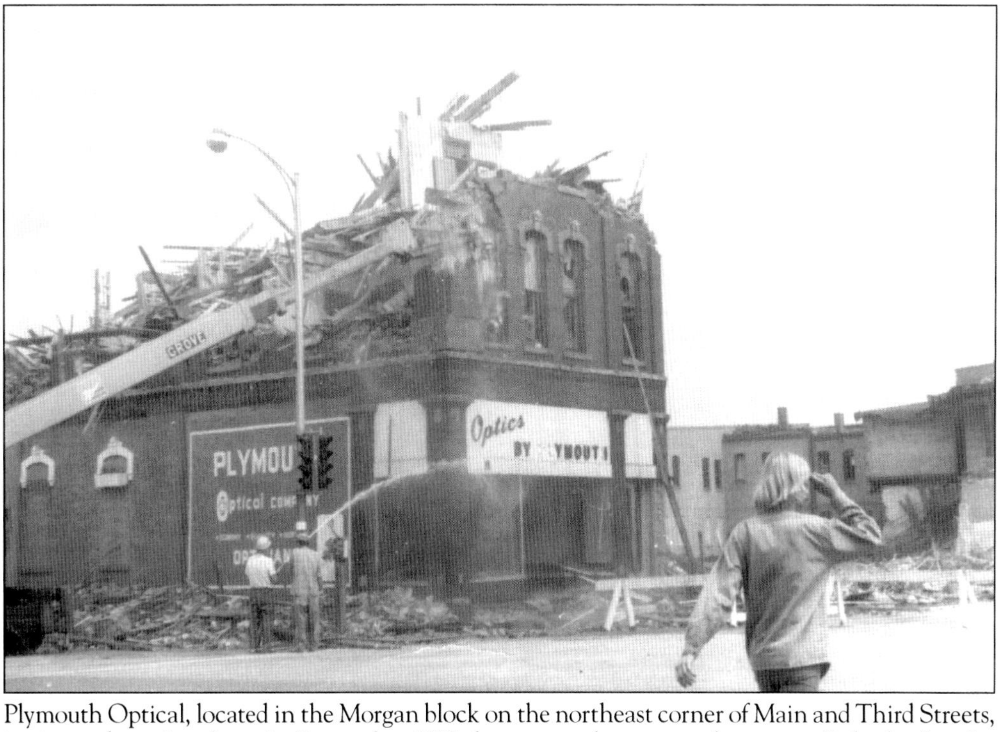

Plymouth Optical, located in the Morgan block on the northeast corner of Main and Third Streets, is pictured coming down in September 1971 due to an urban renewal program. Rebuilt after the fire of 1862, the building had been home to numerous businesses over the years.

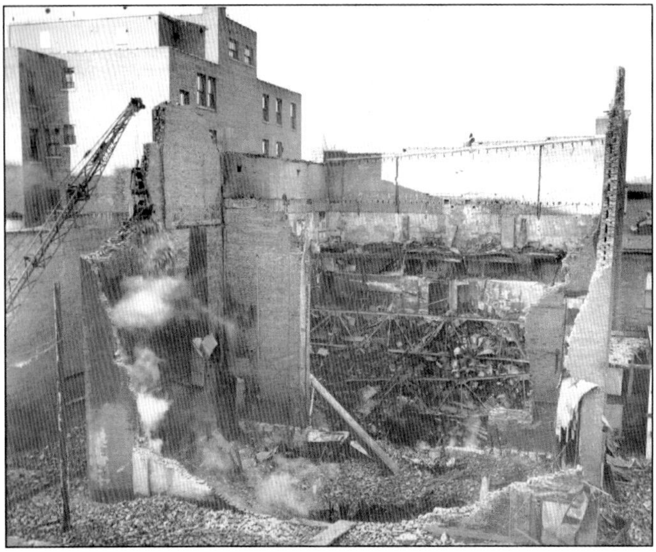

The Latsch Block, along the north side of West Second Street between Center and Main Streets, came down during the summer of 1975. These buildings, constructed between the 1860s and 1900, were part of the John A. Latsch wholesale grocery business, which was active into the mid-1950s.

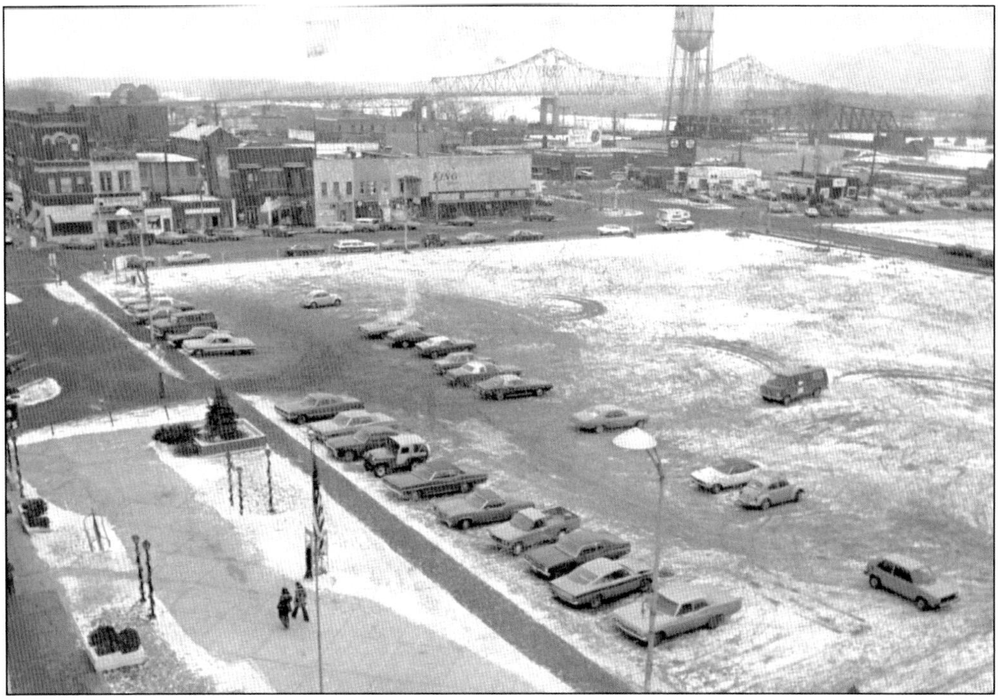

This empty lot, photographed on the afternoon of Christmas Eve 1975, is the former Morgan block, which was cleared during the summer of 1971. To the far right is the former Latsch Block, which was cleared during the summer of 1975. An ice rink was proposed for the former Morgan block during the winter of 1971–1972, but it was rejected because construction would soon be underway. The walkway is a part of Levee Plaza, which extended along Third Street from Main Street east to Lafayette Street. The plaza was dedicated on October 15, 1969. It was not until April 1977 that the Morgan block was replaced with another building. Later the same year, the plaza was rebuilt and a fountain was constructed for Princess Wenonah and her animal friends. Then, during the summer of 1993, the pedestrian mall was torn out and replaced with a street, and the princess went into storage.

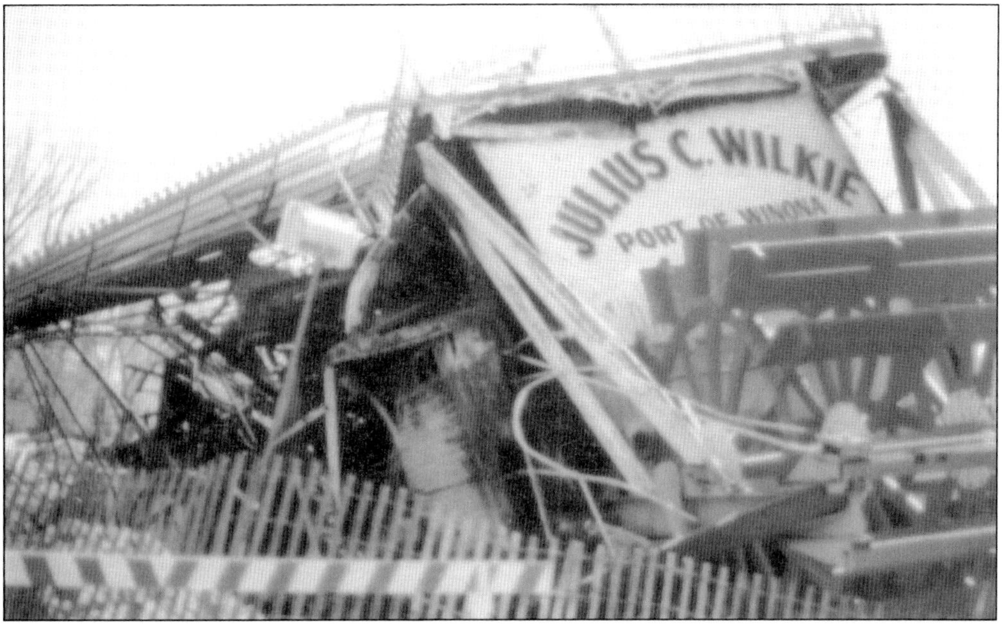

The Julius C. Wilke Steamboat Museum, located in Levee Park, was destroyed by fire on March 12, 1981. Originally, an 1898 vintage wood-hulled paddleboat, the *James P. Pearson*, was brought to Winona in 1956 and put on permanent display in Levee Park. The boat had been moved for a flood control project when it was destroyed.

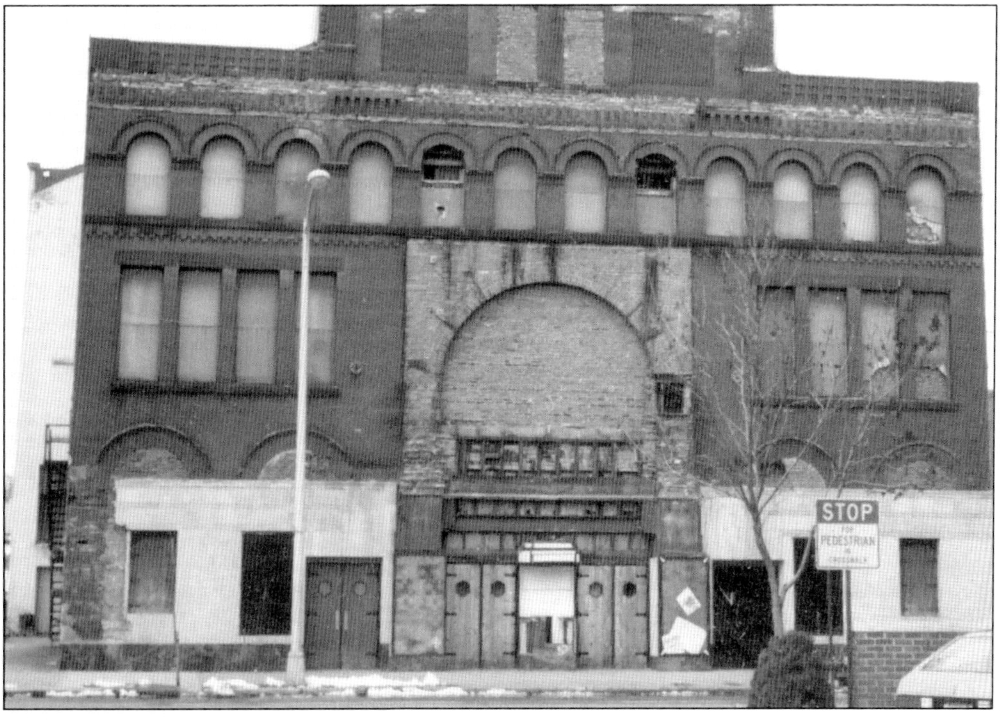

The Winona Opera House, also known as the Winona Theater, had its façade removed in June 1986 in order to inspect its original exterior. Many of the original exterior features were found to be intact with the exception of the balcony that was over the entryway.

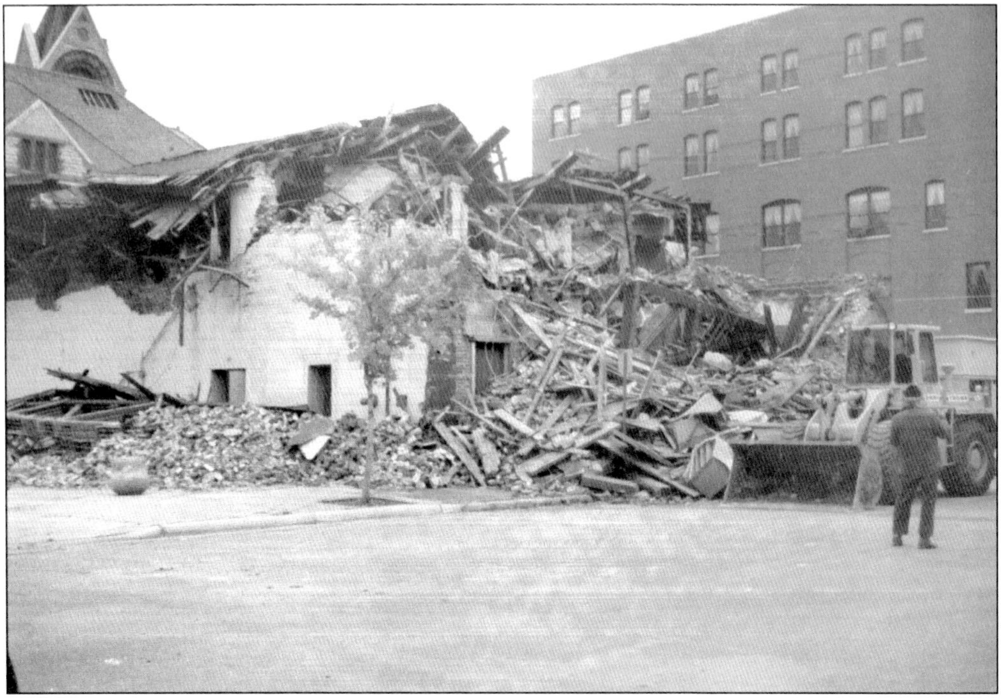

The Winona Opera House came down in mid-October 1990 after a period of agitation to preserve it as a parking garage. The footprint of the old opera house became a parking lot for the residents of the Kensington Apartments, formerly the Hotel Winona.

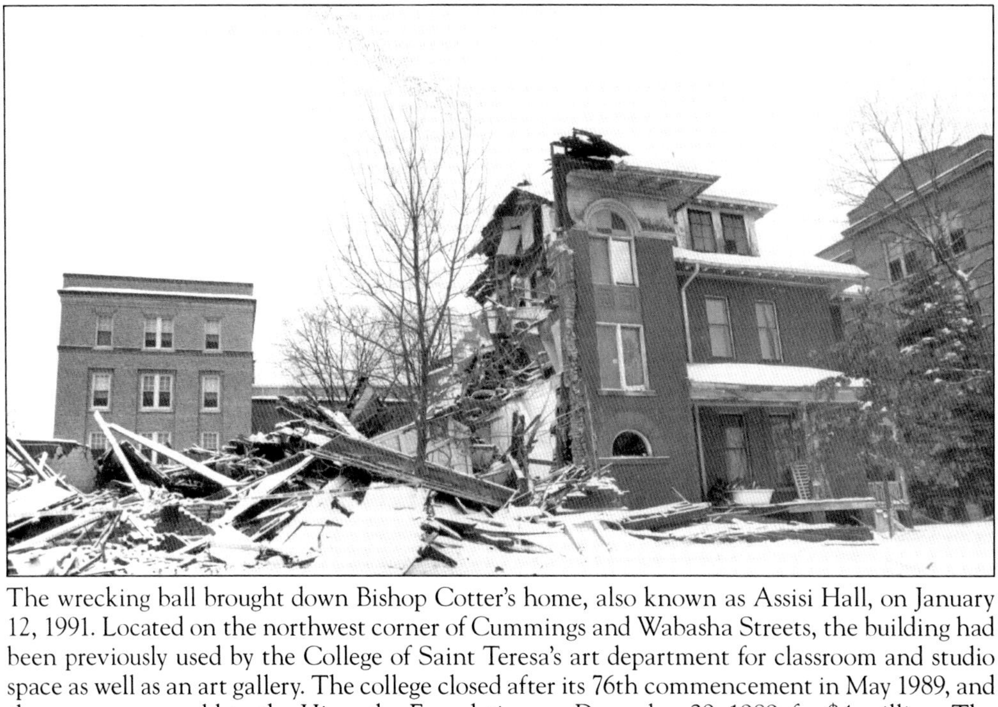

The wrecking ball brought down Bishop Cotter's home, also known as Assisi Hall, on January 12, 1991. Located on the northwest corner of Cummings and Wabasha Streets, the building had been previously used by the College of Saint Teresa's art department for classroom and studio space as well as an art gallery. The college closed after its 76th commencement in May 1989, and the campus was sold to the Hiawatha Foundation on December 29, 1989, for $4 million. The foundation took possession of the campus on June 1, 1991.

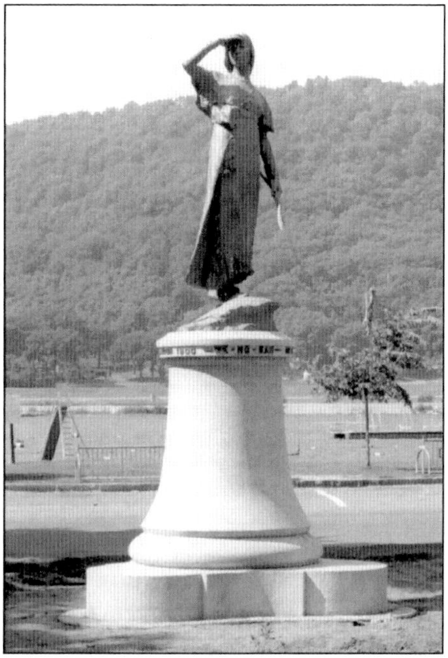

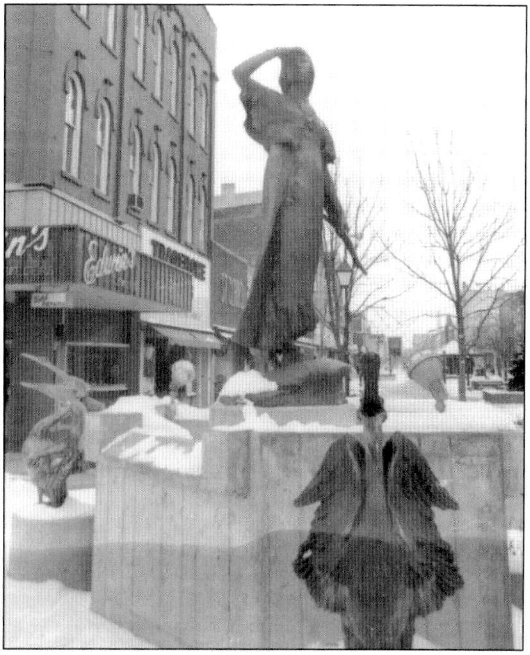

After Princess Wenonah was removed from Central Park, in 1963, she was dropped off in Lake Park in a triangle at the southern end of Main Street (upper left). However, her animal friends were loaned to the state college. In 1977, the princess was reunited with them at the intersection of Third and Center Streets to adorn a small fountain in Levee Plaza (upper right). However, her pedestal was left behind in Lake Park. In 1993, Levee Plaza was removed and Third Street was opened to traffic, so the princess lost her home again. Below, Phillip Feiten (left) and Harland Knight, both members of the city planning commission, headed up a committee to raise funds to build a fountain for the princess and her friends in Windom Park. On September 23, 1993, with water gushing from the pelicans and the turtles, the fountain was dedicated.

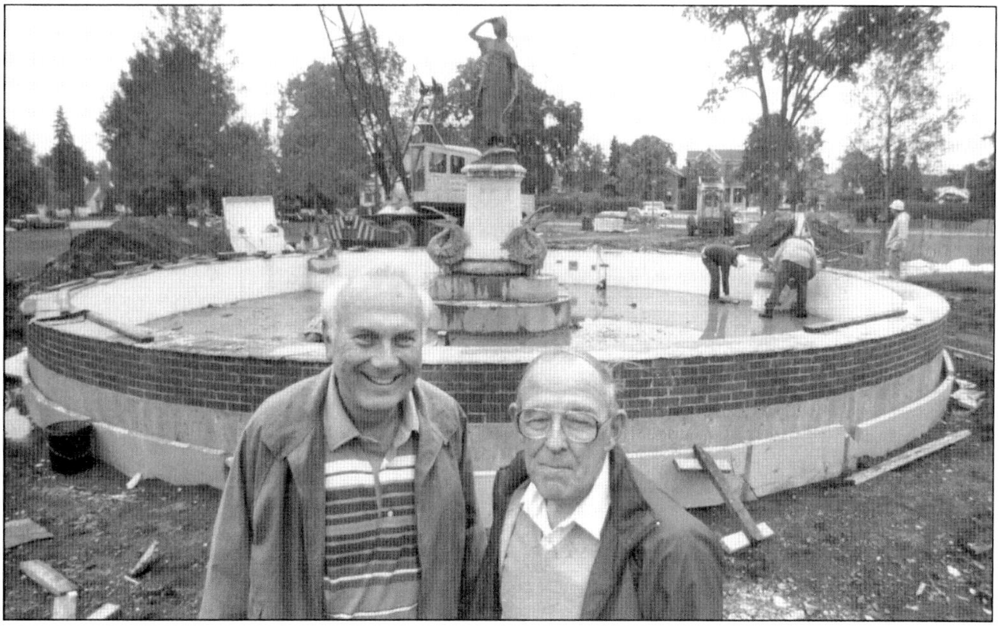

Bibliography

Andreas, Alfred T. *Winona, Minnesota*. Chicago: Chas Shober & Co., Chicago Lithograph Company, 1874.

Bennett, L.G. and A.C. Smith. *Map of Winona County, Minnesota, 1867*. Chicago: Chas Shober & Co., 1867.

Bunnell, Lafayette Houghton. *Winona and its Environs on the Mississippi in Ancient and Modern Days*. Winona, MN: Jones & Kroeger Printer and Publishers, 1897.

Curtis-Wedge, Franklyn, editor. *The History of Winona County Minnesota*. Chicago: H.C. Cooper Jr. & Co., 1913.

Diedrch, Mark. *The Chiefs, Wapahasha: Three Centuries of Dakota Leadership*. Rochester, MN: Coyote Books.

Ellsbury, George N. and Vernon Green. *Winona, Minn*. Chicago: Charles Snober & Company, Lithograph Company.

History of Winona County, Together with Biographical Matter, Statistics, Etc. Chicago: H.H. Hill and Company, Publishers, 1883.

Holbrook, Franklin F. "Fourteenth Minnesota Volunteer Infantry." *Minnesota in the Spanish-American War and the Philippine Insurrection*. St. Paul, MN: Minnesota War Records Commission, 1923.

In the World War—Winona County, Minnesota, 1917, 1918, 1919. St. Paul, MN: Buckbee-Mears Company, 1920.

Kunz, Virginia Brainard. *Sergeant Ramer's Indian War*. St. Paul, MN: Ramsey County Historical Society, 1964.

Portrait and Biographical Record of Winona County, Minnesota. Chicago: Chapman Publishing Company, 1895.

Quinn, Sister M. Bernetta. *Designs in Gold: A History of the College of Saint Teresa, Winona, Minnesota, 1907–1957*. 1957.

Ruger, Albert. *Birds Eye View of the City of Winona, Minnesota*. Chicago: Chicago Lithographing Company, 1867.

Ruggles, C.O. *Historical Sketch and Notes, Winona State Normal School, 1860–1910*. St. Paul, MN: Minnesota Normal School Board, 1910.

"The Gateway City, Winona Illustrated, Historical, Picturesque, Descriptive." Art Publishing Company, Pratt & Owen, Proprietors, 1888.

Upham, Warren. "Volume 1, Description and Explorations." *Minnesota in Three Centuries*. Mankato, MN: Publishing Society of Minnesota, 1908.

Wabasha Prairie. New York: Lithograph by Hermann J. Meyer, 1855.

Wapasha's Cap. From an engraving by Vistus Balch of the drawing by William Momberger. New York: William Pate & Co., 1869.

Younger, Edith Braun, *Winona Training School for Nurses, 1895–1935*. Winona, MN.

INDEX

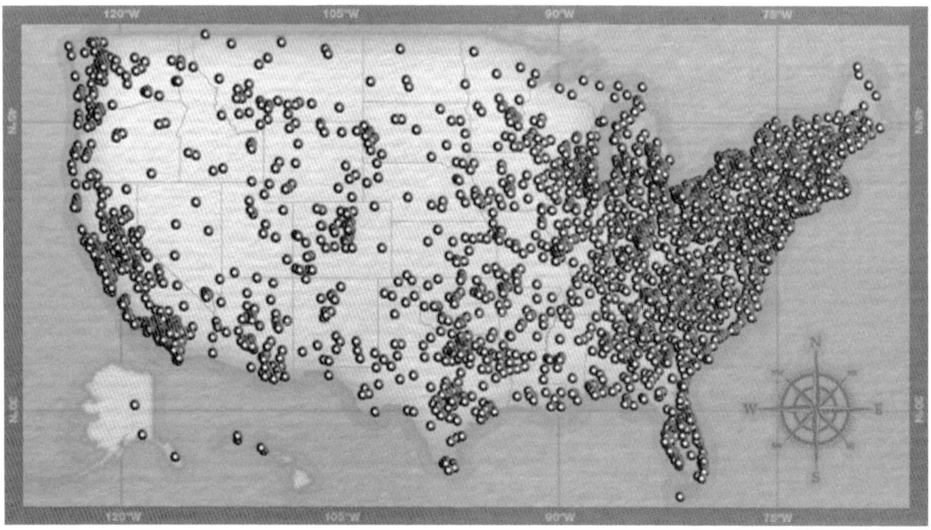